HJ
2348.5
.S53

Simon, Carl P.,
1945-

Beating the system

HJ
2348.5
.S53

Simon, Carl P.
Beating the system

R00028 03967

© THE BAKER & TAYLOR CO.

BEATING THE SYSTEM

BEATING THE SYSTEM

The Underground Economy

CARL P. SIMON
University of Michigan, Ann Arbor

ANN D. WITTE
University of North Carolina, Chapel Hill

with

KELLY EAKIN
ROBIN G. SCHOETTLER
A. L. ZIEGERT

University of North Carolina, Chapel Hill

Auburn House Publishing Company
Boston, Massachusetts

Library of Congress Cataloging in Publication Data

Simon, Carl P., 1945–
    Beating the system.

    Includes bibliographical references and index.
    1. Tax evasion—United States.   2. Informal sector
(Economics)—United States.   I. Witte, Ann D.
II. Title.
HJ2348.5.S53   364.1'33   81-12846
ISBN 0-86569-105-3   AACR2

Printed in the United States of America

ACKNOWLEDGMENTS

In the course of writing this book, we have benefitted greatly from the support and comments of numerous individuals. Our work in this area began when the Joint Economic Committee of the U.S. Congress requested that we complete a paper on the underground economy for the Committee's Special Study on Economic Change. Douglas Ross and Michael Lockerby, who were, respectively, senior economist and research assistant to that committee, provided valuable aid in contacting people in the executive branch of the U.S. government and in completing our first survey of the highly diverse literature in this area. Robert Cozart of the House Committee on Ways and Means and Jack Key of the Senate Permanent Subcommittee on Investigations provided much valuable information.

Due to severe time constraints and the mammoth task of coming to grips with the large and disparate literatures on various sectors of the underground economy, we were able to provide only a partial view of this complex entity for the Joint Economic Committee. After completing our paper for the JEC, we both felt that more needed to be done. Specifically, we felt that we needed to consider many more sectors of the underground economy and that we needed more knowledge of the methods of operation of important sectors if we were to provide a basis for meaningful policy in this area. We approached Edward Zedlewski of the Office of Research and Evaluation Methods of the National Institute of Justice to ask if the Institute would be willing to provide funds to allow the more thorough analysis we envisioned. The Institute agreed to provide a small amount of funds for research assistants, literature acquisition, and other research costs. We would like to thank personnel of the Institute, as without their support this manuscript would not have been completed. Needless to say, points of view and opinions expressed in this document are those of the authors alone and do not reflect the official position or policies of the U.S. Department of Justice.

The Osprey Company of Tallahassee, Florida administered the grant from the National Institute of Justice. Gloria Grizzle and other members of that company provided comments and other aid in completing our work.

On a more informal basis, many members of the executive and legislative branches of the U.S. government provided valuable assistance and greatly enhanced our understanding of various sectors of the underground economy. We have attempted to acknowledge specific help at a number of points in this manuscript. However, we want to take this opportunity to give special thanks to Berj Kenadjian, William Lefbom, and James Swartzwelder of the Internal Revenue Service; Robert Parker of the Bureau of Economic Analysis; and Ralph S. Edwards of the Office of Consumer Goods and Service Industries.

At a number of points, we have received valuable comments from our colleagues. We would particularly like to thank Phillip Cook of Duke University and Richard Porter of the University of Michigan for their aid. Sarah Mason and Betsy Pierce of the Department of Economics at the University of North Carolina and Beth Henderson at the University of Michigan provided expert typing, editorial assistance, and other help without which we could not have completed our tasks. Finally, we would like to thank our families for their patience and understanding.

C.P.S.
A.D.W.

CONTENTS

INTRODUCTION

The underground economy is a term used to describe transactions that involve payment in money or in similar goods but which are not recorded in official economic statistics (such as the taxable income or the unemployment rate). These transactions may not be recorded for a number of reasons. For example, the goods or services sold may be illegal, as are narcotics and prostitution. On the other hand, the provider of these goods may want to avoid paying income, sales, or social security taxes or avoid obeying some frustrating government regulations. Children who sell lemonade in front of their homes, teenagers who babysit for their neighbors, and adults who use garage sales to clean out their attics are all participating in the underground economy if they do not report their income. However, as we will see in later chapters, one of the biggest segments of the underground economy is composed of workers who do not report all the income from their main job or from a secondary job, often demanding payment in cash so that there will be no record of their secret income.

The underground economy is a worldwide phenomenon with different names in different countries. In England it is called "fiddling"; in France, "travail au noir"; in Germany, "schwarzarbeit"; in Japan, "the hidden economy." An estimated six million workers in Italy, one third of the labor force, participate in that country's "lavoro nero." A recent study estimates that the income from this hidden labor was $43 billion in 1979.[1]

During the late 1970s, an increasing number of American financial magazines and journals carried stories describing the surprising size and growth of the underground economy in the United States. In 1976, James Henry pointed out in the *Washington Monthly*[2] that there was a $100 bill in circulation "for every man, woman, and child in the country." He suggested that the main users of these large denominations were people engaged in profit-motivated crime and people evading taxes by demanding cash for their services or products. Using econometric techniques based on the value of these large-denomination bills in circulation, he estimated that the volume of profit-motivated crime and the amount of tax evasion each equaled $30 billion in 1973. He concluded his report with a suggestion that the U.S. Treasury and the Federal Reserve call in all bills of large denominations on very short notice and exchange them for new bills of smaller denominations.

The article that attracted the American media's attention to the underground economy was a three-page report by economist Peter Gutmann in the December 1977 issue of the *Financial Analysts' Journal*.[3] Gutmann estimated the ratio of the amount of currency in circulation to the amount of money in checking accounts each year from the late 1930s to the present. He used the growth of this ratio to estimate that the gross national product of the underground economy was $176 billion in 1976 and $195 billion in 1977. The size of these figures attracted considerable media attention and was reported in detail in all the major newspapers and news magazines in the country.[4] After all, Gutmann's figures indicated that the GNP of the underground economy was a little more than 10 percent of the officially reported GNP—roughly equal to the official GNP of all of Canada, and greater than the entire legal U.S. GNP in the middle of World War II.

Besides the extensive media coverage, Gutmann's work also attracted some heavy criticism from economists and financial analysts.[5] One of these economists, Edgar Feige,[6] used an analysis based on the ratio of the "total transactions in an economy" to the observed income to derive his own estimates. Although he had at first believed that Gutmann's estimates were too high, his own calculations yielded estimates of the underground GNP that were twice as large: $225 to $369 billion in 1976 and $542 to $704 billion in 1978. The 1976 estimates are 13 to 22 percent of the measured GNP, and the 1978 estimates suggest a growth rate of 91 percent or four times the nominal growth rate of 23 percent for the regular sector between 1976 and 1978.

Around the same time, the federal government started deriving its own estimates. The most important of these is a 1979 report by the Internal Revenue Service.[7] This study of the noncompliance with income tax rules estimated that in 1976 $75 to $100 billion of income in the legal sector and $25 to $35 billion of income in the illegal sector were not reported to the IRS. The resulting loss of federal tax revenue was $19 to $26 billion. The IRS study differed from the other projects we have discussed because it used a sector-by-sector approach and was concerned with taxable income rather than the Gross National Product.

These four studies have produced a wide array of estimates for the size of the underground economy. In particular, the estimates of size and growth seem to depend critically on the macroeconomic indices used to measure this size. A number of economists[8] have suggested that what is really needed is a careful, detailed microeconomic analysis of each sector of the underground economy. Not only would such an analysis provide an important alternative to the macroeconomic approaches that have been used, but it should also provide useful information on the "structure" of the underground "economy" whose sectors appear to have very little interaction and relationship with each other. Furthermore, it could pinpoint those sectors that are most dynamic and thus most responsible for the apparent growth of the underground economy. Finally, a careful analysis of the workings of each sector could provide effective policy suggestions on how to halt the growth of the underground economy and on where to concentrate scarce enforcement resources.

The purpose of this book is precisely to carry out such a sector-by-sector study of the underground economy. In the first two parts, written mainly by Ann Witte, we examine the production of *legal* goods which are not properly reported. In the second two parts, written mainly by Carl Simon, we study the sectors involved with the sale and distribution of *illegal* goods and services. Throughout, we discuss the economic organization of these sectors and their size and growth. In contrast to other researchers, we have taken great pains to use national income accounting techniques to estimate the "national income" of the underground economy so that we may validly compare it with the reported National Income. These estimates are summarized in Table 1. We estimate that the total "national income" for the underground economy in 1974 was between $100 and $180 billion, with numbers in the upper portion of this range more likely than numbers in the lower portion.

We used 1974 for the base year of our analysis because, during the period that this book was written (1979–1981), it was the latest year for which there were reliable and comparable figures for all the sectors we wanted to study. However, since our sector-by-sector approach does yield some estimates on the growth rate of most sectors, we carry out in the last chapter of this book an estimate of

Table 1   Estimated National Income for the Underground Economy in 1974

Sector	Estimate (in $ billion)
Tax Evasion and Avoidance	
Federal income and profits tax	56.7–75.7
Excise taxes	0.3–0.5
Illegal Aliens	5.9–7.6
Illegal Transfers	
Stolen goods	5.4–8.9
Fraud arson	0.2
Other fraud	2.2–20.1
Counterfeiting	0.001
Embezzlement	0.1–1.3
Bribery	6.5–13.0
Production and Distribution of Illegal Goods	
Drugs: Heroin	3.2–5.0
Cocaine	5.6–6.2
Marihuana	1.5–2.4
Other drugs	2.8–4.4
Smuggling of goods other than drugs	0.2–0.3
Pornography	1.3–2.0
Production and Distribution of Illegal Services	
Illegal gambling	1.0–2.0
Loan sharking	0.2–3.2
Prostitution	1.7–14.4
Other	5.0–10.0
Total National Income	99.8–177.2

the national income of the underground economy in 1980—$170 to $300 billion. We estimate a 10 percent annual growth rate for the underground economy between 1974 and 1980—just a little slower than the 10.6 percent growth rate of the regular American economy.

Our estimates are in the range of Gutmann's macroeconomic estimates, larger than Henry's, but smaller than Feige's. However, we all agree that the national income of the underground economy is over 10 percent of the reported National Income, an amount that demands the serious attention of American policymakers. Because of the secrecy of the underground economy, official statistics about inflation, unemployment, and productivity are not presenting an accurate view of the American economy. Because the prices are often lower and employment is high in the underground economy, we have overestimated official inflation and unemployment. Feige[9] suggests that if underground prices and employment were included in our official statistics, we might even find a sufficient increase in employment and decrease in inflation to explain away the current appearance of "stagflation" (high unemployment plus high inflation) that has baffled many macroeconomic theorists. In any case, since over $11 billion of major government program expenditures are triggered by inflation and unemployment statistics, the systematic biases in recorded statistics which fail to take into account the underground economy lead to misguided (and probably over-stimulatory) public policy decisions.

Of course, the existence of an underground economy means that federal, state, and local governments are not receiving all the tax revenues that they are due. The $19 to $26 billion of lost federal income tax revenue described by the IRS's 1979 study would almost have been enough to wipe out the $27 billion deficit in the 1979 federal budget. More importantly, the growth of the underground economy is probably related to a growing frustration by many Americans with their higher and higher tax brackets and with government regulations. An underground economy that is over 10 percent of the size of the regular economy implies that those who are resisting the temptation to join the underground economy are paying an inequitable portion of our country's taxes. If this realization spreads, it would certainly weaken the voluntary compliance upon which our tax system is based and at the same time introduce a sense of animosity and non-cooperation between the American people and their government.

The underground economy is an important economic phenomenon in the United States. We can no longer afford to ignore it.

Endnotes

1. See "Cheating on Taxes—A Worldwide Pursuit." 1979. *Newsweek*, October 22, pp. 53, 56. In a working paper, economist Edgar Feige refers to the Italian economist Saba to back up his estimate of six million "underground" workers and adds that their labor produces almost 40 percent of Italy's real income.
2. Henry, James. 1976. "Calling in the Big Bills," *Washington Monthly*, May, pp. 27–33.
3. Gutmann, Peter. 1977. "The Subterranean Economy," *Financial Analysts Journal*, Nov./Dec., pp. 26, 27, 34.
4. Gutmann, Peter. 1978. "Off the Books," *Across the Board*, August, pp. 9–13.

See also Reuter, Peter. 1980. "A Reading on the Irregular Economy," *Taxing and Spending*, Spring, pp. 65–71.

5. Feige, Edgar. 1979. "The Irregular Economy: Its Size and Macroeconomic Implications," Social Systems Research Institute, University of Wisconsin–Madison. See also Garcia, Gillian, and Simon Pak. 1979. "The Ratio of Currency to Demand Deposits in the United States," *The Journal of Finance* 34 (June):703–715.

6. Feige, "The Irregular Economy."

7. U.S. Department of the Treasury, Internal Revenue Service. 1979. *Estimates of Income Unreported on Individual Income Tax Returns*. Washington, D.C.: U.S. Government Printing Office.

8. See Feige, "The Irregular Economy," p. 3; Teeters, Nancy, "Prepared statement before the Subcommittee on Oversight of the Committee on Ways and Means, United States House of Representatives," September 10, 1979; and Reuter, "A Reading on the Irregular Economy," p. 71. Reuter writes: "We should spend some time doing serious micro studies of the various components of the irregular economy before rushing to conclusions about its growth and the need to curb taxes and regulation."

9. "The Outlook." 1980. *Wall Street Journal*. October 20, p. 1.

Part I

ACTIVITY AIMED PRIMARILY AT EVADING TAXES

Part I of our book examines activity aimed primarily at evading taxes, while Part II examines the transfer of people and goods that we, as a society, have declared illegal. Chapter 1 deals with the most important area of nonreporting, and, indeed, the dominant section of the underground economy—nonreporting of income primarily for tax evasion and the evasion of "public benefit loss," such as social security and AFDC (Aid for Dependent Children). While undoubtedly the vast majority of income earned in producing the illegal goods and services discussed in Part II goes unreported, we, like IRS, do not believe that current estimates of income that is not reported to taxing authorities includes much of such income. Current estimates of incomes that escape tax rely mainly on "paper trails" (various nontax sources of income reporting) for discovery, and incomes earned in the production of illegal goods and services generally leave no such "trails." Thus, they are not generally included in estimates of income that escapes taxation. This is important, since if substantial amounts of income from illegal production were included in estimates of income that escapes taxation, we would be "double counting" underground national income when we add estimates of the income that escapes tax to the estimates we obtain in Part II. In Chapter 2 we discuss unrecorded incomes generated by the evasion of excise taxes, particularly taxes on cigarettes.

Chapters in Part II will treat nonreporting due to the illegal status of either the seller or the property sold. Although such nonreporting often involves tax evasion, tax evasion is usually not the main reason for nonreporting. In addition, incomes not reported because of illegal status, like incomes earned by producing illegal goods and services, often leave no "paper trails" and so are not completely included in current estimates of income that escapes taxation.

In each of the areas discussed in detail in Part I we will consider not only the size and trends of the activity but also the costs and benefits of the activity for the individuals directly involved in the transaction, for government units, and for society as a whole. In addition, the chapter on income tax evasion includes a subsection describing some ways in which people earn the income they fail to report; and in Chapter 4, on stolen goods markets, we include a subsection in which we discuss the structure of at least some portions of this industry. We then suggest potentially fruitful topics for policy consideration and for future research.

Chapter 1

UNREPORTED INCOME GAINED BY FEDERAL INCOME TAX EVASION OR BENEFIT FRAUD

Size and Trends

In estimating the size of this sector, we are not interested in tax evasion or benefit fraud per se. Rather we are interested in the total amount of income unreported and thus not reflected in our national statistics. With this in mind we will consider the benefit and income tax programs with the broadest possible coverage. These are the Federal Income Tax, Social Security, the major national welfare programs (Aid for Dependent Children and Food Stamps), and the unemployment compensation program.

Theoretically, there should be some overlap here, with income unreported to benefit-granting agencies often reflected in income tax evasion figures. In practice, we are not at all convinced that current estimates of income (based on IRS's Tax Compliance Measurement Program) reflect all income that is not reported to benefit-granting agencies since these estimates are only for those who file returns. In 1979, estimates of the income of individuals who *do not* file tax returns represented an important expansion of estimates of the income escaping taxation. These estimates undoubtedly capture much, but not all, income that is concealed from benefit-granting agencies. However, our attempts to obtain direct estimates of income not reported to benefit-granting agencies were unsuccessful.

Conversations with personnel of the Quality Assurance Program of the Social Security Administration have indicated that no estimates have been made of the extent of income not reported for purposes of social security benefits. In 1979, in testimony before the Subcommittee on Oversight of the U.S. House of Representatives, the Acting Associate Commissioner for Policy of the Social Security Administration, Lawrence Thompson, estimated that social security trust funds (Old Age, Survivors, and Disability Insurance and Health Insurance) lost "roughly $3 to $4 billion in revenues in 1976" due to unreported self-employment earnings and unreported wages and salaries.[1] This represented more than 5 percent of Social Security receipts in that year. Not surprisingly, the income not reported to the Social Security Administration appears to be less than that not reported to the Internal Revenue Service. Major groups who fail to report large amounts of income to Social Security are the self-employed, independent contractors, and certain types of service workers (for example, domestics).

While we have no estimate of the amount of income which is not reported to the Social Security Administration for benefit fraud purposes, the Division of Quality Control Management of the former Department of Health, Education and Welfare estimates the extent of error in the AFDC programs using a random sample of cases. The 1974 results for this program indicated that approximately one fifth of all errors uncovered resulted from the incorrect reporting of earned income.[2] We were unable to determine what amount of income was not reported or what amount of overpayment of AFDC payments resulted from the failures to report earned income.

Method of Estimating

Given our inability to obtain other direct estimates, we reached our estimate of the national income of this section of the underground economy by using estimates of (1) the amount of income underreported on federal tax returns, and (2) the amount of income earned by individuals who do not file federal tax returns. These estimates undoubtedly include some income which was not reported due to faulty records or lack of understanding of tax laws; however, we believe that the majority of income that is not reported is omitted at least partly for tax evasion purposes.

Using these two types of data and methods detailed in the appendix to this chapter, we estimate that between $60 and $80 billion of income earned by United States residents in legal activity was unreported to the Internal Revenue Service in 1974. If pressed to narrow the range of our estimates, we would estimate that between $70 and $75 billion of income from legal sources was unreported to IRS in 1974.

Using limited time-series data available from IRS's Tax Compliance Measurement Program and more extensive time-series data available from the Bureau of Economic Analysis of the Department of Commerce,[3-5] we estimate that the amount of income that escaped taxes grew at an average annual rate of 3 to 11 percent from 1965 to 1969, 8 to 10 percent from 1969 to 1973, and by approximately 5 percent from 1973 to 1976. These estimates are quite similar to the growth rate of recorded personal disposable income for comparable periods. Comparing the growth rates of recorded disposable personal income to those of income that escaped taxation, we conclude that the latter may have grown slightly more rapidly than reported income in the 1965–1969 period, at approximately the same rate in the 1969–1973 period, and possibly somewhat more slowly than reported income in the 1973–1976 period. These trend figures are consistent with findings by Hansen and Carroll for the IRS (as summarized in Endnote 6). However, we, like IRS in its report, can make no definitive statements concerning recent trends.

As a whole, our results indicate that a large amount of income escapes taxation, making this sector the largest single sector in the underground economy. However, it is wise to put the size and growth of this sector of the underground economy in proper perspective. Our estimate ($70 to $75 billion) of the amount of underreporting in 1974 is about only 6 percent of reported personal income in that year. Moreover, it appears that the size of this sector of the underground economy has grown only moderately relative to reported economic activity during the last decade, and may have actually declined slightly relative to reported activity during the mid and late 1970s.

Who Is Not Reporting and What Incomes Are They Failing to Report?

The simplest answer to "who" is "a lot of us." Studies that ask this question, with varying degrees of anonymity, usually find that 20 to 25 percent of people interviewed will admit to noncompliance with tax laws. See Westat[7] for a recent study and a survey of previous work. Needless to say, it is likely that more actually do fail to

Table 1-1   Estimated Amount of Unreported Income for 1976 as a Percentage of Reportable Amount, by Type of Income ($ billions)

| | *Amount of Income*[a] | | |
| | | *Reported on Tax Returns*[b] | |
Legal-Source Incomes	*Reportable on Tax Returns*	*Total*	*As a Percentage of Amount Reportable*
Self-employment[c]	$ 93–99	$ 60	60–64%
Wages and salaries	902–908	881	97–98
Interest	54–58	49	84–90
Dividends[d]	27–30	25	84–92
Rents and royalties	9–12	6	50–65
Total	$1085–1107	$1021	92–94%

[a] Sum of components may not add to totals due to rounding. Percentages of amounts reportable were computed from unrounded figures.
[b] A small amount of illegal-source incomes are included in the figures in this column. These inclusions will not significantly affect the percentages shown in the right-hand column.
[c] Self-employment income covers net earnings of farm and nonfarm proprietorships and partnerships (at times referred to as unincorporated business income) as well as net earnings of self-employed individuals working outside the context of regularly established businesses in the legal sector.
[d] Dividends include an estimated portion of distributed net profits of qualified small business corporations.

comply with tax laws. However, it is difficult to estimate how many more. In a recent study the General Accounting Office[8] estimated that about 5 million people (approximately 7 percent of those required to file) did not even bother to *file* federal income tax returns in 1972 although they were required to do so.

The 1979 IRS report[9] provides the best available estimates of the types and amount of incomes that are underreported. Table 1-1 contains IRS's estimates of the percent of underreported incomes received for various productive services. As can be seen in this table, reporting is highest for wages and salaries where direct reporting with tax returns is required and withholding widespread; moderate for interest and dividends where information reporting by payors is required; and lowest for self-employment and for rent and royalty income where reporting documents are generally not required. Incomes earned by those who are self-employed comprise the largest amount of incomes unreported ($28 to $38 billion in 1974), with incomes from wages and salaries being the next most important source of unreported income ($14 to $17 billion in 1974).*

---

* See Table A1-2 for amounts of other types of incomes.

Thus, if one is most concerned with tax compliance, it appears that self-employment and rent and royalty incomes are the largest problem; whereas, if the primary concern is with the underground economy, one must be concerned with wage and salary income as well. We will discuss in detail the types of individuals and work that are involved in earning unreported wages and salaries and self-employment income. We will end this section with a briefer discussion of unreported interest, dividend, and rental income.

Our discussion of the types of people who fail to report wage and salary and self-employment income relies heavily on the results of ethnographic work in Detroit[10, 11] and on individual instances of tax evasion. Neither of these sources represents random samples of those underreporting their incomes or failing to file tax returns. Thus, we do not know whether the information can be generalized. We do know that the Detroit study was based mainly on research in working class neighborhoods. As a result it provides far more examples of blue-collar than white-collar underreporting and failure to file.

Underreported Wages of Tax Filers

As we note in the appendix to this chapter, it is useful to divide unreported income into that earned by those who do file tax returns and that earned by those who do not. Unreported wages and salaries for those who do file, which we term underreported income, appears to be mainly cash income earned in second jobs and "off the books" activity. The IRS believes that many workers arrange with employers to report only a portion of their wages and salaries.[12] The portion reported allows the individual to qualify for social security, unemployment, and similar benefits, while taxes and social insurance payments are avoided on the unreported portion. The IRS gives the following examples of workers who fall into this category: crafts persons working in cottage industries; workers for retail establishments such as restaurants and bars; and entertainers such as singers, comedians, and dance band musicians.[13] However, one cannot but wonder if this practice is also not fairly widespread even among high-level employees of small firms. Professional firms where owners are paid salaries would also seem to be an area where such a practice could easily be carried on.

The Detroit study provides the following examples of the types of wage and salary income not reported by those who do file tax returns.[11]

> *Randy Jones is a licensed mason who works as a cement contractor and hires friends of his who are unemployed to do unskilled work such as driving trucks, buying materials, pouring cement, digging and reinforcing foundations, and so forth. He paid them a relatively low wage ($3–4 an hour) in cash which they were happy to use as supplements to their unemployment insurance benefits. He gets the money for the jobs and out of it pays his workers. The rest he officially records as the price of the job. In this way he shows less of a gross profit, can pay his workers less than scale, and does not have to take out insurance, social security, withholding, and so forth. He admits to making good money but says that he needs to use these practices in order to get by in the winter. He feels that he can get by with this type of arrangement because he is a small contractor who offers little or no competition to the 'big outfits.' Most of his jobs are done for individuals rather than companies and he runs little risk of being monitored. (pp. 3.10–3.11)*

> *Don Jenkins has been laid off from his regular job for six months and is drawing $420 a month unemployment compensation. Throughout the period of his unemployment, he has worked sporadically for City Wide Moving Company when they have a big moving job. Don Jenkins did not actively seek employment as a mover; it was offered to him by the owner of the company, who is his drinking buddy. He makes up to $150 a week in cash and does not report it. His pay rate, however, is lower than that which City Wide uses for its full time employees. (p. 3.15)*

> *George Russell is married and has nine children, six of whom are still living at home. He is a licensed electrician who had been unemployed for eight months at the time of our first interview, and his supplementary unemployment benefits had recently expired. While he was drawing both UI and SUB, George had worked intermittently for the contractor who used to be his employer. The contractor would often call him up for short duration jobs and pay him off the books at the hourly rate of $12.50. Some weeks he made as much as $500 under this arrangement. It was risky, however. Had he been discovered, George would have been fined by his union and could have lost his license. (p. 3.15)*

All of these examples point to the fact that wages and salaries that are underreported are generally not reported with the knowledge and aid of the employer involved. Both the employer and employee benefit from "off the books" arrangements.

Unreported Wages of Nonfilers

Individuals who do not file income tax returns earn wages and salaries in a number of ways. Some of the construction laborers in our first example may well not have filed tax returns and thus would fall into this category. Most wage and salary income of nonfilers comes from completely "off the books" employment in small businesses and by households. The IRS believes that completely "off the books" employment occurs in restaurants, construction firms, gas stations, car wash businesses, and taxi-cab companies.[15] The Detroit study indicates that such employment is common among suppliers of personal services (for example, painters, carpenters, television repair persons, yardworkers) to households. In its recent work using the Exact Match File, the General Accounting Office found that laborers and service workers were least likely to file tax returns (an estimated 16 to 17 percent did not in 1972).[16] Of the individuals in these two occupations, GAO estimates that farm laborers and domestic workers were particularly unlikely to file. Specifically, they estimate that 33 percent of all farm laborers and about 64 percent of all private household workers did not file tax returns in 1972.[17]

Again, the Detroit study provides us with examples of the ways in which nonfilers earn wage and salary income.[18]

> *Ralph Peabody is 55 and divorced with no children. He is a recovered alcoholic who is currently receiving a full disability and social security, both of which he would lose should it be discovered that he is working. He earns $125 a week as a dispatcher for a moving company, but is paid in cash and not carried on the books as an employee. He is quite aware that this arrangement is illegal but feels that he has it coming since "the people I used to work for caused me to become an alcoholic and made a million dollars from my labor and by cheating the government." In order to "keep clean," Ralph deposits money in a savings account in another state under an assumed name. Rather than keeping a checking account he periodically buys a few hundred dollars in traveler's checks and carries these around with him. (p. 3.28)*

> *Mr. Peel is a retired assembly line worker in an automobile plant who is now in his late 60s. His pension requires that his reportable yearly income be limited, so he engages in a variety of cash-based exchanges for which no records are kept, and he earns about $4000 a year from them. Two days a week he works as a janitor in a laundromat for $2.50 an hour and is paid in coins from the washers and dryers. He also fills in as a janitor for friends who own a tire company. He also*

takes care of the homes of friends while they are away on vacation and
feeds their animals. (p. 3.24)

Mary Lou Jones is in her early 30s and receives AFDC and some child
support for her two daughters, ages 11 and 12. She works as a bar-
maid in a nearby tavern four days a week, from 2 to 10 p.m. She is
paid in cash weekly and does not report this income. She does not
possess any clerical or secretarial skills and has no desire for factory
work despite the higher wages she might earn from it. She feels
compelled to work in order to finance her daughters' future educa-
tions as both are excellent students. For the most part she enjoys her
work and the opportunity to be around people. By working irregu-
larly, she is able to maintain a decent standard of living, hold a job
which is both flexible and rewarding, and save for her daughters'
educations. (p. 3.22)

Underreported Income of the Self-Employed

As discussed, it appears that the income earned by the self-
employed is quite likely to be underreported and generates a substantial amount of the income of this sector of the underground
economy. IRS believes that underreported self-employment income, like wage and salary income, comes mainly from second jobs
and "off the books" activity. IRS suggests that these second jobs are
likely to be in craft activities such as carpentry and plumbing, and
service work such as small repairs and hairdressing. We believe,
however, that the nonreporting of self-employment income is also
widespread among small business owners and independent professional workers. Individual tax evasion cases indicate that small—
and indeed some large—businesses and independent professionals
use double sets of books, fake invoices, deduct fictitious expenses,
and conceal assets by placing them in the names of friends, relatives, and shell corporations. Bequai provides the following examples of this type of activity:[19] (1) a New England businessman who
avoided taxes by simply not reporting more than $1 million in in-
come, (2) a physician who evaded more than $60,000 in taxes by
maintaining a double set of books, and (3) a New York physician who
evaded more than $30,000 in taxes.[20]

The Detroit study contains the following example of the way in
which unreported professional income is earned.[21]

Ray Ballenger is employed as an advanced auto design engineer for
a major automobile manufacturer. He creates and builds prototypes
for future production. In addition, he is self-employed as a trouble-

*shooter and design mechanic for specialized racing cars. His com-
bined annual income from both jobs is between $75,000 and $100,000
per year. Most of his income from self-employment is irregular in that
he deals primarily in cash and reports only a small fraction for tax
purposes. His irregular activities are not only lucrative but they allow
him a further outlet for his creativity in technical tasks and automobile design. (p. 3.11)*

As would be expected because of the study area, the Detroit
study provides many more examples of the way in which working
class individuals earn self-employment income.

*Dave Samules started working in a steel mill after he got out of the
Navy seven years ago. He earned his high school diploma through
night school, obtained a certificate in refrigeration, and has finished
two years of predentistry with an Associate's degree. In order to pay
for his schooling (he hopes to some day finish a dental degree), he does
roofing in the summer and tiling, carpentry, and minor plumbing in
the winter for people in the neighborhood. His prices are low and he
is paid in cash. Dave is about 35 and has several children, and people
in the neighborhood are proud to help support him in his ambitions
by using his irregular services. He loves the freedom of working
alone, the outdoors, and working with his hands and his tools; and
through the irregular economy, he "can make a decent buck doing it
too." (p. 3.10)*

*Dora French is a licensed beautician who works in a regular beauty
salon three days a week but there is very little business for her there.
She is 23 and lives with her parents, and her father fixed up the
basement as a beauty shop so that she can work for "clear money."
She works primarily for relatives, friends, and neighbors, and often
goes to peoples' homes to do their hair. (p. 3.11)*

*Mr. Thomas is typical of such a worker. His financial situation is
comfortable, with nearly 30 years of employment in the same motor
car company. Not only does he earn a sizeable regular income but his
wife also holds a job. Yet through the years, Mr. Thomas has operated
a vegetable truck and has peddled vegetables and fruits on streets
throughout Detroit, on weekends, during the summer, and whenever
he was laid off. From money earned this way, unreported, he was able
to remodel and pay for a new home, pay for a college education for a
child, buy new cars, and so forth. His combined income from both
regular and irregular sources was well over $45,000 a year. When
Mr. Thomas reached his late forties and he no longer felt he needed
the extra income, he stopped this irregular peddling. (p. 3.11)*

*Sam Russ is 62 years old, married, with eight grown children and
several grandchildren. He has been employed for the past 13 years as
a night janitor at a local recreation center. For the past three years,*

Sam has operated a small ceramics supply center out of his home. He designs and manufactures greenware, bisque, and finishes pieces in his basement, making molds from toys he purchases at garage sales and from pieces manufactured in the regular economy. He also fires pieces in his home for a fee. None of the income from the ceramics activities is reported. Sam's interest in ceramics began as a hobby, stemming in part from his work at the recreation center where ceramics courses are taught. Sam has always needed more than one job in order to support his eight children and states that if they were still young he could not live off his income as a janitor. This is not the first hobby he has transformed into an income-gathering activity. Formerly he dabbled in photography and furniture making. Sam suspects that in a few years his interest will wane and he will drop ceramics and take up something else. He says he would only engage in pastimes that sell enough to pay for themselves but that he wouldn't do it unless it were also fun. (p. 3.12)

Income of the Self-Employed Who Do Not File

The self-employed who fail to file tax returns entirely, like wage and salary nonfilers, appear to be concentrated among service workers, crafts people, and professional people. IRS believes that no more than one third of self-employed nonfilers are in regular businesses and occupations because fixed business operations give too much exposure to the IRS to make it safe to entirely fail to file tax returns. One suspects that those who are in regular businesses run very small operations, often out of their own homes with clients coming by "word of mouth." GAO results indicate that nonfiling by the self-employed is most common in agriculture, construction, transportation, wholesale and retail trade, and nonprofessional services. Self-employed sales workers, operatives, laborers, and service workers were most likely to fail to file tax returns, although 11 percent of professional and technical workers and 12 percent of managers and administrators were also estimated to have failed to file.[22]

Judging from GAO results, individuals whose marriages are not intact are more likely not to file than those who are single or have intact marriages. One suspects, but cannot prove, that many of the self-employed who are failing to file are women, mainly with children, who receive various types of public and private benefits and who run small, part-time businesses out of their homes. The Detroit study provides the following examples of this type of activity.[23]

Mary Jane Folkers is 28 and has two children in elementary school. She has been divorced for five years after marrying at the age of 17.

Mary Jane is a high school dropout but operates a full time irregular interior decorating business out of her home. She had never regarded her skill as a seamstress as a potential income source until a neighbor asked her to make a slipcover for her sofa. The neighbor was so pleased with her work that she then requested Mary Jane to make drapes as well. The business developed gradually as word spread and people began to consult her about colors and choice of fabrics as well as her sewing. Today she is doing "quite well" and has hired a friend to assist with the sewing. She says she eventually plans to open a regular shop but is not anxious to do so at the moment since she would then lose her eligibility for AFDC. (p. 3.23)

Mrs. West is 33 years old, married, and has a 13-year-old daughter. Her husband is employed as an automobile worker, earning about $12,000 a year. She supplements the family income by caring for two children in her home. She earns about $1,000–1,500 a year, tax free. Mrs. West has been babysitting in her home for eight years, and before that time worked regularly at a baby nursery. She says her activities allow her to bring in an income while remaining at home and caring for her daughter. (p. 3.30)

Mrs. Mel is married with two teenage sons. She has been a licensed cosmetician for 15 years. For the past five years she has run a beauty shop in her home. She has worked in a regular beauty parlor but prefers to work at home because her income is untaxed and she does not have to pay rent or other business expenses. Mrs. Mel believes that she realizes a greater profit through irregular work than she could if her business were regular. Her husband earns enough to support the family but she uses her income to provide the family with "extras" such as special clothes, new furniture, and vacations. She enjoys her work and the flexibility of hours it affords. (p. 3.30)

A recent article describes typical types of self-employment available in the "irregular economy" of the ghetto areas of our large cities. The following is an example of the type of transactions that take place in this economy.[24]

Will told David about a 1966 Chevy Impala which he had noticed was for sale at a local gas station. Although the automobile's exterior was in relatively good shape, the engine was in poor condition. The station owner, a southern white who was not an acquaintance of David's, sold him the car for $50. David then removed the engine from the car, working first alone and then with Jimmy's help. Hank was also present though his assistance was not needed. The actual work was accomplished in 3 hours, though several hours were passed as the three men drank beer and conversed.

The engine was eventually sold as junk for $8 at a nearby junk yard. Will sold the engine for David and returned the $8 to him. David then

bought a used Chevy engine for $80 through an advertisement in
Tradin' Times, a local trade journal. In order to make the purchase
he borrowed $50 from Jenny. David worked alone for two days on the
installation and tuning of the "new" engine. However, after that time
its performance had still not met with his satisfaction. He asked
Pete to come over and take a look, and together they worked another
day on the car. It was necessary for David to use several of Pete's tools
in order to finish the work.

The fifth and final day of labor David worked alone mending seat
covers, cleaning the interior, and washing and polishing the exterior
of the car. He then placed an advertisement in Tradin' Times *asking*
$400 for the car. There had been no response to the ad when a week
later the car was sold to a Puerto Rican neighbor who had heard
about the car through a Mexican-American friend of Jenny's. The
negotiated price of the car was $350. (p. 123)

In this study David and Pete are listed as auto repair workers and
Will is listed as a junk dealer in the "irregular economy." None of
the three have jobs in the regular economy and one suspects that
they do not file tax returns. The Detroit study provides the following additional examples of how likely nonfilers earn income through
self-employment.[25]

Don Parsons is retired at the age of 66 from a job as an upholsterer for
an automotive corporation which he held for 37 years. Both he and
his wife held steady jobs from which they made $20,000 a year before
their retirement and they have no children. They both receive pen-
sions and social security and are well fixed financially. Before he
retired he did carpentry and home improvement tasks for himself and
a few friends, but was not involved in irregular activities. After he
retired, however, he had a lot of spare time for doing these things and
he knew several people who could use his skills. He restricts his work
to general home repair such as carpentry and painting and prefers
small jobs of short duration. He only likes to work three or four hours
a day and he has to turn down half of the jobs he is offered. He
attributes his success to three factors: (1) he is very skilled; (2) his
prices are very low; and (3) he does small jobs that bigger companies
don't want to do. Economically he is not faced with the need to work
and his only reasons for doing so are because he enjoys it, it keeps him
busy and "out of his wife's hair." (p. 3.25)

Jimmy Jones is 34 years old, married, and has two very young chil-
dren. Three years ago he developed a work-related kidney problem
and was forced to leave his job with an automobile manufacturer. His
wife works full time as a clerical and Jimmy cares for the children.
He receives disability payments of about $100 a week. Since he
was forced to quit his job, Jimmy has dedicated himself to being

> an all-around "fixit" man. He buys, repairs, and resells just about anything mechanical that he can get his hands on—air conditioners, washing machines, dishwashers, radios, television sets, and, especially, automobiles. He earns about $100 a week from these activities. Although Jimmy has repair facilities in a garage behind his home, his disability precludes long hours of steady exertion. However, irregular work allows him to supplement the family income and to keep busy, at a pace he can handle. (p. 3.27)

Dividend and Interest Income

As can be seen in Table 1-1, the proportion of dividend and interest income which is not reported is not particularly high. However, both IRS and Department of Commerce research seems to indicate that the rate of noncompliance in the reporting of interest income has risen markedly in recent years.[26, 27] One suspects that reporting of both dividend and interest income will increase markedly as IRS develops its Income Information Document Matching Program. This program attempts to match, among other things, payor reports of dividend and interest payments against the returns of individual filers. (Owens provides a discussion of this program,[28] and the report of a House of Representatives hearing provides a discussion of current efforts and results.[29]) Processing of these "information documents" has increased markedly in recent years as has the percentage of matches with returns. Forty percent of information documents received in 1974 were processed and 35 percent matched. Eighty percent of such documents were processed in 1978 and 74 percent matched.[30] However, a 1969 study estimated that 32 percent of all payors were delinquent in filing form 1099 (the form on which dividends and interest, as well as other income, is reported).[31] Improvements in the use and matching of information documents, together with passage of the Department of the Treasury's proposal to increase penalties for failure to file form 1099, should greatly increase compliance in reporting dividends and interest income. However, there are certain types of interest income receipts that even perfection of the Information Returns program will not capture: (1) interest earned on "bearer" securities, and (2) interest on informal loans between private individuals. (We use IRS's definition of bearer securities, which includes unregistered debt instruments covered by book entry systems where ownership is denoted on a hierarchy of records by issuing and distributing agencies.) IRS estimated that at year end 1977, the household sector owned $118 billion worth of bearer securities and earned $8 billion in interest on these securities during 1977.[32] Interestingly, both the largest holdings of and largest earnings on bearer assets were U.S. Treasury securities. In 1979, IRS explored the feasibility of a program for reporting interest paid on corporate bearer and government obligations.[33] As far as we are aware, a program has yet to be implemented.

IRS also believes that substantial dividend and interest income is not reported or misreported through the use of tax havens and tax shelters. IRS conducted a large-scale investigation of the use of tax havens in the late 1970s and early 1980s, but results have not yet been published as far as we are aware.

While underreporting of dividends and interest income of the type discussed above seems to be amenable to IRS action, underreporting of interest payments on informal loans between private individuals is largely beyond the reach of normal IRS efforts. IRS estimated interest income on these types of loans to be $0.3 billion in 1976.[34]

As is reflected in the figures of Table 1-1, rental income tends to be less completely reported than any other types of income, with only 50 to 65 percent of rental income estimated to have been reported to IRS in 1976. We know little about the nature of this underreporting in recent years, but an older study by Groves[35] provides some interesting insights. Groves found that rental income was relatively completely reported (estimated 86 percent) for multiple-unit rental buildings, but was much less completely reported for rooms (estimated 68 percent), single units (estimated 65 percent), sublet lodgings (estimated 30 percent), and garages (estimated 39 percent). Groves's results seem to indicate that those who reported any rental income tended to do so quite accurately. It was those who filed but reported no rental income, and those who failed to file, that accounted for the bulk of rental income that was not reported in his study. As a whole, Groves's work seems to indicate that it is mainly the owners of single rental units or those who rent a portion of their own homes who fail to report their rental income. The Detroit study discussed above provides two examples of situations in which such rental income is earned.[36]

Connie Brant lives alone at the age of 77, a widow of her first husband and divorced from her second. Her daughter lives ten miles away in the suburbs and her son is dead. Her daughter visits occasionally when she is in town for major shopping and doctor's appointments and

Connie visits her on holidays and birthdays. She suffers from severe arthritis which has gotten much worse in the last few years and this has severely circumscribed her activities. She is fiercely protective of her independence and is fighting to retain her home, which is paid for in full. She lives off her social security check and money from roomers. In addition to renting out rooms for about $20 a week, she rents her garage for $7 a month, and in very tight times she has sold various household antiques from her grandmother. (p. 3.24)

Mrs. Scruth is 53 years old, divorced, unemployed, and ill. She is receiving AFDC and public assistance. She is physically unable to care for her home, and a housekeeper is provided once a week through a social service agency. She has housed at least two roomers over the last five years. They are charged monthly rent for room and board and the income is not reported for tax purposes. Mrs. Scruth requires her tenants to pay their rent promptly as this income is vital to her. (p. 3.21)

Costs and Benefits of Tax Evasion

Economists have been actively building models that detail the costs and benefits of tax evasion to the taxpayer.* Most of these models define the costs and benefits involved quite narrowly. According to these models, the benefit to the taxpayer who successfully avoids taxes is the increase in personal wealth. The cost to the taxpayer who fails is the penalty imposed. Other economists have recently suggested that one must consider the moral and ethical position of the taxpayers as well as the monetary gains and losses involved.† This suggestion seems particularly relevant in light of the finding of Schwartz and Orleans.[37] These authors, in cooperation with the IRS, were allowed to conduct an experiment to determine which was more effective in improving tax compliance, sanctions or moral appeals. The results of the experiment indicate that moral appeals may be more effective than sanction threats in obtaining tax compliance.

A second line of research, simulation studies,‡ provides further interesting insights into the way in which individuals react to different tax strategies. A recent study found that "the fraction of earned income reported becomes very elastic with respect to the tax

---

* For examples, see Endnotes 50 through 54.
† For examples, see Endnotes 40, 55, and 56.
‡ For examples, see Endnotes 57 and 58.

rate."[38] In other words, as tax rates become higher and higher, the fraction of income unreported increases even more quickly. Furthermore, these researchers found that large fines tend to be more effective deterrents than frequent audits. This is contrary to IRS's beliefs: "IRS considers the audit of returns to be the greatest stimulus to voluntary compliance."[39] Finally, this study found that the determinants of the decision to underreport and the actual amount of underreporting are quite different and that personal characteristics are important in both decisions. This latter conclusion is further supported by preliminary IRS research and by sample surveys. In the most recent survey finding for the United States, Spicer and Lundstedt found that perceptions of inequity, the number of tax evaders known personally, and a previous audit experience tended to *increase* tax evasion. This finding is quite startling. Spicer and Lundstedt hypothesize that this may be the result of a negative reaction to the audit experience.[40] Strümpel has also noted that stringent assessment may lower compliance and willingness to cooperate.[41] This seems to contradict the results of a GAO survey which indicated that 70 percent of the audited taxpayers surveyed reacted favorably to their audit experience.[42] IRS research seems to indicate that audits do have a positive effect on future compliance for lower income groups although most positive effects appear to dissipate by two years after the audit. For higher income classes, IRS concluded that their "model was too simplified and required further refinement."[43] At the least, this points up the need for additional research on the determinants of the extent and amount of tax avoidance. This is also a recommendation of a GAO study of IRS.[44] In 1978, the Internal Revenue Service requested proposals for the development of methods to determine the relative impact of factors, both within and outside IRS control, on compliance with individual income tax laws. The contractor that was selected, Westat, Inc., suggested that IRS conduct a series of experimental studies to determine the effect of various types of IRS actions on individual compliance.* As far as we are aware, IRS at the time of this writing has no plans to conduct these studies.

A relatively recent development with major tax evasion possibilities is the large-scale reintroduction of barter in the United States. Barter, which goes under the formal name of "the reciprocal trade

---

* See Endnote 59. Westat, Inc. (Endnote 60) also developed a statistical design to estimate taxpayer response to IRS audit coverage.

business," facilitates the exchange of large quantities of goods and services between businesses and individuals. The size of this sector is difficult to determine, but *Purchasing World,* a trade publication, estimates that 48 percent of purchasing agents in the United States engage in some form of barter. The service sector is the major user of reciprocal trade services although manufacturers are increasingly using this sector for stock liquidation purposes. Barter and other noncash trading agreements are used extensively in trade with Eastern European and Third World countries.* The self-proclaimed largest firm in this new and growing industry is Atwood Richards, Inc., which estimates that it handled over $100 million worth of goods and services during fiscal year 1976–1977. While large firms such as Atwood Richards undoubtedly pay all taxes due, the growth of the industry and participation of individuals as well as firms in the business make one suspicious that one of the attractions of this area is the ease with which such transactions can be kept from the eyes of prying tax agents. IRS conducted a study involving a random audit of barter exchange members in the Los Angeles area in the late 1970s and early 1980s. Preliminary results indicate that returns with bartering transactions were approximately twice as likely to require tax changes as were returns without such transactions. In addition, the percentage of individuals with bartering transactions whose returns required tax changes increased from 62 percent in 1976 to 74 percent in 1977.[45] While the emergence and growth of this sector is cause for concern, we believe that at present barter transactions account for less than 1 percent of tax evasion. Thus, we estimate (or perhaps better stated, guess) that as much as $1 billion of income from barter transactions may have escaped taxation in 1974.

The benefits to the taxpayer of avoiding taxes vary directly with the tax rates applicable on the income. The increasing progressivity of tax rates coupled with the movement of families into higher marginal tax rate brackets as a result of inflation has undoubtedly increased incentives for tax evasion for many individuals. As mentioned above, research seems to indicate that the rate of tax avoidance rises at an increasing rate with the overall tax rate. This provides an additional argument against very high tax rates. Not only do they decrease the incentive to work and thus the GNP (the Laffer curve), but they also may lead to rapid decline in tax compliance rates.

---

* See Endnote 61 for a discussion.

A study of the Belgian situation seems to indicate that tax evasion may also serve to alter income distribution.[46] This study found that the lowest and highest income classes benefit most from tax evasion. This is consistent with what we know about tax evasion in the United States and may be a further factor firing revolt and discontent among middle-income taxpayers.

The cost of tax evasion to the government is the loss of revenue plus the cost of compliance programs. The revenue loss to the federal government depends upon the amount of income on which taxes are evaded and the applicable tax rate. IRS estimates that individual underreporting and failure to report legal income resulted in a $13 to $17 billion income tax revenue loss in 1976.[47] In addition, we estimate that the failure to accurately and completely report corporate profits resulted in a further federal tax loss of around $5 billion in that year. Thus, the total federal tax loss from all failures to report appears to have been between $18 and $22 billion in 1976. Compliance costs added approximately $1 billion to this cost. Thus costs to the federal government of income tax evasion and other failures to report were probably around $20 billion in 1976, an amount which is approximately equal to the federal budget deficit in 1974. To look at it slightly differently, the federal government could have paid all veterans benefits and service costs in 1976 with these funds had they been collected. Other levels of government with income and profit taxes also lost substantial revenue, although it would be difficult to estimate the size of this loss.

The social costs of tax evasion are far larger and much more difficult to judge. As a result of tax evasion, taxpaying citizens must either pay higher taxes or forego the public services that would otherwise be available. Assuming that tax evaders are just as much members of "society" as those who comply with tax laws, this is not a social cost, but only a transfer. Tax evasion does generate efficiency loss, but this loss comes through effects on work incentives, the cost of compliance programs, the cost of evasion itself, and, most importantly, the effect on social mores. As the President's Commission expressed it, tax evasion affects the "moral climate of our society."[48] The extensive tax evasion in some European countries (such as France and Italy) further warns us that public attitudes toward taxes are extremely important.

Endnotes

1. U.S. House of Representatives, Subcommittee on Oversight, Committee on Ways and Means. 1980. *Hearings on the Underground Economy.* Washington, D.C.: U.S. Government Printing Office, p. 253.
2. U.S. Department of Health, Education and Welfare, Social and Rehabilitation Service. 1975. *Quality Control in AFDC: National Findings, January-June 1974 Reporting Period.* Washington, D.C.: SRS Regional Commissioners, p. 23.
3. Lehman, S. C. 1976. "Relationship Between Personal Income and Taxable Income, 1947–74," *Survey of Current Business* 56 (December), 17–19:27.
4. Park, Thae. 1978. "Reconciliation of BEA Personal Income with SOI-AGI," Working Paper Government Division, Bureau of Economic Analysis, U.S. Department of Commerce.
5. U.S. Department of the Treasury, Internal Revenue Service. 1979. *Estimates of Income Unreported on Individual Income Tax Returns.* Washington, D.C.: Department of the Treasury, Publication 1104.
6. U.S. Department of the Treasury, Internal Revenue Service. 1978. "IRS Work Statement for the Factor Study," request for proposal for a study of the factors affecting tax compliance.
7. Westat, Inc. 1980. "Self-Reported Tax Compliance: A Pilot Survey Report." Unpublished report to the Internal Revenue Service by Westat on Contract No. TIR-78-50.
8. Comptroller General of the United States. 1979. *Who's Not Filing Income Tax Returns?: IRS Needs Better Ways to Find Them and Collect Their Taxes.* Washington, D.C.: General Accounting Office.
9. U.S. Department of the Treasury, Internal Revenue Service. 1979. *Estimates of Income Unreported on Individual Income Tax Returns.* Washington, D.C.: U.S. Department of the Treasury, Publication 1104 (9-79).
10. Dow, Leslie M., Jr. 1977. "High Weeds in Detroit: The Irregular Economy Among a Network of Appalachian Migrants," *Urban Anthropology* 6(2):111–128.
11. Ferman, Louis A., Louise Berndt, and Elaine Selo. 1978. "Analysis of the Irregular Economy: Cash Flow in the Informal Sector," report to the Bureau of Employment and Training, Michigan Department of Labor.
12. U.S. Department of the Treasury, *Estimates.*
13. *Ibid.*, p. 129.
14. Ferman et al., "Analysis of the Irregular Economy."
15. U.S. Department of the Treasury, *Estimates.*
16. Comptroller General of the United States, *Who's Not Filing Income Tax Returns?*
17. *Ibid.*, p. 8.
18. Ferman et al., "Analysis of the Irregular Economy."
19. Bequai, A. 1978. *White-Collar Crime: A 20th-Century Crisis.* Lexington, Mass.: Lexington Books.
20. *Ibid.*, pp. 123–124.
21. Ferman et al., "Analysis of the Irregular Economy."

22. Comptroller General of the United States, *Who's Not Filing Income Tax Returns?*, p. 109.
23. Ferman et al., "Analysis of the Irregular Economy."
24. Dow, "High Weeds in Detroit," p. 123.
25. Ferman et al., "Analysis of the Irregular Economy."
26. Lehman, "Relationship Between Personal and Taxable Income."
27. Park, "Reconciliation of BEA Income."
28. Owens, J. I. 1978. "The IRS Information Returns Program," *The Tax Adviser* 9 (June):359–362.
29. U.S. House of Representatives, *Hearings on the Underground Economy*, pp. 49–51.
30. *Ibid.*, p. 49.
31. *Ibid.*, p. 50.
32. U.S. Department of the Treasury, *Estimates*, p. 90.
33. *Ibid.*, p. iv.
34. *Ibid.*, p. 125.
35. Groves, H. M. 1958. "Empirical Studies of Income Tax Compliance," *National Tax Journal* 11 (December):291–301.
36. Ferman et al., "Analysis of the Irregular Economy."
37. Schwartz, R. D., and S. Orleans. 1967. "On Legal Sanctions," *University of Chicago Law Review* 34 (Winter):274–300.
38. Friedland, N., S. Maital, and A. Rutenberg. 1978. "A Simulation Study of Income Tax Evasion," *Journal of Public Economics* 10 (August):107–116.
39. Comptroller General of the United States. 1976. *How the Internal Revenue Service Selects Individual Income Tax Returns for Audit*. Report to the Joint Committee on Internal Revenue Taxation. Washington, D.C.: General Accounting Office, p. 20.
40. Spicer, M. W., and S. B. Lundstedt. 1976. "Understanding Tax Evasion," *Public Finance/Finances Publiques* 31(2):295–305.
41. Strümpel, B. 1969. "Contribution of Survey Research," in A. Peacock (ed.), *Quantitative Analysis in Public Finance*. New York: Praeger, pp. 29–32.
42. Comptroller General of the United States. 1976. *Audit of Individual Income Tax Returns by the Internal Revenue Service*, report to the Joint Committee on Internal Revenue Taxation. Washington, D.C.: General Accounting Office.
43. U.S. Department of the Treasury. "IRS Work Statement," Attachment B, p. 23.
44. Comptroller General of United States, "How IRS Selects Individual Returns for Audit," p. 56.
45. U.S. House of Representatives, *Hearings on the Underground Economy*, p. 120.
46. Frank, Max, and Daniele DeKeyser-Meulders. 1977. "A Tax Discrepancy Coefficient Resulting from Tax Evasion or Tax Expenditures," *Journal of Public Economics* 8 (July-Aug.):67–78.
47. U.S. Department of the Treasury, *Estimates*.
48. President's Commission on Law Enforcement and Administration of Justice. 1967. *Task Force Report: Crime and Its Impact—An Assessment*. Washington, D.C.: U.S. Government Printing Office, p. 104.
49. Tullock, G. 1971. *The Logic of the Law*. New York: Basic Books.

50. Allingham, M. G., and A. Sandmo. 1972. "Income Tax Evasion: A Theoretical Analysis," *Journal of Public Economics* 1 (November):323–338.

51. Kolm, S. C. 1973. "A Note on Optimum Tax Evasion," *Journal of Public Economics* 2 (July):265–270.

52. Singh, B. 1973. "Making Honesty the Best Policy," *Journal of Public Economics* 2 (July):257–263.

53. Yitzchaki, S. 1974. "A Note on Income Tax Evasion: A Theoretical Analysis," *Journal of Public Economics* 3 (May):201–202.

54. McCaleb, T. S. 1976. "Tax Evasion and the Differential Taxation of Labor and Capital Income," *Public Finance* 31(2):287–294.

55. Block, M. K., and J. M. Heineke. 1975. "A Labor Theoretic Analysis of the Criminal Choice," *American Economic Review* 65 (June):314–325.

56. Witte, A. D. 1980. "Estimating the Economic Model of Crime with Individual Data," *Quarterly Journal of Economics* 94 (February):57–84.

57. Friedland, N. J., J. Thibault, and L. Walker. 1973. "Some Determinants of the Violation of Rules," *Journal of Applied Social Psychology* 2:265–270.

58. Thibault, J., N. Friedland, and L. Walker. 1974. "Compliance with Rules: Some Social Determinants," *Journal of Personality and Social Psychology* 30:792–801.

59. Westat, Inc. 1980. "A Research Design for the Study of Individual Income Tax Compliance," report submitted to the Internal Revenue Service.

60. Westat, Inc. 1980. "A Procedure for Estimating Taxpayer Response to Changes in IRS Audit Coverage," report submitted to the Internal Revenue Service.

61. Weigand, Robert E. 1977. "Special Report: Barter Arrangements Can Overcome Barriers to Deals with Eastern Europe and the Third World," *Harvard Business Review* 55 (November/December):28–30, 34, 38, 42, 166.

Appendix

ESTIMATING INCOME UNREPORTED TO THE INTERNAL REVENUE SERVICE

Table A1-1 contains IRS estimates of "factor income" unreported by individuals *who filed tax returns* in 1965, 1969, and 1973. These estimates were derived from IRS's Tax Compliance Measurement Program (TCMP) results. By "factor income" we mean income derived from the provision of the services of factors of production (land, labor, capital). This is the only income that enters reported national income and which we will enter in our estimates of underground national income to ensure comparability. Such income specifically excludes transfers, such as alimony, tax refunds, and income from asset sales (a stock) such as personal capital gains. It also excludes income from most nonmarket production, such as housework of a wife or husband.

IRS established the Tax Compliance Measurement Program in 1962 when it began to place increased emphasis on measuring taxpayer compliance. The United States Department of the Treasury provides an extended discussion of the TCMP program,[1] and the 1979 IRS report provides a shorter description.[2] In a recent report, Susan Long provides both a description and an evaluation of the program.[3] Since 1962 twenty TCMP studies have been conducted covering different tax areas (phases) and tax years (cycles). Long provides a list of these studies,[4] which cover timely payment of taxes (Phase I), return filing requirement (Phase II), and correct reporting of tax liability on filed returns (Phases III-VII). For present purposes, we are concerned only with the correct reporting of liabilities on individual (Phase III) and corporate (Phase IV) returns.

Table A1-1   TCMP Estimates of Underreporting of Income by Type

	Income Underreported ($ millions)			Percent Increase	
Type	1965	1969	1973	1965–1969	1969–1973
Wages and salaries	1,683.0	1,954.8	2,891.0	16.1	47.9
Dividends	369.7	544.6	908.0	47.3	66.7
Interest	264.6	471.7	917.3	78.3	94.5
Nonfarm business income	4,001.3	7,131.0	9,805.8	78.2	37.5
Farm business income	1,352.3	2,071.6	3,353.5	53.2	61.9
Rents	867.4	1,235.6	2,102.2	42.4	70.1
Royalties	62.2	62.1	85.2	0.0	37.2
Partnership income	1,081.5	1,460.8	2,060.3	66.1[a]	45.6[a]
Estate and trust income	25.2	82.4	152.5	327.0	85.1
Small business corporation income	N.A.[b]	335.5	555.6	N.A.	65.6
Other[c]	286.9	344.6	405.0	20.1	17.5
Total	9,994.1	15,694.7	23,236.4	51.0	48.1

SOURCE: TCMP Phase III, Cycles 2, 3 and 5. This data was supplied to the Subcommittee on Oversight in the House Ways and Means Committee by IRS and was kindly made available to us by Robert Cozart, a staff attorney for that Subcommittee.

[a] Rate of change is for Partnership Income and Small Business Corporation Income.
[b] N.A. indicates that an item was not available. This particular item was included in Partnership Income for this year.
[c] The figures given for this category assume that 75 percent of the income classified as "other" is transfer payments. See Endnote 2, p. 7, footnote 6.

Currently, estimates of underreported factor income on individual returns are available for 1963, 1965, 1969, and 1973. Results for tax year 1976 are being processed and should be available in the fall of 1981. These estimates are based on an intensive audit of a relatively small (50,000 returns in 1976) random sample (stratified, cluster design) of returns filed. As Long has pointed out, this method is subject to a number of difficulties: (1) only items detectable in a thorough audit will be uncovered, and what is detected will vary with the skill of the auditor and the thoroughness of the audits; (2) accuracy and quality control of audits, although improving over time, is not all that would be desired; and (3) TCMP results report only auditors' findings, not findings that will ultimately result after taxpayer appeal. In spite of the weaknesses of TCMP results, they still provide us with the most reliable data available on certain types of income underreporting. Comparing TCMP estimates of underreported factor income for 1965, 1969, and 1973 (see Table A1-1), one notes rapid growth in estimated unreported income during this period. Indeed, the percentage increase for underreported factor income exceeded the percentage increase for reported personal income by 15 percent in the 1965 to 1969 period and by 5 percent from 1969 to 1973. These estimates support the claims that this sector of the underground economy has been growing rapidly in recent years and is increasing even relative to reported economic activity. During 1969 to 1973, the rate of increase in underreported income was greatest for interest and estate and trust income. Perhaps most disturbing was the marked increase in unreported wage and salary income during this period. It is interesting to note that the rate of growth of the estimated underreported income slowed down in the early 1970s.

The comparisons reported in the previous paragraph should be viewed with considerable caution. The increase in income underreporting noted may well be the result of the increased thoroughness of TCMP audits rather than increased underreporting. Between 1963 and 1973, the average length of a TCMP audit doubled.[5]

In its 1979 report, the Internal Revenue Service noted that a small portion ("guesstimated" to be 5 percent for wages and salaries and 1 percent for self-employment income) of unreported wage and salary and self-employment income uncovered by TCMP comes from illegal sources.[6] To avoid double counting when adding estimates from the various parts of this book, we exclude this proportion of underreporting from TCMP estimates to obtain our estimate of wage and salary and self-employment underreporting for 1973: $2.7 billion for wages and salaries and $15.1 billion for self-employment income (that is, income from farm and nonfarm business and partnerships).

The TCMP unreported income estimates cited above substantially underestimate the actual amount of unreported individual income for a number of reasons. First, IRS acknowledges that TCMP fails to capture much cash-wage and self-employment income such as income from moonlighting, tip income, and wage of household, agricultural and "off the books" workers. Second, TCMP does not capture the income of those who fail to file.

In its 1979 report, IRS estimated that TCMP results failed to capture between $5 and $7.4 billion of wages and salaries that were underreported and $3.5 to $8.8 billion of underreported self-employment income in 1976.[7] Both the IRS and the General

Accounting Office have obtained estimates of the amount of income earned by those who do not file federal income tax returns. To do this they used primarily the 1973 Exact Match file developed by the Social Security Administration and the Bureau of the Census. This file merges data from the Current Population Survey, Social Security files, and the IRS Master File for approximately 100,000 persons aged 14 or older. Kilss and Scheuren discuss the process of linking data, and the strengths and weaknesses in the resultant data files.[8] In its report, issued in July of 1979, the GAO estimated that of the 68 million required to file, about 5 million people, with taxable incomes of $26 to $35 billion, did not file returns in tax year 1972.[9] Most of these nonfilers earned low incomes with 52 percent of the total nonfiler population making less than $5,000. However, many high-income self-employed managers, administrators, and crafts persons also failed to file. IRS made a number of adjustments to GAO's work, particularly in the way in which the incomes of nonfilers and the taxes lost were calculated. IRS results indicate that between $30 and $37 billion worth of factor income should have been reported by delinquent nonfilers in 1972. However, IRS estimates that $6.4 billion of this income was later reported by late filers and that approximately $12 billion of this income was subject to withholding. Thus, IRS's techniques would estimate that only $15 to $17 billion of nonfiler factor income was actually unreported in 1972.

IRS believes that estimates of income earned by nonfilers obtained using the Exact Match file must be supplemented by estimates of nonfiler income earned from unreported cash wages and self-employment income. For 1976, they estimate this income to have been between $5 and $12 billion.

To obtain an estimate of the total amount of factor income that was not reported to IRS in 1974, the year we are attempting to estimate total underground national income, we must: (1) move forward to 1974 appropriately adjusted 1973 TCMP figures for unreported income of filers and 1972 Exact Match file estimates of income of nonfilers; and (2) move backward to 1974 the 1976 IRS figures for unreported income not captured by either TCMP or Exact Match file estimates. We do this by assuming the same growth factor (generally based on statistics of income growth for the line item and the year under consideration) for each line item, as does IRS. Table A1-2 reports our results. We estimate that between $50 and $75 billion worth of 1974 individual factor income was not reported and forms part of the underground economy in that year.

Table A1-2 Estimated Factor Income Unreported to IRS in 1974 ($ billions)

| Type of Income | Underreported by Filers | | Not Reported by Nonfilers | | Total |
	TCMP	Other Sources	Exact Match	Other Sources	
Wages and salaries	$3.0	$4.2–6.1	$4.4–5.0	$2.1–2.7	$13.7–16.8[a]
Self-employment income	16.6	2.9–7.3	6.0–7.0	2.1–7.0	27.6–37.9
Dividends	1.0		0.5		1.5–3.9
Interest	1.0	1.3	1.6		3.9–6.9
Rents and royalties	2.3		0.5		2.7–5.3
Estate and trust income	0.2		0.1		0.3
Small business corporation income	0.6				0.6
Other	0.4				0.4
Total					$50.7–$72.1

[a] Our estimates of wage and salary underreporting is lower than IRS's—even considering the difference in years—because we do not include income unreported by illegal aliens, but estimate this income separately in Chapter 3.

Note that our estimate is for individuals and a few small corporations and does not include the underreporting of most small corporations or any large ones. Theoretically, one could obtain such estimates by using large corporate audit results, but as far as we are aware this has not been done. IRS is currently trying to improve its estimates of the amount of income underreporting by corporations. Fortunately, the Bureau of Economic Analysis has estimated underreporting of this type of income using national income accounting and other data.[10] The Bureau estimates that $6 billion of such income was underreported in 1974 and $11.6 billion in 1976.

Incorporating all of the preceding information, we estimate that the national income of this sector of the underground economy was between $60 and $80 billion in 1974. Note that in obtaining our estimate we rely heavily upon IRS's 1979 report. The methods used by IRS are not definitive and have been subject to a number of criticisms. (See U.S. House of Representatives' *Hearings on the Underground Economy.*[11]) However, this criticism has been most stringent concerning areas omitted by IRS and IRS estimates of incomes in the illegal sector, not IRS estimates of unreported legal incomes. We feel that it is only prudent to rely heavily on IRS for estimates of income unreported to the taxing authorities as IRS has access to much relevant information and technical knowledge that would not be available to an independent researcher.

Endnotes

1. U.S. Department of the Treasury, Internal Revenue Service, Office of the Assistant Commissioner. 1977. *Tax Compliance Measurement Program Handbook*. Washington, D.C.: Department of the Treasury, Document 6451 (9–77).
2. U.S. Department of the Treasury, Internal Revenue Service. 1979. *Estimates of Income Unreported on Individual Income Tax Returns*. Washington, D.C.: U.S. Department of the Treasury, Publication 1104, Appendix C, pp. 54–57.
3. Long, Susan B. 1981. "The Internal Revenue Service: Measuring Tax Offense and Enforcement Response." Washington, D.C.: Bureau of Social Science Research.
4. *Ibid.*, pp. 56–57.
5. *Ibid.*
6. U.S. Department of the Treasury, *Estimates*.
7. *Ibid.*
8. Kilss, B., and F. Scheuren. 1978. "The 1973 CPS-IRS-SSA Exact Match Study: Past, Present, and Future," paper presented at the Social Security Administration Workshop on Policy Analysis and Social Security Research Files, March 15–17, Williamsburg, Va.
9. Comptroller General of the United States. 1979. *Who's Not Filing Income Tax Returns?: IRS Needs Better Ways to Find Them and Collect Their Taxes*. Washington, D.C.: General Accounting Office.
10. Parker, Robert. 1980. "Audit Profits," working draft, Bureau of Economic Analysis, U.S. Department of Commerce.
11. U.S. House of Representatives, Subcommittee on Oversight, Committee on Ways and Means. 1980. *Hearings on the Underground Economy*. Washington, D.C.: U.S. Government Printing Office, pp. 136–148, 261–265.

Chapter 2

UNREPORTED INCOME GAINED BY EVADING EXCISE TAXES

Size and Trends

In this chapter, as in the previous one, we are not so much interested in tax evasion per se, but rather in the incomes earned by those who evade excise taxes on goods. An excise tax is a tax levied on specific goods or services sold in the taxing jurisdiction. The tax may be levied directly on the manufacturer, wholesaler, retailer, or consumer. The United States has made extensive use of excise taxes at various points in its history. Excise taxes have been levied at the federal, state, and local levels. The number of excise taxes used at the federal level has been reduced sharply in recent years and excise receipts now generally comprise only approximately 5 percent of federal budgetary receipts. (Due and Friedlaender contains a list of major federal taxes and receipts,[1] and Pechman provides a summary of federal excise tax changes from 1913 to 1970.[2]) Currently, the most lucrative federal excise taxes are those on alcohol, gasoline, and tobacco. Excise levies by state and local government vary markedly both as to what goods are taxed and as to tax rates. In general, excise taxes are not a major source of revenue for either state or local government. One of the most important items upon which state and local governments levy excise taxes is cigarettes, and we will discuss variations in tax rates for this item extensively.

Any time a government levies a tax on specific goods and services, an excise tax, or sets up special distribution systems for cer-

31

tain items, there is a potential for illegal incomes to be made avoiding those taxes or providing alternative, lower-cost distribution systems. In the United States, excise taxes are levied on a wide variety of goods by all three levels of government, federal, state and local. However, receipts from taxes on the "traditional" excise goods (tobacco products, alcoholic beverages and petroleum products) made up over 50 percent of total receipts in recent years.[3] In this chapter, we discuss the evasion of excise taxes on two of these goods, tobacco products and alcohol. Until recently evasion of taxes on petroleum products is believed to have been very limited. Some farmers apparently abuse their right to use untaxed fuels for nonhighway use of vehicles, but one would expect the incomes in such activities to be small. However, the relatively large increases in such taxes in recent years may make this a growth sector for the underground economy in the 1980s.

Excise tax evasion appears to be more common the further down the distribution system the tax is levied. That is, excise taxes are evaded less often by manufacturers than by wholesalers, retailers, or consumers. This is mainly due to the fact that there are generally fewer manufacturers of a good than wholesalers, retailers, or consumers, and thus the taxing authorities can more easily check on their compliance. Furthermore, the higher the excise tax and the greater the variation in rates among taxing jurisdictions, the more profitable is excise tax evasion.

Current research seems to indicate that substantial incomes are currently earned only by people who evade state and local taxes on cigarettes. Evasion of excise taxes on alcohol was more important in past years than it appears to be today. When taxes are levied on the manufacturer at the federal level, as are some alcohol excises, evasion requires either international smuggling, the cooperation of "legitimate" manufacturers, or illegal production. Like many other native U.S. industries, moonshining has fallen on bad times in recent years. This industry's decline has stemmed from three primary factors: (1) the decline in the number of "dry" areas; (2) the lowering of the drinking age and lessening of other restrictions on the sale of alcoholic beverages; and (3) the rise in the drug culture. The number of still seizures declined from 10,685 in 1952 to 481 in 1977. Interestingly, approximately two-thirds of the 1977 seizures occurred in Alabama, Georgia, and North Carolina, which still have dry counties. One interesting trend is the industry's movement toward "mammoth" stills. Another is a movement from the "piney woods" to more urban settings. For example, the Distilled Spirits Council reports that one producer purchased a large house, ostensibly for use as a nursing home, to locate a still. Given the current small size and the continual decline of the moonshining industry, we estimate that it made a very small contribution to the underground economy and could not possibly have fueled its growth.

Cigarette Smuggling Since the Mid-Sixties

Cigarette smuggling has been a problem at least since the early 1950s, but only became a serious problem in the mid-1960s when differences in state cigarette tax rates widened markedly.[4,5] On January 1, 1965, state tax rates ranged from none to 9 cents per pack, while by January 1, 1976, they ranged from 2 cents a pack in North Carolina to 21 cents a pack in Massachusetts and Connecticut.[6] (See Figure 2-1 for a complete illustration of state excise taxes on cigarettes, and Table 2-1 for a listing of local rates.) An "old wives' tale" suggests that large-scale cigarette smuggling becomes profitable when interstate price differences reach 10 cents a pack.[7] However, one would suspect that profitability would depend on transportation costs between jurisdictions, the extent of law enforcement effort, and the penalties applied if apprehended.

As far as we are aware, the most comprehensive effort to date that estimates the amount of cigarette smuggling is the work of the Advisory Commission on Intergovernmental Regulations. The Commission estimated per capita sales gains and losses for each state using a multiple regression approach to estimation. Specifically, the Commission assumed that per capita cigarette sales in a state in 1975 were a function of state and local tax rates, per capita income, the amount of tourism, the age structure of the population, the weighted price differential with bordering states, a religious index to account for adherence to religions opposed to smoking (such as the Mormons), a regional binary to account for the fact that easterners smoke more, and two binary variables for states believed to be large sources of smuggled cigarettes (one for New Hampshire and one for Kentucky and North Carolina combined). Using the coefficients from this regression and assuming a price elasticity of demand of 0.34, the Commission obtained its estimates of state per capita sales gains and losses. (See Endnote 4 to the appendix for details.)

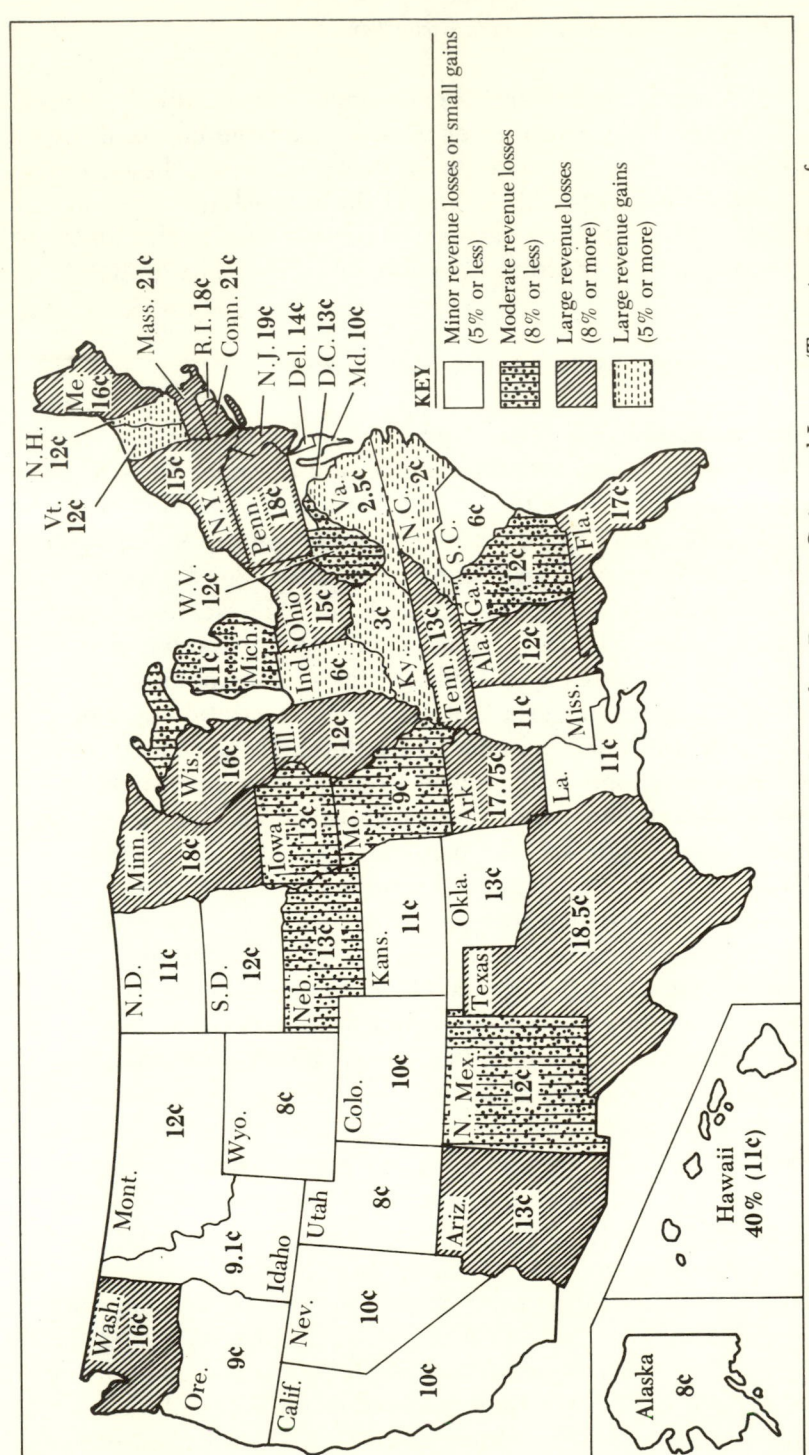

Figure 2-1 State Cigarette Tax Rates and Cigarette Smuggling Revenue Gains and Losses (Tax rates are as of July 1, 1976; revenue gains and losses are based on ACIR staff estimates, 1975 data. Estimates of dollar revenue gains and losses are presented in Table 2-2. *Source: Advisory Commission on Intergovernmental Relations, Cigarette Bootlegging: A State and Federal Responsibility, 1977, p. 2.*)

Table 2-1 Municipal Cigarette Tax Rates for Selected States, FY 1975

State	Number of Jurisdictions Levying Tax	Tax Rate (cents)	Weighted Average Tax Rate (cents)	Total Revenue	Number of Packs Taxed Locally (in thousands)	Per Capita Sales in Taxing Localities (Packs)	Per Capita Sales in Localities as Percent of State Average
Alabama[a]	237	1–5	NA	$8,617,135	NA[b]	NA	NA
Missouri	101	1–10	4.9	18,711,066	383,458	105.7	77.9%
Illinois	2[c]	5	5	18,331,618	366,632	112.2	85.1
New Jersey	1[d]	3	3	247,323	8,244	190.0	155.4
New York	1[e]	4, 7, 8[f]	6	45,410,075	755,483	99.8	80.5
Tennessee	2[g]	1	1	912,462	91,246	125.6	107.0
Virginia	21	2–10	6.5	13,004,215	198,723	97.6	63.9

SOURCE: ACIR staff compilation from data provided by the Tobacco Tax Council, Inc., Richmond, Va., published in Advisory Commission on Intergovernmental Relations, *Cigarette Bootlegging: A State and Federal Responsibility*, Washington, D.C., 1977, p. 69.

NA = Not available

[a] Some Alabama data is for fiscal year 1974.
[b] Jurisdictions taxing cigarettes represent 75.3 percent of State population.
[c] Chicago and Rosemont.
[d] Atlantic City.
[e] New York City.
[f] Eight cents effective January 1, 1976.
[g] City of Memphis and Shelby County.

The estimates of income of those who evade cigarette taxes indicated that changes in state per capita sales due to smuggling ranged from increases of 125.6 packs in New Hampshire to losses of 23.2 packs in Connecticut. (See Table 2-2.) Using these estimates and population figures, one may obtain estimates of the extent of smuggling between the various states. Table 2-2 presents these estimates. As can be seen in this table, the Advisory Commission on Intergovernmental Relations (ACIR) estimates imply that over 100 million packs of cigarettes were smuggled into California, Florida, Illinois, New Jersey, New York, Ohio, Pennsylvania, and Texas in 1975. States estimated to have had over 100 million packs smuggled out are Kentucky, New Hampshire, and North Carolina.

Combining the information in Table 2-2 with other information about cigarette smuggling, one obtains the following picture of the industry. First, there appear to be mainly two types of smuggling: (1) casual smuggling for one's own and friends' use, from nearby states or while traveling; and (2) large-scale organized cigarette smuggling for profit. ACIR believes that casual bootlegging on a large scale exists only where tax rates in adjacent states differ by more than 2 or 3 cents per pack and that large-scale smuggling operations begin when price differences exceed 7 cents per pack.[8] Considering state tax differentials (see Figure 2-1), the estimated amount of cigarettes smuggled, and the findings of a Battelle-LEAA survey,[9] it appears that large-scale organizations are likely to be involved in smuggling cigarettes into Florida, Louisiana, Massachusetts, Connecticut, New York, Pennsylvania, Texas, Wisconsin, Illinois, New Jersey, Ohio, and Washington. In most other states smuggling appears mainly to be small-scale or of the casual variety.

The most serious bootlegging problem appears to have developed in the Northeast in the last decade. Cigarettes are shipped from low-tax, tobacco-producing southern states (North Carolina, Kentucky, and Virginia) to the high-tax states of the Northeast. Organized crime involvement is most prevalent in New York State, but there is evidence that a criminal element is involved in cigarette smuggling in a dozen states.[10] J. Robert Murphy, president of the National Tax Association, has estimated that "organized crime handles 80 percent of the illegal cigarettes."[11] Other large-scale smuggling efforts are believed to exist in the Middle West, Florida, and Texas.

Table 2-2   **Estimated Per Capita Sales Change in Number of Packs of Cigarettes Smuggled and Revenue Loss for 1975**

State[a]	Estimated Per Capita Gain or Loss in Sales (in packs)	Estimated Number of Packs of Cigarettes Smuggled[b] (in millions)	Estimated Revenue Change (in $ millions)
Alabama	− 12.3	− 44.5	− $6.9
Alaska	5.7	2.1	0.2
Arizona	− 10.0	− 22.1	− 3.4
Arkansas	− 17.3	− 36.5	− 6.5
California	− 5.8	− 122.9	− 16.0
Colorado	1.3	3.3	0.3
Connecticut	− 23.2	− 71.9	− 15.1
Delaware	− 2.4	− 1.4	− 0.2
District of Columbia	2.8	2.0	0.2
Florida	− 21.3	− 176.3	− 35.7
Georgia	− 5.4	− 26.6	− 2.8
Idaho	3.5	2.8	0.3
Illinois	− 12.8	− 143.3	− 21.7
Indiana	10.6	56.3	4.0
Iowa	− 9.3	− 26.6	− 4.0
Kansas	− 5.5	− 12.5	− 1.6
Kentucky	78.5	265.9	13.3
Louisiana	− 4.3	− 16.4	− 2.1
Maine	− 12.2	− 12.9	− 2.1
Maryland	0.5	2.1	0.2
Massachusetts	− 13.0	− 75.6	− 12.1
Michigan	− 5.8	− 52.8	− 6.9
Minnesota	− 17.2	− 67.4	− 12.2
Mississippi	− 4.4	− 10.3	− 1.3
Missouri	− 8.0	− 38.1	− 5.0
Montana	− 3.5	− 2.6	− 0.3
Nebraska	− 7.8	− 12.0	− 1.7
Nevada	6.1	3.6	0.4
New Hampshire	125.6	102.0	11.3
New Jersey	− 18.7	− 137.1	− 26.0
New Mexico	− 5.9	− 6.7	− 1.0
New York	− 21.0	− 379.6	− 72.3
North Carolina	75.9	413.0	16.6
North Dakota	− 3.2	− 2.0	− 0.2
Ohio	− 10.5	− 112.7	− 16.9
Oklahoma	− 3.5	− 9.5	− 1.2
Oregon	7.3	16.7	1.5
Pennsylvania	− 16.7	− 198.1	− 35.6

Table 2-2   (Continued)

State[a]	Estimated Per Capita Gain or Loss in Sales (in packs)	Estimated Number of Packs of Cigarettes Smuggled[b] (in millions)	Estimated Revenue Change (in $ millions)
Rhode Island	−2.6	−2.4	−0.3
South Carolina	5.9	16.6	1.4
South Dakota	−1.0	−0.7	−0.1
Tennessee	−12.2	−50.9	−7.8
Texas	−19.0	−232.5	−43.1
Utah	2.0	2.4	0.3
Vermont	18.0	8.5	1.0
Virginia	7.9	39.3	2.5
Washington	−19.6	−69.8	−13.2
West Virginia	−7.5	−13.5	−1.9
Wisconsin	−16.5	−75.7	−13.6
Wyoming	7.7	2.9	0.2

[a] Information for Hawaii was not available.
[b] A negative number indicates that cigarettes were smuggled into a state and a positive number indicates that they were smuggled out.

Cigarette smuggling takes a large number of forms. One simple operation is for an enterprising individual to rent a truck—generally in a high-tax state—and drive the truck to a low-tax state. When the individual arrives in the low-tax state he or she purchases cigarettes from a legitimate wholesaler or retailer. The smuggler then returns to the high-tax state and sells the cigarettes to "legitimate" wholesalers and retailers. The profits from such an operation can be substantial. An individual using a one-ton panel truck between New York and North Carolina could expect to earn approximately $5000 per trip. (This figure is based on a method used by Weintraub.[12] We assume that the panel truck will hold 41,000 packs of cigarettes, that cigarettes were purchased in North Carolina for 36 cents and sold in New York for 50 cents, and that travel and other costs were around $500.) More complicated schemes often involve the use of counterfeit tax stamps and large-scale warehousing facilities. (See Endnote 4, pp. 23–24, for a description of one such scheme.)

Using methods described in detail in the appendix to this chapter, we estimate that between $100 and $200 million of income was earned by cigarette smugglers in 1975. People who smuggled cigarettes into New York ($30 to $50 million), Texas ($15 to $25 million), and Pennsylvania ($15 to $20 million), earned the largest incomes. We estimate that incomes totaling over $5 million were also earned by individuals who smuggled cigarettes into Connecticut, Florida, Illinois, New Jersey, Ohio, and Wisconsin. (See Table A2-1 for additional details.) The major states of origin of smuggled cigarettes in the Northeast are North Carolina and New Hampshire. Cigarettes from North Carolina are smuggled mainly into Pennsylvania, New York, and New Jersey, while cigarettes from New Hampshire are smuggled into Maine, Connecticut, and Massachusetts. In the Midwest, cigarettes are shipped mainly from Kentucky and Indiana into Illinois, Ohio, Minnesota, and Wisconsin. Many illegal cigarettes in Texas and Florida appear to come from outside the United States.

As estimates of the amount of cigarette smuggling have only recently been attempted, it is difficult to develop definitive estimates of trends in cigarette smuggling. However, we will suggest likely trends based on tax rate differences, the opinion of experts, and enforcement efforts. ACIR believes that cigarette bootlegging did not become a serious problem until the late 1960s. Indeed, in 1960, the largest difference in cigarette taxes between any two states was 8 cents per pack, and the largest variation in the retail price for a pack of cigarettes was about 10 cents. The largest tax difference was between Oregon and North Carolina (8 cents per pack, no state tax) and Louisiana, Montana, and Texas (16 cents per pack). Weighted average price per pack ranged from $.206 in Oregon and North Carolina to $.303 a pack in Louisiana. (See Cnossen,[3] p. 74, for details.) The price differential between North Carolina and New York was only 6 cents per pack.

By 1965, the largest variation in cigarette tax rates had increased to 11 cents per pack and variations in retail price to 13 cents. The largest variation in retail prices now occurred between North Carolina and New York, and it seems likely that large-scale smuggling from North Carolina to New York developed during this period.

A combination of more negative public attitudes toward smoking (sparked at least in part by the 1964 Surgeon General's report) and the fiscal problems of many northeastern and midwestern states led to further large increases in tax rates in the 1965–1973 period. Meanwhile, tobacco-producing states maintained their low tax rates, due mainly to pressures from tobacco manufacturers and workers. As a result, by 1970 the high- and low-tax states were separated by 16 cents—2 cents tax in North Carolina and 18 cents tax in Pennsylvania. Between 1970 and 1973, 26 states increased their tax rate on cigarettes still further. However, since 1973, increases in taxes in high-tax states have been less common, with only one high-tax state increasing taxes between 1973 and 1975. Indeed, the New York State Special Task Force on Cigarette Bootlegging even called for a reduction in state taxes of 2 cents per pack and for the New York City tax on cigarettes to be eliminated to combat bootlegging.[13] While New York has not followed this task force's recommendations, it also has not raised its tax on cigarettes since 1975.

In its 1977 report, the Advisory Commission on Intergovernmental Relations recommended that smuggling of cigarettes be made a federal offense, and a federal law was signed in December of 1978. Under this law, anyone caught smuggling more than 300 cartons of cigarettes faces five years in prison and a $100,000 fine. This law, combined with more rigorous law enforcement efforts in high-tax states—which began in 1977—is probably responsible for the 3 to 5 percent drop in cigarette revenues that North Carolina has experienced in recent years.

Taken as a whole, these facts suggest that cigarette smuggling probably began in the 1950s and grew slowly until the mid 1960s, when large increases in tax rates occurred in a number of states. The greatest growth in cigarette smuggling probably occurred in the 1965–1973 period, with much slower, if any, growth occurring since then.

Costs and Benefits of Cigarette Smuggling

The benefits to those smuggling cigarettes are, of course, the profits they earn, which we estimated to be between $100 and $200 million in 1975. One expert, Morris Weintraub, has suggested that cigarette smuggling is second only to narcotics in providing funds to organized crime.[14] Benefits to consumers come in the form of lower prices; and, while these benefits are substantial for consumers as a group, they do not appear large for any individual consumer. The size of an individual consumer's benefit will depend on the price difference between legal and illegal cigarettes and the quantity of cigarettes which he or she smokes. For a consumer in New York City with a pack-a-day habit, benefits are likely to be between $15 and $40 per year—certainly not a substantial amount for most budgets.*

The costs to cigarette bootleggers include the cost of purchasing cigarettes in low-tax states, transportation costs to high-tax states, the costs of efforts to avoid arrest and punishment (for example, bribes to enforcement officials, devious routes, camouflages), and the cost of legal process and penalties if apprehended. Efforts to avoid arrest appear to be extensive. Cigarettes are often transferred a number of times on their way from a low- to a high-tax state. Trucks often carry an armed guard as well as a driver to ward off hijacking attempts. Camouflage attempts can be relatively sophisticated. There was even one instance in which a truck used to smuggle cigarettes was camouflaged as a logging truck. The amount of bribes paid is, unsurprisingly, difficult to estimate. However, one report suggests that New York tax agents investigating cigarette smuggling had received more than $100,000 a year in payoffs.[15] Until recently the costs of legal process and penalties do not appear to have been substantial. Cigarette smuggling was not a federal offense until 1979, and state laws were generally relatively lenient and not strictly enforced until the early 1970s. Currently, both state laws in high-tax states and the new federal laws are much more stringent and rigorously enforced.

The cost to the consumer of using illegal cigarettes is generally very low. Although many states have laws against the possession of untaxed cigarettes, most laws require that a large number of cigarettes be possessed to be illegal. For example, Ohio requires a wholesale value of $60 or more; Wisconsin requires 20 packs of cigarettes or more.[16] Pennsylvania is an interesting exception. In Pennsylvania, the possession of any pack of cigarettes with intent to evade taxes is a felony punishable by imprisonment of not over five years and a fine of not more than $5,000.

The cost of cigarette bootlegging to the government is the loss of revenue plus the cost of compliance programs. Revenue loss to the federal government is apparently minor and has not, as far as we are aware, been estimated. The Advisory Commission on Intergovernmental Relations estimates of the tax loss to the state and

---

* This figure was obtained using the same mark-up assumptions used in Table A2-1. These mark-ups indicate that consumers in New York City pay from 4 cents to 10 cents less a pack for smuggled than for legal cigarettes.

local governments are contained in Table 2-2. In 1975, the estimated net loss to all states was $337.1 million and the estimated
gross loss to losing states was $390.8 million. States with revenue
losses exceeding 8 percent of current cigarette tax revenues are
blackened in Figure 2-1. States with revenue losses exceeding 15
percent of current revenues are Arkansas, Connecticut, Florida,
New Jersey, New York, Texas, and Washington. Three states receive large increases in tax revenues as a result of smuggling: Kentucky, New Hampshire, and North Carolina. Compliance costs
occur at both the state and federal levels, but there has been no
compilation of these costs as far as we are aware.

The social costs of cigarette smuggling are far larger and much
more difficult to judge. In tax-losing states, law-abiding citizens are
forced to pay higher taxes or forego public services, while in tax-
gaining states the reverse occurs. This is, of course, merely a transfer payment to the extent that gains equal losses. However, gains do
not equal losses because of the higher taxes in revenue-losing states.

ACIR lists the following additional losses due to cigarette smuggling: (1) legitimate cigarette wholesalers and retailers are driven
out of business, (2) political and law enforcement officials are cor-
rupted, (3) trucks are hijacked and warehouses raided, and (4) people are injured and killed. Most of these losses, like the state revenue loss, represent equity, not efficiency, problems. Most of the
losses suffered by legitimate wholesalers and retailers are merely
transferred as gains to illegal cigarette distributors. We as a society
may well condemn this, but it does not represent a major efficiency
problem. Cigarette smuggling does generate efficiency loss, but this
loss comes through effects on work incentives, the cost of compliance programs, increased costs of doing business illegally, and,
most importantly, the effect on public mores.

Endnotes

1. Due, John F., and Ann F. Friedlaender. 1977. *Government Finance: Economics of the Public Sector.* Homewood, Ill.: Richard D. Irwin, p. 366.
2. Pechman, J. A. 1971. *Federal Tax Policy.* New York: W. W. Norton, pp.
   260–263.
3. Cnossen, Sijbren. 1977. *Excise Systems: A Global Study of the Selective Taxation of Goods and Services.* Baltimore, Md.: Johns Hopkins, p. 154.
4. National Tobacco Tax Association. 1965. *Proceedings.*
5. National Tobacco Tax Association. 1966. *Proceedings.*

6. Advisory Commission on Intergovernmental Relations. 1977. *Cigarette Bootlegging: A State and Federal Responsibility.* Washington, D.C.: Advisory Commission on Intergovernmental Relations.

7. U.S. House of Representatives, Subcommittee 1, Committee on the Judiciary. 1972. *Hearings on the Elimination of Cigarette Racketeering.* Washington, D.C.: U.S. Government Printing Office, pp. 42, 77.

8. Advisory Commission, *Cigarette Bootlegging,* p. 43.

9. U.S. Department of Justice, Law Enforcement Assistance Administration. 1972. *Combatting Cigarette Smuggling.* Washington, D.C.: U.S. Department of Justice.

10. Larch, Edward, and J. Winters. 1975. "An Analysis of Untaxed Cigarette Smuggling." Working paper, Intelligence Division of the New York City Police Department.

11. Advisory Commission, *Cigarette Bootlegging,* p. 105.

12. Weintraub, Morris. 1966. "The Bootlegging of Cigarettes Is a National Problem," in *Proceedings, 1966, of the National Tobacco Tax Association,* p. 23.

13. New York State Special Task Force on Cigarette Bootlegging. 1976. *Report.* Albany, N.Y.: Department of Taxation and Finance.

14. Advisory Commission, *Cigarette Bootlegging,* p. 112.

15. *Ibid.,* p. 21, 22.

16. *Ibid.,* p. 35.

Appendix

ESTIMATING UNREPORTED INCOME EARNED FROM CIGARETTE SMUGGLING

Table A2-1 contains our estimates of income earned by cigarette smugglers by state of sale. We obtained these estimates in the following manner. First, we assumed that only in those states with large revenue losses are cigarettes smuggled in for profit. Figure 2-1 indicates which states experience large revenue losses. Next, we assumed that 80 percent of the cigarettes smuggled into states believed to have large-scale smuggling operations—Connecticut, Illinois, Massachusetts, New Jersey, New York, Ohio, Pennsylvania, Texas, and Wisconsin—were smuggled for profit; 50 percent of the cigarettes smuggled into states with some organized smuggling operations—Alabama, Arkansas, Florida, Maine, Minnesota, Tennessee, and Washington—were smuggled for profit; and 25 percent of the cigarettes smuggled into states with only small-scale smuggling operations—only Arizona—were smuggled for profit.

In order to determine the state of origin of cigarettes smuggled into each state, we considered knowledge of smuggling routes and our estimates of the number of cigarettes smuggled out of each state (refer to Table 2-2). We attempted to make total shipments from a state equal total receipts from that state. This was possible for all states but Kentucky and North Carolina. For these two states, total receipts by other states exceed total shipments by approximately 80 million and 200,000 million packs, respectively. There are at least two possible explanations for this discrepancy. First, it seems that substantial amounts of cigarettes are smuggled into Texas and Florida from abroad. (See Footnote e to Table A2-1 for details.) Having

Table A2-1   Estimation of Incomes Earned from Cigarette Smuggling in 1975

State of Sale	State of Origin (millions of packs)	Tax Difference per Pack ($)	Estimated Profit per Pack ($)	Total Estimated Profit ($ million)
Alabama[a]	North Carolina (11.1) Kentucky (11.1)	North Carolina (.10) Kentucky (.09)	North Carolina (.052–.087) Kentucky (.047–.078)	$1.1–$1.8
Arizona[b]	Utah (2.4) Nevada (3.1)	Utah (.05) Nevada (.03)	Utah (.026–.044) Nevada (.016–.026)	0.1–0.2
Arkansas[a]	Kentucky (18.25)	Kentucky (.15)	Kentucky (.077–.128)	1.5–2.4
Connecticut[c]	North Carolina (35.95) New Hampshire (21.57)	North Carolina (.19) New Hampshire (.09)	North Carolina (.099–.165) New Hampshire (.047–.078)	4.6–7.6
Florida[a,e]	North Carolina (88.15)	North Carolina (.15)	North Carolina (.078–.130)	6.9–11.5
Illinois[c]	Indiana (16.89) Kentucky (97.71)	Indiana (.06) Kentucky (.09)	Indiana (.031–.052) Kentucky (.047–.078)	5.1–8.5
Massachusetts[c]	New Hampshire (56.18) Vermont (4.3)	New Hampshire (.09) Vermont (.09)	New Hampshire (.047–.078) Vermont (.047–.078)	2.8–4.7
Maine[a]	New Hampshire (6.45)	New Hampshire (.04)	New Hampshire (.021–.035)	0.1–0.2
Minnesota[a]	Kentucky (22.44) Indiana (11.26)	Kentucky (.15) Indiana (.12)	Kentucky (.078–.130) Indiana (.062–.104)	2.4–4.1
New Jersey[c]	North Carolina (99.68) Virginia (10.0)	North Carolina (.17) Virginia (.165)	North Carolina (.088–.148) Virginia (.086–.144)	9.6–16.2
New York[c,d]	North Carolina (267.38) Virginia (14.3) New Hampshire (17.8) Vermont (4.2)	North Carolina (.13–.21) Virginia (.125–.205) New Hampshire, Vermont (.03)	North Carolina (.068–.113; .109–.183); Virginia (.065– .109; .107–.178); New Hampshire, Vermont (.016–.026)	28.7–48.1

Ohio[c]	Kentucky (73.27)	Kentucky (.12)	Kentucky (.062–.104)	5.3–7.9
	Indiana (16.89)	Indiana (.09)	Indiana (.047–.078)	
Pennsylvania[c]	North Carolina (139.38)	North Carolina (.16)	North Carolina (.083–.139)	12.9–21.6
	Virginia (15.0)	Virginia (.155)	Virginia (.081–.135)	
	Maryland (2.1)	Maryland (.08)	Maryland (.042–.070)	
	D.C. (2.0)	D.C. (.05)	D.C. (.026–.044)	
Tennessee[a]	Kentucky (25.45)	Kentucky (.10)	Kentucky (.052–.087)	1.3–2.2
Texas[e]	North Carolina (81.4)	North Carolina (.165)	North Carolina (.086–.144)	15.2–25.1
	Kentucky (81.3)	Kentucky (.155)	Kentucky (.081–.135)	
	South Carolina (16.6)	South Carolina (.125)	South Carolina (.065–.109)	
	Colorado (3.3)	Colorado (.085)	Colorado, Nevada (.044–.074)	
	Nevada (0.5)	Nevada (.085)	Wyoming (.055–.091)	
	Wyoming (2.9)	Wyoming (.105)		
Washington[a]	Oregon (5.6)	Oregon (.07)	Oregon (.036–.061)	0.2–0.4
	Idaho (1.0)	Idaho (.069)	Idaho (.036–.060)	
Wisconsin[c]	Kentucky (49.3)	Kentucky (.13)	Kentucky (.068–.113)	3.9–6.6
	Indiana (11.26)	Indiana (.10)	Indiana (.052–.087)	
Total Estimated Income				$101.7–$169.1

[a] We assumed that 50 percent of the estimated number of cigarettes smuggled into these states were smuggled for profit.

[b] We assumed that 25 percent of the estimated number of cigarettes smuggled into this state were smuggled for profit.

[c] We assumed that 80 percent of the estimated number of cigarettes smuggled into these states were smuggled for profit.

[d] We assume that 80 percent of the cigarettes coming from North Carolina and Virginia were sold in New York City where the combined city and state tax was 23¢ on January 1, 1976. Due to the difficulty of allocating sales in other states with local excise taxes on cigarettes, we have ignored the effect of such taxes. This means that we slightly underestimate smugglers' profits.

[e] Large allocations of shipments from North Carolina to Florida and Texas meant that the estimated flow of smuggled cigarettes out of North Carolina exceeded our estimate by more than 200 million packs. Similarly, assuming a flow of cigarettes from Kentucky to Texas made our consumer-based estimate of smuggled cigarettes out of Kentucky exceed our producer-based estimate by approximately 80 million packs. We suspect, but cannot prove, that much of this excess was probably smuggled in from abroad. Shrimp and other commercial fishing boats are reported to smuggle large amounts of cigarettes into Florida and Texas either by using duty-free purchases or by buying cigarettes in port cities of Puerto Rico, the Dominican Republic, and the Panama Canal. See National Tobacco Tax Association *Proceedings* (1965, pp. 37–38; 1966, pp. 8–9) for details.

no detailed information on these smuggling operations, but believing them to be quite profitable, we assigned these sales to North Carolina and Kentucky. Second, it is possible that some cigarettes shipped from those two states are completely "off the books" and thus not reflected in per capita sales. Column 2 of Table A2-1 lists the states of origin and amounts for each state of sale.

In order to convert packs sold into profits earned, we assumed that smugglers' profits are 52 to 87 percent of the tax difference between the state of origin and state of sale. The first figure reflects smugglers' profit per pack in a 1966 New York City operation,[1] and the second figure represents smugglers' profits per pack in a more recent New York City operation.[2] Multiplying the profit per pack for each state of origin by the number of packs emanating from that state and summing over all origin states, we obtain an estimate of the incomes earned in each state of sale. Summing those estimates over all states of sale, we obtain our estimate of the total income earned in cigarette smuggling—$102 to $170 million in 1975.

To check the reasonableness of our estimate, we compared it with the Council Against Cigarette Bootlegging's estimates of illegal profits in eight eastern states. The Council estimated that profits from bootleggers in Connecticut, Delaware, Maryland, Massachusetts, New York, New Jersey, Pennsylvania, and Rhode Island were $97.9 billion in 1975–1976. The estimated profits for these states obtained from Table A2-1 would be between $58.6 and $98.2 million. The closeness of these figures gives us some additional faith in our estimate.

Our estimate of the profit from cigarette bootlegging assumes that only casual cigarette smuggling occurs from Indian reservations and military Post Exchanges. Realizing that this is somewhat unrealistic, we raise the upper bound of our estimate to $200 million. Moving our 1975 estimate back to 1974 by assuming a 10 percent growth rate in income from cigarette smuggling, we estimate that income from cigarette smuggling was between $90 and $180 million in 1974.

Endnotes

1. Weintraub, Morris. 1966. "The Bootlegging of Cigarettes Is a National Problem," in *Proceedings* of National Tobacco Tax Association, p. 22.
2. Advisory Commission on Intergovernmental Relations. 1977. *Cigarette Bootlegging: A State and Federal Responsibility.* Washington, D.C.: Advisory Commission on Intergovernmental Relations, p. 112.

Part II

ILLEGAL TRANSFERS
OF PEOPLE AND GOODS

Chapter 3

ILLEGAL IMMIGRATION

Illegal immigration to the United States has been a public concern since the country first closed its borders almost 100 years ago. The first major exclusionary immigration laws, passed in 1882, were the Chinese Exclusion Act and the Immigration Law of 1882. (Earlier restrictions on immigration were the Alien and Sedition Act, the prohibition of the importation of Oriental slave labor, and the pro- hibition against prostitutes and alien convicts.) Since the mid 1970s the government has considered illegal immigration to be a major problem, and thus the size of and trends in such immigration has attracted a substantial amount of research interest. Yet there is still much to be learned. Because of their illegal status, it is hard to get reliable information about illegal aliens. Major studies on the char- acteristics of the illegal alien population have greatly increased our knowledge of the characteristics of such aliens. North and Houston interviewed a large sample of apprehended illegals, both Mexican and non-Mexican.[1] Samora[2] and Villalpando[3] conducted a large number of interviews with apprehended Mexican illegals. Bustamante,[4] Cornelius,[5] and, more recently, Reichert and Massey[6] have interviewed villagers from communities in Mexico from which illegals have come. These studies have gathered a large amount of information about different subsamples of the illegal population. None of the studies use random samples of the illegal population, and thus the generalizability of findings is problematical. Our use of these studies requires much subjective judgment. Realizing the difficulties with existing studies, the Immigration and Naturaliza- tion Service (INS) awarded a contract in 1977 to study a more

---

Note: This chapter was written in major part by Kelly Eakin.

representative population sample. However, due to contractual disputes between the consulting firm and INS, the results of this study have not been released at the time of this writing. Indeed, our conversations with INS led us to believe that the results of this study may never even be analyzed.

There have also been increasing statistical efforts to count the illegal aliens in the United States. Recent work in this area uses existing sources of population statistics to estimate the number of illegal aliens. These works make varying assumptions about characteristics of the illegal population to produce a range of estimates.

There is uncertainty in making informed judgments about illegal immigration. Despite the obvious limitations, we attempt to utilize information at hand to make some estimates about illegal immigration and the underground economy. We make and accept several assumptions about the illegal alien population in making our estimates. We feel that the assumptions we opted for are reasonable, and as the topic is more thoroughly investigated our set of assumptions can be fine-tuned or scrapped.

The Number and Some Characteristics of Undocumented Immigrants

Actually counting the number of illegals in this country is impossible, barring substantial infringements on civil liberties. As a result, researchers have attempted to estimate the number of illegal aliens in the country and trends in this population using a number of disparate techniques (see Table 3-1). A study by Korns found no evidence for a sustained increase in the size of the undocumented population employed in the nonagricultural sector between 1969 and 1975. Korns's primary interest was to establish a plausible explanation for the differences in cyclical behavior between the Census Bureau's Current Population Survey and the Labor Department's payroll survey. His conclusion about illegal immigration is secondary. He explains that his technique is a "somewhat ambiguous indicator of such changes [in the illegal alien population], because it is also sensitive to other factors."[7] A study by Lesko and Associates using different and highly criticized methods estimates that there were 4 to 11 million illegal aliens in 1975.[8] (See Keely[9] for an excellent critique of the Lesko study and a survey of most of the efforts to count the illegal population.) Lancaster and Scheuren,

Table 3-1   Estimates of Illegal Alien Population in the United States

Source	Year(s) Estimated for	Estimated Number of Illegals
INS	1974 (Chapman)	955,000[a]
INS	1975 (Chapman)	4–12 million[b]
INS	1977 (Graham)	3.67 million[a]
Lesko and Associates	1975	4–11 million 8 million
Lancaster and Scheuren	1973	2.9–5.7 million 3.9 million
Robinson[c]	1960–1975	177,000–4.67 million 2.6 million[d]
Heer[c]	1970–1975	425,000–1.2 million 600,000[d]
Korns[c]	1969–1975	no evidence of increase in nonagricultural sector

[a] Estimate of employed illegal aliens in agriculture, heavy industry, light industry, service, and construction, as reported in "Special Report: Illegal Immigration," *The Environmental Fund* 2 (November, 1978).
[b] Source: Leonard Chapman, INS Commissioner, Prepared statement before House Judiciary Subcommittee, February 4, 1975, p. 32.
[c] Estimates of net increases during the period.
[d] Preferred estimates by source.

using Exact Match file data* and a capture-recapture technique, estimated 3.9 million illegals 18–44 years of age (prime working years) in April of 1973.[10] Heer estimates a net increase of 600,000 illegal Mexican aliens in the United States from 1970 to 1975 through the use of the Current Population Survey.[11] Robinson uses age-specific death rates to estimate the illegal population.[12] His "composite 1" estimate of 2.6 million assumes a (U.S.) death rate for male illegal aliens 18–24 that is below the death rate for white males of the same age group, as aliens are assumed to go home if they are ill. He also assumes that the bulk of the illegal alien population is contained in ten states: Arizona, California, Colorado, Florida, Illinois, Michigan, New Jersey, New Mexico, New York, and Texas. These ten states were the intended residence of 73.8 percent of

---

* This method is based upon two estimates of the population. One estimate, an adjusted 1970 census count, is assumed to exclude the illegal alien population. The other estimate uses the Current Population Survey matched with Internal Revenue Service data and Social Security Administration data and is assumed to include the illegal population. The difference between these two estimates is the estimate for the number of illegal aliens.

the legal immigrants in 1974 and 96 percent of the legal Mexican immigrants that year (see Table 3-2). Robinson's methods estimate increases in the illegal population for 1960–1970 and 1970–1975. If one is to use the sum of these increase estimates to judge the total illegal population, one must assume a small illegal stock in 1960.

The studies by Heer, Robinson, and Lancaster and Scheuren are by far the best efforts to date to estimate the number of illegals. Each of these three efforts has generated a wide range of estimates by varying assumptions. However, these estimates, with certain reasonable assumptions, are relatively close. While the ranges offered by these studies are substantial, all three studies indicate that earlier guesses above 4 million are most likely too high. Heer's "preferred" estimate is a net flow of 600,000 illegals for 1970–1975. Robinson's "composite 1" estimate of net increase during this period is 1.6 million. Robinson's estimate of 2.6 million illegal male aliens 18–44 years old is close to the lower end of Lancaster and Scheuren's range ("anything from 2.9 million to 5.7 million"). The results of these three studies suggest that the less sophisticated "estimates" made in the early and mid-seventies were too high. For our purposes in this paper we will use 4 million as a reasonable estimate of the illegal alien population in 1974.

The characteristics are as unknown as the actual size of the illegal population. However, the work of North and Houston gives us some insights which allow us to make informed guesses about certain characteristics. Their work, *The Characteristics and Role of Illegal Aliens in the U.S. Labor Market: An Exploratory Study*, is the summary of findings from interviewing 793 apprehended illegal aliens. Apprehensions are a function of enforcement efforts and therefore are not a random sample of illegal aliens. However, weighting apprehension data by a proxy for likelihood of being apprehended, we can get a rough estimate of the proportion of illegal aliens coming from Mexico. (This technique and its limitations are discussed on page 87 of North and Houston. The likelihood proxy is

$$\frac{\text{average Mexican's prior apprehensions}}{\text{average non-Mexican's prior apprehensions}} \times \frac{\text{average Mexican's time in U.S.}}{\text{average non-Mexican's time in U.S.}}$$

The average number of prior apprehensions are from North and Houston's study. This proxy is multiplied by the ratio of non-

Table 3-2   Distribution of Illegal Alien Population Among Ten States, and Lost Income Tax Revenues Associated with Illegal Alien Population

State	Percentage of Legal Immigrants in 1975 Claiming State as Intended Permanent Residence[a] — All Immigrants	Non-Mexican Immigrants	Mexican Immigrants	Individual Income Tax Revenue[b] — As a Percentage of Total State Revenue	As a Percentage of Total State Tax Revenue	Assumed Tax Rate Applicable to Illegal Aliens (Per Dollar Earnings)[c]	Estimated Number of Illegal Aliens Residing in the United States in 1974[d]	Estimated Number of Illegals Employed[e]	Range of Estimated Lost State Income Tax Revenue (in millions)[f]	Estimated Lost Local Income Tax Revenue (in millions)[g]
Arizona	1.1	.5	3.9	3	16	.05	47,696	42,926	3.5–4.5	—
California	22.0	16.4	47.1	14	27	.06	953,929	858,536	84.6–108.5	—
Colorado	.6	.5	.7	15	33	.05	26,016	23,414	1.9–2.4	—
Florida	4.9	5.8	.8	0	0	0	212,466	191,219	0	—
Illinois	6.3	5.7	8.8	15	25	.025	273,171	245,854	10.1–12.9	—
Michigan	2.6	3.0	.7	15	30	.046	112,737	101,463	7.7–9.9	2.5–3.2
New Jersey	6.3	7.6	.1	2	4	.02	273,171	245,854	8.1–10.4	—
New Mexico	.4	.2	1.3	5	10	.04	17,344	15,610	1.0–1.3	—
New York	22.3	27.1	.6	21	40	.05	966,938	870,244	71.5–91.7	21.4–27.5
Texas	7.3	1.9	31.9	0	0	0	316,531	284,878	0	—
Ten-State Total	73.8[h]	68.8[i]	96.1[j]			.04	3,199,999	2,879,998	188.4–241.6	23.9–30.7
All-State Total	100	100	100				4,000,000	3,600,000	235.5–302.0	29.9–38.4

[a] Source: INS, 1974 Annual Report, Table 12.
[b] Source: Tax Foundation, *Facts and Figures*, 1977, Table 150.
[c] Source: Tax Foundation, 1977, Table 155. We had to do some extrapolating to get some of the tax rates.
[d] We multiplied column 1 (in percentage) by 80/73.8 and then multiplied that by 4 million.
[e] We multiplied the previous column by .9.
[f] We multiplied the estimate of employed illegal aliens by .27 (those in the underground economy) then by $117/wk × 52 wk/yr × the applicable tax rate to get the smaller figure. The larger figure is $150/$117 times the smaller.
[g] Source: Tax Foundation, 1977, Table 201. For New York City we multiplied the estimated number of illegal aliens in New York by .75, then by .27 × $117/wk × 52 wk/yr × .02 (the New York City tax rate) to get the smaller figure. The larger figure is $150/$117 times the larger. The applicable tax rate for Michigan is .015. We assume that the lost local tax revenues of New York City and Michigan account for 80% of lost revenues due to illegal aliens in the underground economy.
[h] 291,290 of 394,851.   [i] 222,527 of 323,275.   [j] 68,763 of 71,586.

Table 3-3 Distributions of the Illegal Alien Population in 1974

	1974 Apprehensions[a]	Assumed Average Prior Apprehensions[b]	Assumed Average Duration of Stay (years)[c]	Improved Estimate of Distribution (%)[d]	"Revised" Estimate (%)[e]
Country of Origin					
Mexican	709,959	0.8	2.4	55	60
Other	78,186	0.1	2.6	45	40
Western Hemisphere	44,310	0.1	2.5	28	25
Eastern Hemisphere	33,876	0.1	3.1	17	15
Total	788,145			100	
Method of Entry					
EWl[f,g]	693,084	0.7	2.2	60	70
Visa Abuser[f]	95,061	0.1	3.2	40	30
Total	788,145			100	
Occupation[h]					
Agriculture	25,462	1.1	1.8	36	
Nonagriculture	22,485	0.38	2.6	64	
Total	47,947			100	

[a] INS 1974 annual report, Table 27b.
[b] North and Houston, p. 87.
[c] North and Houston, p. 85.
[d] See description of method on pages 54 and 57.
[e] These are subjective corrections.
[f] Table III.2, North and Houston, p. 50.
[g] EWl is entering illegally without going through immigration procedures.
[h] This is unpublished INS data gathered in a sample study. We found this information in North and Houston, Table V-II, p. 120. We are assuming that the sample is representative of the total apprehended population.

Table 3-4   Estimates of Employed Illegal Aliens by Category of Employment

Industry	Number Estimated in 1974[a]	Number Estimated in 1977[b] (percent of total employed)	Percent Increase 1974 to 1977
Agriculture	335,000	1,200,000 (33%)	258
Heavy industry	105,000	176,000 (5%)	68
Light industry	214,000	1,000,000 (27%)	367
Service	301,000	990,000 (27%)	229
Construction		300,000 (8%)	

[a] Estimate submitted to Congress by Leonard F. Chapman, Commissioner, Immigration and Naturalization Service (INS), September 18, 1974 as reported in "Special Report: Illegal Immigration," *The Environmental Fund*, 2 (November, 1978), p. 7.
[b] Estimated by Janet Graham, Public Affairs Office, INS, February, 1977 as reported in "Special Report: Illegal Immigration."

Mexican apprehensions to Mexican apprehensions to give an improved distribution estimate. Limitations include the possibility of a nonrepresentative sample of apprehended illegals and less than truthful answers by the respondents.) Using the same technique, the "other" population can be distributed between "other Western Hemisphere" and "Eastern Hemisphere." Similarly, distribution by violation and occupation can be obtained. (See Table 3-3.) We can roughly guess that 60 percent of the illegal population is from Mexico. This is also the conclusion of several other researchers (see Endnote 62, p. 133). Approximately 70 percent of the illegal aliens enter without going through immigration procedures. The other 30 percent are visa abusers. We also guess that 36 percent of the working illegal population is employed in agriculture. This is about the same percentage as that estimated by the INS in 1977, 33 percent. (See Table 3-4.)

Illegal Aliens' Contribution to the Underground Economy

Only that part of the illegal population which is working and whose product or income is not reported form part of the underground economy. While no reliable estimates of the number of illegal aliens employed in the United States are currently available, we can use information from studies of illegal aliens to guess the number of working aliens. North and Houston[13] report that their respondents had been in the United States an average of 2.5 years and employed an average of 2.1 years. This implies an average unemployment rate among illegals of about 15 percent. However, a sample of apprehendees probably has an upward bias in unemployment vis-à-vis total illegal population. A more appropriate figure is probably around 10 percent. Assuming that there were 4 million illegal aliens and that 90 percent of them were employed at any given time, then there was an average of 3.6 million illegal aliens employed in the United States in 1974. The INS in 1977 estimated 3.66 million illegal aliens employed in 1977 (see Table 3-4).

The next question is: How many of these employed illegals work in the underground economy? Three major studies—North and Houston, Cornelius, and Villalpando—all indicate that around 70 percent of the illegal aliens have social security and income taxes deducted from their wages. We will assume that 73 percent of the illegals have income taxes withheld and therefore are not a part of the underground economy. (This is the percentage that North and Houston found from their study of a sample of apprehended illegal aliens from many national origins. We chose this finding by North and Houston over the other studies—which interviewed only Mexicans—because of the broader sample.) These studies also consistently indicate a low average wage for Mexican illegals ($2.33 to $2.42/hr). North and Houston found that the average gross weekly wage for illegals was $117.[14] A 1974 INS study indicated that the average weekly wage of these individuals was $150.[15] We shall use these two figures to obtain our estimate that illegal aliens added $5.9 to $7.6 billion dollars to the underground economy in 1974. This range is extremely close to the range estimated by the IRS for 1976. The Internal Revenue Service estimated $5 to $6.6 billion worth of income attributable to illegal aliens went unreported in 1976.[16] (See IRS Table F.1 and footnote 11, pp. 98 and 100.) Assuming that the number of illegal aliens has probably been increasing since 1975, especially the number of illegals from the Caribbean, this portion of the underground economy has undoubtedly grown as well. Unfortunately, we have no data that would allow us to estimate the rate of growth.

The Migration Decision and Participation in the Underground Economy

There are several steps that an individual must take before reaching the decision to immigrate to the United States. First, the individual must decide whether to migrate. Then there is a choice between internal or international migration. If one decides to immigrate to the United States, a choice between legal entry or illegal entry must also be made. The decision to migrate is basically an economic one. Cornelius states that 84 percent of the respondents in the North and Houston, Villalpando, and Cornelius studies went to the United States "to find a job or increase family income."[17] The decision between legal and illegal migration is heavily influenced by U.S. immigration policies.

Economic theory predicts that an individual considering immigration compares the costs and benefits of living and working in his or her native country and in the U.S. (For a development of the theory upon which this discussion is based, see Sjaastad.[18] Greenwood provides a survey of work on migration in the United States[19] and Todaro provides a similar survey for less developed countries.[20]) One would expect several factors to contribute to heavier immigration: the larger the amount by which wages in the United States exceed wages in the potential immigrant's native country, the larger the amount by which the immigrant's native country's unemployment rates exceed U.S. rates, the closer the immigrant's native country to the United States, and the smaller the amount by which cost of living in the United States exceeds that of the native country.

It is difficult to check the hypothesis about differences in employment rates because the prevailing problem in Mexico is underemployment.[21] However, recent research on Mexican migration to the United States indicates a positive relationship between immigration and the wage differential between the United States and Mexico.[22, 23] It should be noted that both the studies emphasize that it is the "push" factors that most significantly influence migration from Mexico. As Jenkins states, "In general, economic conditions in Mexico pushing immigrants out have had far more to do with migration than have pulls exercised by the U.S. agricultural economy."[24]

One of the major sources of the economic "push" from Mexico has been rapid industrialization and implementation of capital intensive

Table 3-5 Selected Economic Indicators for Mexico and Haiti, 1970–1978

| Year | Consumer Price Index[a] | | Average Monthly Manufacturing Wages[a] | | Daily Minimum Wage for Agriculture[c] | | Index of Per Capita Gross Domestic Product[a] | | Population (in millions)[b] | |
	Mexico	Haiti	Mexico (in pesos)	Haiti	Mexico (in pesos)	Haiti	Mexico	Haiti	Mexico	Haiti
1970	100	110	1703	NA	21.20	NA	100	100	50.69	4.24
1971	105	110	1851	NA	21.20	NA	100	104	52.45	4.31
1972	111	114	1956	NA	24.94	NA	103	104	54.27	4.37
1973	124	140	2202	NA	27.40	NA	108	108	56.16	4.44
1974	153	162	2804	NA	37.79	NA	110	111	58.12	4.51
1975	176	188	3412	NA	46.10	NA	110	121	60.15	4.58
1976	204	200	4285	NA	56.55	NA	NA	NA	62.33	4.67
1977	264	214	5619	NA	NA	NA	NA	NA	64.59	4.75
1978	310[b]	NA	NA	NA	NA	NA	NA	NA	66.94	4.83
Total Increase 1970–1978	210%	114%[d]	230%[d]		168%[e]		10%[f]	21%[f]	32%	14%

NA = not available.
[a] U.N. Statistical Yearbook, 1978, Tables 181, 183, 184.
[b] International Financial Yearbook (1979), International Monetary Fund.
[c] Wilkie and Reich, *Statistical Abstract of Latin America*, 1980, Table 1403.
[d] 1970–1977.
[e] 1970–1976.
[f] 1970–1975.

technologies. Alba has shown that productive technologies in Mexico "have a tendency toward lesser work-force absorption" especially in the farm and "other services" sectors.[25] Witte found that "for manufacturing as a whole, relative factor costs (capital costs/labor costs) declined by an average annual rate of 5 percent in Mexico" for the years 1945–1965.[26] Witte's work indicates that this has led to increased substitution of capital for labor, which undoubtedly contributed to Mexico's employment problems. Additionally, the growth of Mexico's GNP has not been able to keep up with its population increase. Table 3-5 indicates greater than 200 percent inflation in Mexico in the last ten years. Evans and James explain that wages have kept up with inflation only due to government action, which has further increased capital substitution for labor.[27] While increasing wages eases the impact of inflation for those employed, it only exacerbates the condition of the unemployed and underemployed who are the most likely to migrate. Table 3-5 also shows some of the gloomy economic conditions of Haiti. Recent economic statistics on Cuba are difficult to obtain and the accuracy of those that do exist is questionable.[28] Agricultural products are a major part of the Cuban economy and consequently Cuba's economy is subject to considerable fluctuation. Table 3-6 indicates the fluctuation in Cuban tobacco and sugar exports. Additionally, Cuba was plagued by hurricanes in 1978 and 1979, which undoubtedly destroyed many crops. The recent influx from these Caribbean countries, including many illegal entries, is most likely due as much to economic conditions as to political repression. (The U.S. views immigrants from Cuba as political refugees, while those from Haiti are viewed as fleeing from poverty. In the spring of 1980, special treatment was offered to 130,000 immigrants from Cuba and Haiti by the Carter Administration with the expectation that Congress will pass legislation accepting them as refugees.[29])

Push and pull forces often work together to encourage immigration to the United States (for example, low wages in Mexico and

Table 3-6 Exports of Selected Cuban Crops (in thousands of tons)

Year	Raw Sugar	Refined Sugar	Molasses	Tobacco
1963	3,521	623	499	13.0
1970	6,065	592	950	13.9
1974	4,812	375	581	15.6
1975	5,197	242	443	14.2

SOURCE: Council for Mutual Economic Assistance, *Statistical Yearbook*, 1978, p. 358.

high wages in the United States). When the peso was devalued in 1976, the buying power of workers in Mexico decreased, while the value in pesos of wages received in U.S. dollars doubled. One action, peso devaluation, caused an increase in both the push and pull factors leading to Mexican immigration to the United States. One would suspect that illegal immigration would have increased as a result of these increased incentives. Indeed, apprehension statistics show that Mexican apprehensions increased almost 23 percent in 1977.[30] Whether the devaluation should be considered as predominantly a push or pull force is not important. It is important to recognize the existence of both forces in order to formulate any effective policy to reduce the migration pressures. Most research on push and pull forces has been done in Mexico. Their relative importance in causing illegal immigration from other parts of the world is an area for future research.

The forces behind immigration are primarily economic ones. In addition, the migration literature has indicated that migration to any country increases with the size of the migrant stock already in that country. Researchers have suggested that this effect is due to improved knowledge of opportunities as well as the reduced psychic and real costs of movement when friends and relatives are in the country to which one immigrates. Thus, one would expect more immigration to the United States from countries where large numbers of individuals have migrated to the United States in recent years.

Given that an individual has decided that immigration is potentially beneficial, the individual next has to decide whether legal immigration is possible and consider the costs involved. In general, legal immigration is most feasible for highly skilled individuals from Western European nations. Immigration for other nationalities and for the less skilled has become increasingly difficult. The termination of the Bracero (guest worker) Program in the 1960s and the 1965 amendments to the Immigration and Nationality Act limited immigration from Mexico and the Western Hemisphere to a total of 120,000. Changes in immigration laws in 1976 extended the per-country limitation of 20,000 and the preference system to the Western Hemisphere. These changes reduced the number of immigrant visas available to Mexican nationals from 62,205 in fiscal year 1975 to 57,863 in fiscal year 1976 and 44,079 in fiscal year 1977.[31]

Even if it is possible to obtain a visa, there are still costs involved. One must apply at a U.S. consulate's office, which exist only in the larger cities and at some points of entry. Also, much time is involved. Mexicans must wait an average of two and a half years to be approved for a U.S. visa, and the 1976 amendments to the Immigration Act probably have increased this period.[32] The time and travel involved in obtaining a visa and the probability of being refused are all factors in the cost of legal immigration.

Given that immigration is potentially beneficial and that legal immigration is impossible or perceived as too costly, the individual may consider illegal immigration. There are also costs to illegal immigration. Wage discrimination and lack of fringe benefits due to one's illegal status are costs only if the individual has a choice of legal or illegal immigration, or enjoys those benefits in his or her native land. Discrimination and prejudice in the United States are psychological costs. Avoiding detection and deportation are also costly. A significant number of illegal entrants are having to rely on smugglers to get them into the United States. The price that must be paid to the smugglers varies but is usually around $150 to $225. (This is the finding of Cornelius.[33] North and Houston found the average payment to be $234, with $1200 the highest response.[34] More recently, it was reported that a group from El Salvador paid $2500 each to be smuggled into the United States. Their journey ended in tragedy.[35]) Once the individual has successfully entered the country, he or she is subject to additional uncertainty due to the possibility that in any given period the individual will be deported and thus not earn the income expected. If the deported individual plans to minimize his time out of the U.S. labor force (that is, he or she will attempt to reenter as soon as possible), then the cost of deportation is directly related to the distance the individual's homeland is from the United States. Thus, to an experienced border-hopper living just across the border, deportation does not present the same fear that it does to a person who has traveled 2,000 miles. Indeed, many "locals" that are apprehended merely agree to leave the country. Finally, there is the possibility of losing some wages due to deportation. It is unknown how often employers refuse to pay wages owed to apprehended illegal alien workers. However, it is a possibility, and the laws have given the deportee little recourse.[36]

While it is obvious that there are costs involved with illegal immigration, these costs can be expected to decrease with successive illegal trips to the United States. There seems to be a definite learning curve for illegal aliens. Those who have made prior illegal trips to the United States have a much lower chance of being apprehended.[37] Therefore the probability of being deported decreases, and so do the costs associated with deportation. Additionally, if an illegal immigrant has sound employment contacts (as a result of an earlier trip), the period of transitional unemployment is reduced and expected income is increased. While the use of smugglers might not decrease,* it is likely that smuggling costs will decrease. This is true for two reasons. First, the illegal alien repeaters have more contacts with and knowledge about smugglers and can "shop around." Second, it is reported that U.S. employers often are the contractor with the smuggler.[38] To the extent that an employer pays part of the smuggling fee, costs to the illegal alien are reduced.

Potential immigrants weigh the costs and benefits of immigration. Most of these motivating forces concern economic conditions. Whether to immigrate legally or illegally is largely a function of U.S. immigration policy. Those who are prohibited from immigrating legally then must weigh the costs and benefits of illegal immigration against those of not immigrating. By and large, for the low-skilled migrant from Mexico there is an increasing likelihood that he or she will illegally enter the United States.

Once the immigrant has decided upon illegal immigration, one final decision is faced—whether to participate in the regular or the underground economy. This choice is constrained by the employment opportunities available to the illegal alien. From the alien's point of view, participation in the underground economy offers a number of advantages. First, the probability of detection and deportation should be lower for individuals in the underground economy than for those in the regular economy, since records are minimal and the employer as well as the employee has an incentive to maintain secrecy. Second, the illegal alien can avoid paying taxes, social security, and other deductions. The evasion of such taxes is desirable to the illegal alien, as he or she is unlikely to utilize many public services or benefits for one reason or another (particularly fear of discovery and deportation). North and Houston found low levels of use of public services and benefits. Twenty-seven percent of their respondents had used hospitals or clinics, only 3.7 percent had children in U.S. schools, 1.3 percent obtained food stamps, and 0.5 percent received welfare assistance.

---

* Cornelius found 36 percent of his respondents were smuggled in the first time they came to the U.S., while 41 percent were smuggled in on their most recent trip.[59] Furthermore, as the border is "tightened" through increased surveillance and enforcement, the incidence of smuggling will likely increase.

Table 3-7 Unemployment Compensation Programs as a Percent Tax of Taxable Wages by State and Year

State	1971	1973	1975	1977
California	1.94	3.1	3.15	3.47
Florida	0.81	0.7	0.98	2.73
Illinois	0.88	2.1	1.06	2.99
New York	2.11	2.7	1.12	3.46
Texas	0.26	0.7	0.35	0.97
All states average	1.41	2.0	1.98	2.85

SOURCE: Tax Foundation, *Facts and Figures,* Table 178 (1979, 1977, 1975, 1973).

For the employer, not reporting illegal aliens hired has become increasingly attractive in recent years. By not reporting such hirings the employer can forego employer contributions to private health and retirement plans as well as social security, unemployment insurance, and workmen's compensation payments. The size and coverage of these payments have grown markedly in recent years (see Table 3-7), making evasion increasingly attractive. The expected benefits to the employer of not reporting employment of illegal aliens is higher than for regular employees, because detection is less likely due to the alien's desire for anonymity. Nevertheless, the studies by Cornelius, Villalpando, and North and Houston all found that around 70 percent of working illegal aliens have social security and income tax withheld, and, therefore, are in the regular economy. This indicates that aliens' job opportunities outside the regular economy are limited and that most employers who hire illegal aliens for some reason prefer to operate "on the books." The legal consequences faced by an employer who hires illegal aliens "off the books" are relatively minor. Currently there is no federal law prohibiting the hiring of illegal aliens. In California, it is unlawful to hire illegal aliens "if such employment would have an adverse effect on lawful resident workers." The punishment is a fine from $200 to $500 for each offense (California Labor Code Section 2805). Thus the lack of federal legislation and the weakness of existing laws reduce the employer's incentive for secrecy in avoiding the regular economy.

More substantial costs of hiring aliens off the books are a damaged reputation among business associates, labor problems (as has been the case with the California farm workers), and a guilty conscience for knowingly breaking the law. The high percentage of illegal aliens employed in the regular economy might also be due in part to a shifting of illegal employment away from agriculture to companies with large work forces. Economies of scale in the cost of keeping records on employees, along with a greater potential damage from loss of reputation and strikes faced by larger companies, will reduce the incentives to go "off the books."

Costs and Benefits to Society

The United States has obviously benefited from immigration. It has been said that the history of the immigrant is the history of the United States. Immigrant labor played major roles in the development of the United States. They have worked on canals and railroads, on farms and in factories, and have supplied labor during wartime shortages. Today they fill some jobs that U.S. residents do not want. In times of prosperity they are welcomed, while in times of recession they are blamed for the plight of American citizens.

During the Depression of the 1930s there was much public concern over aliens in the labor force, especially Mexicans. (See Divine[39] for a study of American immigration policy and public attitudes toward immigration during the first half of this century.) During World War II they supplied labor, but after the Korean War was over, "Operation Wetback," a massive effort by the Immigration and Naturalization Service to remove illegal Mexican aliens, was carried out. It peaked in 1954 with the apprehension of over a million illegal Mexican aliens. Similarly, the mid-1970s were characterized by increased concern over illegal immigration. It was asserted that illegal immigration cost U.S. society $13 billion dollars and over one million jobs.* Enforcement efforts have been increasing.

The presumption that the illegal alien is necessarily a burden to society seems to be invalid. Those illegal aliens who work in the regular economy pay all normal taxes. As mentioned earlier, studies have shown that the overwhelming majority of illegal alien workers have income taxes and social security deducted from their earnings.

---

* These frequently cited figures seem to be inaccurate. The estimate of $13 billion was made in 1975 by a consulting firm (Inner City Fund) hired by the INS. Their conclusions apparently were based upon the findings of the Lesko Study (see Keely[9] and Bustamante[61] for a critique of these findings). The assertion that illegal aliens take away 1 million jobs was made by INS Commissioner Chapman in 1975 before a House of Representatives' Subcommittee.[62] In a *Reader's Digest* article in October, 1976, Chapman claimed that with adequate enforcement, unemployment could be cut almost in half.

In addition, state and local sales taxes and user fees cannot be avoided even by those in the underground economy. Property taxes affect the illegal alien the same as any other renter. These taxes form a substantial part of the state-local tax base. We calculate the loss of federal tax revenue due to participation in the underground economy by illegal aliens to have been $473 million to $606 million in 1974. (We arrive at this figure by assuming there were 3.6 million aliens employed (90 percent), earning between $117 and $150 per week. We further assume that 27 percent of these employed illegal aliens do not have income taxes withheld and the applicable tax rate is .08. That is, 4 million aliens in 1974 × .9 employed × .27 in underground economy × $117/week × 52 weeks/year × .08 tax dollars/wage dollars = $473 million dollars in 1974; $473 million in 1975 × $150/$117 = $606 million in 1974.) In its recent report, IRS[40] estimates revenue loss from illegal aliens to be between $400 million and $519 million in 1976.* We assume that 80 percent of the illegal alien population is located in ten states and that illegal immigrants are divided among these states in the same proportion as legal immigrants. We use the same ten states that Robinson did. Due to our belief that Mexican illegals are the bulk of the illegal alien population, we assume that approximately 80 percent of the illegal alien population is included in these states. Thus the percentage of illegal population residing in each state is estimated by multiplying the percentage of legal immigrants who intended to permanently reside there by 80/73.8. We use methods similar to those explained earlier to estimate lost state income tax revenue. We can estimate the total amount of state income taxes avoided by illegal aliens participating in the underground economy. We estimate that from $235 million to $302 million dollars of state income tax is not paid (see Table 3-2). The loss of local income tax revenue is roughly estimated at $30 million to $40 million. (Only two states of the ten, New York and Michigan, have local income taxes. We assume that three fourths of the illegal population in New York lives in New York City—the only locality with an income tax in New York—and that half of the illegal population in Michigan lives in

---

* This figure is generated rather than actually reported. IRS estimates $27.5–$35.6 billion goes unreported due to nonreporting (Table 3 of IRS report). Of this total they estimate $5–$6.6 billion comes from illegal aliens not reporting (Table F.1 of IRS report). They estimate the loss due to total nonreporting to be $2.2 to $2.8 billion. Multiplying this range by 5/27.5 to 6.6/35.6 gives us our generated IRS estimate of $400 and $519 million (i.e., 2.2 billion × 5 billion ÷ 27.5 billion = 400 million; 2.8 billion × 6.6 billion ÷ 35.6 billion = 519 million).

Detroit. The applicable tax rates are 2 percent for New York City and Detroit and 1 percent for the rest of Michigan. We further assume that this represents 80 percent of the lost local income tax revenue due attributable to illegal aliens. We use methods similar to those we used in calculating loss of federal tax revenue.) Thus total lost income tax revenue from this section of the underground economy is from $738 million to $948 million.

As previously mentioned, the illegal alien tends to underutilize social services and programs. One study in San Diego county concluded that illegal aliens there used about $2 million worth of services while contributing almost $50 million in income taxes.[41] These studies indicate that less than 30 percent use medical services, 4 percent claim unemployment, 4 percent have children in U.S. schools, about 1 percent receive food stamps, and less than 1 percent receive welfare. (These are very similar to the findings of North and Houston discussed earlier.)

The most significant impact of illegal immigration to the United States is on the labor market. It is generally concluded that illegal immigration increases native unemployment (especially in the secondary labor market) and depresses the wages of U.S. citizens. Due to the lack of accurate data on labor market participation by illegals,[42] it has not been possible to empirically estimate the validity and magnitude of these effects, although theoretical approaches to the problem have been developed by INS.[31, 43] Briggs argues that high unemployment, low wages, low per capita income, low union activity, and high level of welfare assistance in South Texas "are signs of labor surplus which is one indication of the presence of sizeable numbers of illegal aliens," but says additional "soft data" is necessary (such as "personal interviews, newspaper accounts, and INS activities in the local market").[44] Piore, emphasizing the importance of the structure of relative wages, argues that increasing the wage of the migrant (by decreasing the supply of migrant labor through increased border control) will bring about labor pressure to raise other wages. Thus "on the macro level . . . we must anticipate as a consequence of curtailing migration not simply a decline in living standards, adjustments in the balance of payments, slower growth and higher unemployment. We probably must anticipate a certain amount of inflationary pressures as well."[45]

Others argue that illegal immigrants do not displace native workers because they take jobs that native workers do not want and will not take. Villalpando documented the inability of two government programs in Southern California to fill jobs vacated by apprehended aliens with native workers.[46] He also points out that the revenue maximizing native worker is better off on welfare than earning the wages paid to illegal aliens, and, thus, employing illegal aliens has institutionalized support. Job displacement probably is a result of the employment of illegal aliens. However, the magnitude of this displacement currently cannot be estimated and is the subject of considerable controversy.

Data limitations have also prevented much empirical testing of the wage depression hypothesis. Smith and Newman, by gathering data from field survey work, did find evidence of real wage differences between Houston and the South Texas border area.[47] They estimated a $719 per year differential (11 percent) for Mexican Americans and a $580 (7 percent) differential for non-Mexican Americans.

The labor market effects discussed above are caused by any increased immigration—legal or illegal. Fogel argues that illegal immigration uniquely lowers labor standards.[48] Due to their illegal status, these workers cannot seek enforcement of labor standards. Furthermore, the illegal alien tends not to unionize[49] and this has "a significant deleterious impact on labor standards because one of the functions of a union is to see that these standards are observed."[50]

The balance of payments is also affected by illegal immigration. North and Houston found that illegal aliens they surveyed made average monthly payments abroad of $105.[51] Mexican illegals averaged $129 per month or about 30 percent of their monthly income, while other Western Hemisphere illegals averaged $76 and Eastern Hemisphere illegals $37 per month abroad. Cornelius found the Mexicans he studied to remit an average of $162 per month or 42 percent of monthly income,[52] and Villalpando found a similar figure of $138 per month or 37 percent of monthly wages.[53] Weighting these averages by the number of respondents in the respective studies and by the assumed distribution of the illegal population, we estimate that the average illegal immigrant remitted approximately $125 to $156 per month.* Thus in 1975 we estimate that a total of

---

* North and Houston interviewed 481 Mexicans, while Villalpando interviewed 217 Mexicans, and Cornelius's results were taken from a 25 percent sample of 1,000 interviews. Weighting the findings of these studies by the number of respondents, we estimated that the average Mexican illegal alien sent $162 home every month. Then accepting North and Houston's findings for the non-Mexican illegal alien population, we got a weighted average of approximately $122 per month (i.e., 60% Mexican illegals × $162/mo + 25% other Western Hemisphere illegals × $76/mo + 15% Eastern Hemisphere × $37/mo ≅ $122/mo; $122/mo × $150/$117 = $156/mo.

approximately $6 to $7.5 billion was exported from the United States by illegal aliens. However, this figure is not a "net" figure, since immigrants bring money into the United States. In Bustamante's study, illegal aliens spent an average of $70 to migrate to the U.S.[54] (This is derived by weighting the finding of Bustamante (his Table 5) by the number of respondents. Of course, expenditures are directly related to the distance that the immigrant must travel to reach the United States.) It is not possible to determine what portion of these monies are spent in the United States. However, the amount of money brought into the United States somewhat offsets the effect of illegals sending money out of the United States.

There are several positive partial consequences of illegal aliens working in the U.S. economy. The cheap labor provided by illegals lowers operating costs for producers. Consequently, some businesses probably avoid collapse, and consumer prices should be lower than they would be without the presence of illegal aliens. Aggregate demand in the United States is increased approximately $15–$20 billion since the illegal population appears to spend around 70 percent of the earnings in the United States. (We arrived at this figure by the following formula: 4 million illegal aliens $\times$ .9 employment $\times$ $117/wk $\times$ 52 wk/yr $\times$ .7 domestic consumption rate $\cong$ $15 billion; $15 billion $\times$ $150/$117 $\cong$ 20 billion dollars.) Furthermore, it is often contended that illegals make good workers because they are "docile." Thus, illegals might be more productive (in units/time) than native Americans in the same job.

These positive aspects are not without negative counterparts. The more productive, docile, illegal worker might tolerate dangerous working conditions. Furthermore, Marshall has documented a case where the practice of paying labor on a piecemeal basis has prevented basic management innovations, since inefficiency is most costly to the workers and not to the producers.[55] As noted above, native unemployment and lower wages for those already receiving low pay are also likely results. There are some indications that among the native population the benefits from illegal immigration are skewed in favor of the more wealthy, while the lower-class native population absorbs most of the negative impact. Cheswick has done recent work on the redistribution of wealth associated with illegal immigration.[56]

There are other social consequences of immigration. Sending countries often benefit from emigration to the United States. It is argued that illegal immigration to the United States is an escape valve for internal political pressure in Mexico.[57] The high level of agrarian revolt in Mexico during the mid-1970s (which, incidentally, happened during the tightening of the United States-Mexican border) indicates the real threat rural underemployment poses to the Mexican government. Illegal immigration to the United States is an alternative to revolt, and, thus, is not discouraged by the government of Mexico. Many officials of the U.S. executive branch realize that high levels of illegal immigration from Mexico preserve stability in Mexico.* Indeed, now and in the foreseeable future, any unilateral effort by the United States to merely tighten the border (that is, increased enforcement) will contribute to internal unrest in Mexico. Likewise, the current emigration from Cuba is welcomed by the government there and it is the United States that is seeking to curtail the flow.

A more long-term problem that illegal immigration causes is the potential creation of an underclass of residents. North and Houston find that "Mexican respondents were much more likely to travel in and out of the United States than those from other parts of the world."[58] Since the Mexican respondents on average had been here a shorter period of time, this could indicate that Mexican illegals are more temporary than those from other areas. If the illegal alien becomes a permanent rather than a temporary U.S. resident, then the practice of denying this resident legal status and other institutional discrimination will create an underclass. Compounding this problem, Texas has engaged in litigation to require the payment of public school tuition for the children of illegal aliens,† even though Texas has no income taxes and supports schools by property and sales taxes, which illegal aliens pay.

---

* "Memorandum for the President, Subject: Undocumented Aliens," April 27, 1977, p. 34, from the Secretaries of Labor, State, and HEW, and the Attorney General: "We must recognize that the imposition of effective legislation restrictions will shut off an important escape valve for our Latin neighbors and could lead to destabilizing social, economic, and political pressures there." We found this citation in National Lawyers Guild, Immigration Project, *Immigration Law and Defense*, New York, 1979.

† One such case (INRE: Alien Children Education Litigation, MDL Docket Number 398, Southern District of Texas, Houston Division) was decided in Federal District Court on July 22, 1980. The decision went against the State of Texas, but the Texas Attorney General has appealed the case to the Supreme Court, and the writ of *certiorari* has been granted, but at the time of this writing, no final judgment has been reached.

Endnotes

1. North, David S., and Marion Houston. 1976. *The Characteristics and Role of Illegal Aliens in the U.S. Labor Market: An Exploratory Study.* Washington, D.C.: Litton and Co., Public Document PB-252-616.
2. Samora, Julian. 1971. *Los Mojados: The Wetback Story.* Notre Dame, Ind.: University of Notre Dame Press.
3. Villalpando, M. Vic, et al. 1977. *A Study of the Socioeconomic Impact of Illegal Aliens on the County of San Diego.* San Diego, Cal.: San Diego County Human Resources Agency.
4. Bustamante, Jorge. 1977. "Undocumented Immigration from Mexico: Research Report," *International Migration Review* 11:149–177.
5. Cornelius, Wayne A. 1977. "Illegal Mexican Migration to the United States: A Summary of Recent Research Findings and Policy Implications," Congressional Record, Vol. 123, No. 118, 95th Congress, 1st Session, July 15, 1977, pp. 22726–22732.
6. Reichert, Josh, and Douglas Massey. 1979. "Patterns of U.S. Migration from a Mexican Sending Community: A Comparison of Legal and Illegal Migrants," *International Migration Review* 13 (Winter):599–623.
7. Korns, Alexander. 1977. "Coverage of Issues Raised by Comparisons between CPS and Establishment Employment," American Statistical Association, *Proceedings,* Social Statistics Section, pp. 60–69.
8. Lesko and Associates. 1975. "Final Report: Basic Data and Guidance Required to Implement a Major Illegal Alien Study During the Fiscal Year 1976." Prepared for U.S. Immigration and Naturalization Service, Washington, D.C.
9. Keely, Charles B. 1975. "Counting the Uncountable: Estimates of Undocumented Aliens in the United States," *Population and Development Review* 3 (December):473–481.
10. Lancaster, Claire, and F. Scheuren. 1977. "Counting the Uncountable Illegals: Some Initial Statistical Speculations Employing the Capture-Recapture Techniques," American Statistical Association, *Proceedings,* Social Statistics Section, pp. 530–533.
11. Heer, David M. 1979. "What Is the Net Flow of Undocumented Mexican Immigrants to the United States?" *Demography* 16 (August):417–423.
12. Robinson, J. Gregory. 1979. "Estimating the Approximate Size of the Illegal Alien Population in the U.S. by Comparative Trend Analysis of Age-Specific Death Rates." Paper presented at Population Association of America Annual Meeting, April 26–28.
13. North and Houston, *Characteristics and Role of Illegal Aliens,* pp. 85, 99.
14. *Ibid.,* Table V-14, p. 125.
15. *New York Times.* 1979. "Illegal Aliens in New York: A Life of Fear, Costly to All." March 18, pp. 1, 40.
16. U.S. Department of the Treasury, Internal Revenue Service. 1979. *Estimates of Income Unreported on Individual Income Tax Returns.* Washington, D.C.: U.S. Department of the Treasury. Publication 1104 (9–79).
17. Cornelius, "Illegal Mexican Migration," p. 22726.
18. Sjaastad, L. 1962. "The Costs and Returns to Human Migration," *Journal of Political Economy* 70 (October):80–93.

19. Greenwood, Michael J. 1975. "Research on International Migration in the United States: A Survey," *Journal of Economic Literature* 13 (June):397–433.
20. Todaro, M. 1977. *Internal Migration in Developing Nations: A Review of Theory, Evidence, Methodology and Research Priorities.* Geneva: International Labor Organization.
21. Evans, John S., and D. James Demerus. 1979. "Conditions of Unemployment and Income Distribution in Mexico as Incentives for Mexican Migration to the United States: Prospects to the End of the Century," *International Migration Review* 13 (Spring):6–8.
22. Jenkins, J. Craig. 1977. "Push/Pull in Mexican Migration to the U.S.," *International Migration Review* 11 (Summer):184–185.
23. Frisbie, Parker. 1975. "Illegal Migration from Mexico to the United States: A Longitudinal Analysis," *International Migration Review* 9 (Spring):11.
24. Jenkins, "Push/Pull in Mexican Migration," p. 183.
25. Alba, Francisco. 1978. "Mexico's International Migration as a Manifestation of Its Development Pattern," *International Migration Review* 12, 4 (Winter):502–513.
26. Witte, Ann D. 1973. "Employment in the Manufacturing Sector of Developing Economies: A Study of Mexico and Peru," *Journal of Developmental Studies* 10 (October):33–49.
27. Evans and James, "Conditions in Mexico as Incentives for Migration," pp. 10–11.
28. Mesa-Lago, Carmela. 1970. "Availability and Reliability of Statistics in Socialist Cuba." Center for Latin American Studies, University of Pittsburgh, Occasional Papers, No. 1 (January).
29. *Newsweek.* 1980. "The New Immigrants." July 4, p. 28.
30. Immigration and Naturalization Service. 1977. *Annual Report.* Washington, D.C.: INS, U.S. Department of Justice, p. 14.
31. Jasso, Guillermina. 1978. "A Framework for the Study of Displacement." Washington, D.C.: U.S. Immigration and Naturalization Service, p. 3.
32. Cornelius, "Illegal Mexican Migration," p. 22730.
33. *Ibid.*, p. 22727.
34. North and Houston, "Characteristics and Role of Illegal Aliens."
35. *Newsweek.* 1980. "The Salvadorian Aliens: Death in the Desert." July 21, p. 55.
36. Samora, *Los Mojados*, pp. 99–100.
37. Cornelius, "Illegal Mexican Migration," p. 22727.
38. Stoddard, Ellwyn. 1976. "A Conceptual Analysis of the 'Alien Invasion': Institutionalized Support of Mexican Aliens in the United States," *International Migration Review* 10 (Summer):172.
39. Divine, Robert. 1957. *American Immigration Policy, 1924–1952.* New Haven, Conn.: Yale University Press.
40. *Estimates of Income Unreported.*
41. Villalpando, "Socioeconomic Impact."
42. Briggs, Vernon M., Jr. 1976. "Illegal Immigration and the American Labor Force: The Use of 'Soft' Data for Analysis," *American Behavioral Scientist* 19 (January/February):356–359.
43. Cheswick, Barry. 1978. "Methodology for Estimating the Impact of Immigra-

tion on Unemployment in the United States." Report prepared under the Immigration and Naturalization Service Contract, CO-78-525 (July 14), Washington, D.C.
44. Briggs, "Illegal Immigration and the American Labor Force," p. 360.
45. Piore, Michael. 1979. *Birds of Passage: Migrant Labor and Industrial Societies.* New York and London: Cambridge University Press.
46. Villalpando, "Socioeconomic Impact," p. 62.
47. Smith, Barton, and Robert Newman. 1977. "Depressed Wages Along the U.S.-Mexico Border: An Empirical Analysis," *Economic Inquiry* 15 (January):51–67.
48. Fogel, Walter A. 1977. "Illegal Aliens: Economic Aspects and Public Policy Alternatives," *San Diego Law Review* 15 (December):63–78.
49. Briggs, "Illegal Immigration and American Labor Force."
50. Fogel, "Illegal Aliens," p. 66.
51. North and Houston, *Characteristics and Role of Illegal Aliens,* p. 80.
52. Cornelius, "Illegal Mexican Migration," p. 22729.
53. Villalpando, "Socioeconomic Impact."
54. Bustamante, "Undocumented Immigration from Mexico," pp. 168–169.
55. Marshall, F. Ray. 1975. "Economic Factors Influencing International Migration of Workers." Paper presented at the Conference on Contemporary Dilemmas of Mexican-U.S. Border, Weatherhead Foundation (April).
56. Cheswick, Barry. 1978. "Immigrants and Immigration Policy," in W. Fellner (ed.), *Contemporary Economic Problems, 1978.* Washington, D.C.: American Enterprise Institute, pp. 285–325.
57. Briggs, Vernon M., Jr. 1978. "Labor Market Aspects of Mexican Migration to the United States in the 1970's," in *Views Across the Border,* Stanley Ross (ed.). Albuquerque, N.M.: University of New Mexico Press, p. 213.
58. North and Houston, *Characteristics and Role of Illegal Aliens,* p. 86.
59. *Business Week.* 1977. "What Illegal Aliens Cost the Economy," June 13, pp. 86–88.
60. Bustamante, "Undocumented Immigration from Mexico," p. 151.
61. Chapman, Leonard. 1975. Prepared statement before the Subcommittee on Immigration, Citizenship and International Law, Committee on the Judiciary, House of Representatives, 94th Congress, 1st Session, February 4, p. 32.
62. Domestic Council Committee on Illegal Aliens. 1976. "Preliminary Report." Washington, D.C.: Department of Justice.

Additional References

BRIGGS, VERNON M., JR. 1975. "Illegal Aliens: The Need for a More Restrictive Border Policy," *Social Science Quarterly* 56 (December):477–484.
The Environmental Fund. 1978. "Special Report: Illegal Immigration." Special Report No. 2 (November), Washington, D.C.
Immigration and Naturalization Service. 1974. *Annual Report.* Washington, D.C.: INS, U.S. Department of Justice.
Immigration and Naturalization Service. 1975. *Annual Report.* Washington, D.C.: INS, U.S. Department of Justice.

ROCHIN, REFUGIO. 1978. "Illegal Aliens in Agriculture: Some Theoretical Considerations," *Labor Law Journal* (March), pp. 149–167.
WASSERMAN, JACK. 1979. *Immigration Law and Practice*. 3rd edition. Philadelphia: American Law Institute–American Bar Association.

Chapter 4

NONREPORTING DUE TO ILLEGAL STATUS OF GOODS

In this part we will consider the failure to report transactions in goods because of their status—stolen. Although closely related to transactions in illegal goods and services, the goods and services discussed in this section are different because it is only their status which makes the transactions illegal and not the nature of the goods themselves.

Size and Trends

There are many transactions of stolen goods in the United States at both the wholesale and the retail level. Stolen goods originate, of course, with a theft, and a number of researchers[1, 2] have suggested that we view the thief—whether shoplifter, burglar, robber, or pilfering employee—as the "producer" in this section of the underground economy.

Although many thieves keep a portion of the "loot" for themselves and/or fence the goods they steal themselves, most thieves, particularly professional or large-scale thieves, work with a "fence" in order to turn the goods they steal into money. The fences are the wholesalers and retailers of this sector of the underground economy.

It is very difficult to obtain estimates of the size of this sector of the underground economy because of the limited amount of previous research and the diversity of the sector. Some economists (for example, James Henry[3]) would not even count this sector as part of the underground economy because it adds no value, but rather represents a mechanism for illegal transfer of ownership. While we are sympathetic to this position and, indeed, adhere to it when estimating the social costs of stolen goods markets, we believe that the incomes earned in this sector should be included in the national income of the underground economy. There are at least two possible lines of argument that might lead to their inclusion. The first, discussed above, sees the thief as the producer in the stolen goods industry and the fence as the wholesaler and retailer. The second argument is that the thieves and fences expend their energies and other resources to transfer, albeit illegally, money and goods; and, like the incomes of secondhand dealers and government workers administering transfer payments, the income of these "workers" should be included in the national income of their economy.

Given that we feel that incomes generated in this sector should be included in underground national income, we are left with the problem of estimating these incomes. Both direct and indirect approaches to the problem are possible and have been used in the past. Direct approaches estimate the incomes of thieves and fences by considering the value of property stolen, fences' purchase and sale prices, and the costs of doing business for thieves and fences. Indirect approaches seek to estimate trends in stolen goods markets by observing the movement of series believed to be related to the size of the stolen goods market (for example, value of goods stolen, youth unemployment rates, truck hijackings). We believe that the direct approach provides more reliable estimates of the size of stolen goods markets and we have employed it to obtain estimates of incomes earned in these markets in 1974. Using the incomes approach to national income estimation, this gives us our estimate of the amount of underground national income generated by stolen goods markets. We have used the indirect approach to estimate trends in this market.

Using the methods and data described in detail in the appendix to this chapter, we estimate that $28.8 billion worth of property was stolen in 1975. Most of this property was not stolen by traditional strong-arm tactics (such as robbery or burglary), but is business lost through shoplifting and employee theft. Indeed, only approximately $6 billion of the total $28.8 billion loss occurred as a result of the traditional property offenses (robbery, burglary, larceny). Further, it appears that while the rate of growth in traditional theft has slowed considerably since the late 1960s, the rate of increase in such nontraditional areas as employee theft has actually accelerated.

In order to estimate national income for the stolen goods industry, we need to know not the value of goods stolen, but rather the incomes earned by the thieves and fences who operate in this industry. In order to do this, we made a number of assumptions. We briefly describe our assumptions here and give additional details in the appendix. First, we needed to obtain estimates of the incomes earned by the thieves and fences employed in the stolen goods industry. We decided that cash stolen by thieves and goods kept by thieves for their own uses represent largely a "transfer" payment, and thus we include only 10 percent of the values of those items in our estimate of the national income of this sector. We see this 10 percent as the thieves' pay for "productive services" rendered. As explained in the appendix, we estimate that stolen money and goods which thieves used for their own purposes was worth $5.8 to $7.6 billion in 1975. To obtain estimates of the incomes earned by thieves and fences from goods that are fenced, we assumed that fences pay thieves, on the average, 25 percent of the value of the goods they steal. Fences, in turn, eventually sell these goods to the ultimate consumer for between 50 and 75 percent of their value. We estimate that the thieves' "cost of doing business" averages 10 percent of their gross income, and that fences incur costs averaging 25 percent of their gross income. Using all of the above assumptions, we estimate that thieves who fenced goods earned a net income of $3 to $3.4 billion in 1975 and the fences earned a net income of between $2.4 and $5.6 billion in that year. Summing all of the above income estimates, we obtain an estimated national income for the stolen goods industry of between $6.0 and $9.8 billion in 1975. Moving this 1975 figure backward in time, using the consumer price index as a deflator, we obtain an estimated 1974 national income for the stolen goods industry of between $5.4 and $8.9 billion.

Trends in the size of the stolen goods industry are hard to estimate. However, assuming that the size of the traditional strong-arm portion of this industry moved at approximately the same rate as the value of stolen goods reported to the police, we estimate that this portion of the industry grew by approximately 11 percent per annum in the 1960–1969 period and by approximately 8 percent per annum during 1970–1975 period. The growth rate of this traditional stolen goods industry exceeds that for reported GNP by approximately 4 percent per annum in 1960–1969 and was below that for reported GNP by approximately 1 percent per annum in 1970– 1975. As mentioned above, and explained in more detail in the

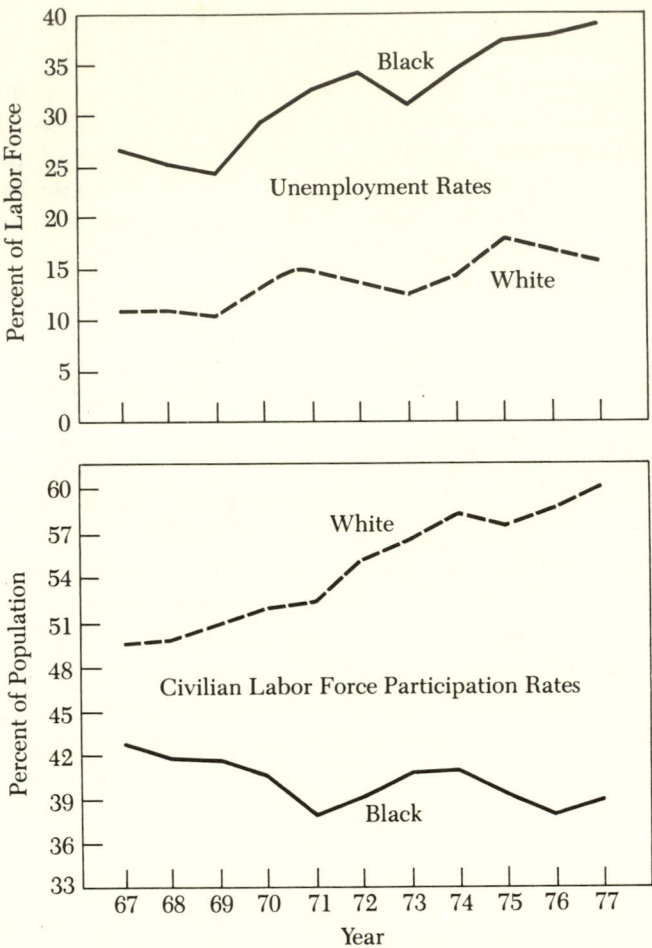

Figure 4-1 Unemployment Rates and Civilian Labor Force Participation Rates for those 16 to 19 Years Old. *(Source: U.S. Department of Labor, 1978, p. 71.)*

appendix to this chapter, many thefts are not reported to the police. Perhaps the largest amount of such theft is employee theft from businesses. Using Bureau of Domestic Commerce figures for business loss from all property offenses we estimate that this portion of the stolen goods market may have been the most dynamic in recent years, growing by approximately 15 percent per annum in the 1971 to 1976 period. Thus, it appears that while the "traditional" portion (burglary, robbery) of the stolen goods industry may have actually declined relative to reported economic activity in the early 1970s, non-traditional sectors of this industry (such as employee theft) may have grown markedly.

A number of economists, the first of whom is Becker,[4] have suggested that it is mainly those who are unemployed or not participating in the legitimate labor market who form the "labor force" for the traditional sector of the stolen goods industry. Recent surveys of empirical work testing this proposition have generally found that higher rates of unemployment and lower rates of labor force participation are associated with higher rates of *reported* property offenses.[5] As it is predominantly young males who participate in property crime, one would expect the unemployment rate and labor force participation rates for such individuals to be directly related to the size of the labor force available for traditional theft activities. Figure 4-1 presents unemployment rates and labor force participation rates for individuals 16 to 19 years old during the 1967–1977 period. As can be seen in this figure, the trends for black and white teenagers diverged markedly in the post-1974 period. While white teenager labor force participation rates increased and unemployment declined, the opposite was generally true for nonwhites. Although recent data on school attendance is not available, data from the 1970 census seems to indicate that the proportion of teenagers not in the labor force who were attending school has probably either remained relatively stable or perhaps declined. (A table for 1960 and 1970, which gives the percentage of males, by race, not in the labor force and not enrolled in school, is shown in Levenson,[6] pp. III–16.) As a whole, the above data seems to indicate that the labor force for the traditional sectors of the stolen goods industry is increasingly nonwhite. This contrasts markedly with the labor force for employee theft, which current research seems to indicate is predominantly Caucasian. (See Clark *et al.*[7] for a discussion of the characteristics of thieves who steal from their employers.)

The Structure of the Industry

Given the covert nature of both theft and fencing industries and the relatively limited amount of previous research, our description may well only reflect the way in which selected portions of these two industries operate. Indeed, one reason these two industries are difficult to describe is their extreme diversity. Our descriptions are based on research which has described these industries in general and on studies of auto, securities, and art portions of those industries. We chose to study these particular portions of the industry in detail because we feel that quite different techniques and quite distinct labor forces are used in them. Auto theft is believed to be the most widespread and costly of all property crimes. Theft of motor vehicles, their contents, and accessories accounted for approximately 50 percent of all reported larcenies in 1977. This amounted to 968,400 motor vehicle thefts reported, 998,100 reports of content theft, and 1,210,700 thefts of accessories for a total valuation of $2.3 billion (vehicles alone were valued at $1.93 billion). (See Trepel[8] for an excellent discussion of the auto theft industry.) People who steal cars range from juvenile joyriders to highly organized professional theft rings. Both security and art theft are much more specialized and less common offenses. However, due to the sophistication of techniques and personnel and the international redistribution systems often used, we felt knowledge of these two sectors would expand our understanding of the "specialty" portion of the stolen goods industry. (See the U.S. Senate *Hearings on Organized Crime*[9] for a detailed discussion of securities theft; see Bossard,[10] Clamen,[11] and Mason[12] for discussions of art theft.)

As is so often the case in criminal justice research, we tend to know more about the "losers" than the "winners" in theft and fencing businesses because much research relies on criminal justice system records. This appears likely to much more seriously damage our description of the fencing than the theft industry since most thieves, even "good" thieves, are believed to have relatively substantial contact with the criminal justice system at one or more points in their careers.

Fortunately, there have been a number of ethnographic studies that provide detailed descriptions of a narrow portion of these two industries by observing how they actually operate. By merging results from this research with data from criminal justice system records, we hope to both expand and deepen our understanding of the stolen goods industry.

The Theft Industry

The theft industry can be broken into two sectors—traditional and nontraditional. We define the traditional sector as including the property offenses one normally encounters in police department files—for example, robbery, burglary, and shoplifting. Most research has concentrated on this sector of the theft industry. However, as we have already noted, it is theft from business that has grown most rapidly in recent years. Much theft from business is of a non-traditional sort (for example, employee theft) which rarely shows up in police files. Relatively little research has been conducted on employee theft in this country, although it has been a topic of considerable interest in Britain for some time. Following is a description of, first, traditional offenses and then nontraditional theft activities.

Traditional Theft. The classic work in this area is Edwin Sutherland's *The Professional Thief.*[13] Gibbons[14] and Petersilia *et al.*[15] provide surveys of more recent work. Gibbons suggests the following typology for this category of property offenders: (1) professional thieves, (2) professional "heavy" criminals, (3) semiprofessionals, and (4) occasionals. In their study of habitual offenders, Petersilia *et al.* used a similar but simpler typology: intensives and intermittents. We will merge these two typologies and discuss three types of thieves: professional thieves, intensives, and intermittents.

Professional thieves are the elite in this area of the stolen goods market. These individuals are relatively well trained, tend to specialize in one or a few types of property offenses, and earn their livelihood from their criminal activity. Most, if not all, crime carried out by professional thieves is nonviolent, and professional thieves are only infrequently incarcerated. Popular areas for professional thieves are shoplifting, pickpocketing, auto theft, and professional robbery and burglary. Consider Gibbons' description of the career for this type of offender:[16]

> *Professional thieves enter into grifting relatively early in life. Some become involved in learning experiences as beginning grifters in their teens; others enter into thievery at a later age from occupational backgrounds on the outskirts of the criminal underworld. Professional theft is a way of life pursued over an extended period of time and in a relatively uninterrupted fashion. Because of the skilled nature of their criminality, professional grifters are rarely found in prison populations. It is likely that many thieves ultimately retire voluntarily as they come to regard the frequent traveling and other features of theft behavior as overly burdensome. Still, professional theft is a form of criminality that probably represents an atypically long career pattern.* (p. 275)

Table 4-1 presents estimates of the working hours of some types of professional thieves, while Table 4-2 gives estimates of incomes. As can be seen if one disregards the fact that hours are relatively short and that all income is tax-free, the incomes of professional burglars, pickpockets, and bank robbers do not seem much, if any,

Table 4-1   Typical Working Hours for Professional Thieves

Day burglar (apartments, homes)	11 A.M.–2 P.M.
Night burglar (hotel)	6:30 P.M.–11 P.M. (dinner and theater hours)
Night burglar (house)	12 A.M.–5 A.M.
Booster (department store shoplifter)	12 P.M.–2 P.M. (crowded lunch hour)
Auto thief	Anytime

SOURCE: Plate, Thomas, *Crime Pays: An Inside Look at Burglars, Car Thieves, Loan Sharks, Hit Men, Fences and Other Professionals in Crime*, p. 96. Copyright 1975 by Thomas Plate. Reprinted by permission of Simon & Schuster, a Division of Gulf & Western Corporation.

Table 4-2   Estimated Salaries of Professional Thieves

Profession	*City*	*Estimated Annual Gross Income (Tax Free)*
Hotel burglar (pick man)	New York	$20,000
Pickpocket	Miami	$20,000
House burglar	Long Island	$25,000
Burglar (industrial)	Westchester County	$75,000
Bank robber	East Coast	$24,000
Shoplifter (booster)	Washington	$15,000
Securities thief	East Coast	$100,000

SOURCE: Plate, Thomas, *Crime Pays*, p. 92. Copyright 1975 by Thomas Plate. Reprinted by permission of Simon & Schuster, a Division of Gulf & Western Corporation.

higher than the incomes earned by individuals working in the lower-skilled legitimate professions. Based on these estimates and on the facts that barriers to entry are few and competition relatively strong, we feel that this portion of the professional theft operation is probably monopolistically competitive or competitive. Incomes for more highly skilled and specialized professional thieves (such as an industrial burglar or security thief) are much higher. Indeed, judging by the information in Table 4-2, the incomes for such thieves seem comparable to, if not above, those available to members of such legitimate professions as law and medicine. Judging from this, we feel that this type of professional theft is probably oligopolistic, with cartels forming and dissolving from time to time.

Although many professional thieves appear to be "loners," they will often operate with "rings" from which appropriate "working crews" will be selected for particular thefts. Professional burglary rings appear to range from 30 to 100 individuals, with working crews ranging from 2 to 6 specialists.[17] The size of the working crew and the degree of specialization of its members will depend upon the geographic location of the building to be burglarized, upon the construction of the building and the construction of the enclosure wherein the valuables are secured (that is, the vault, safe, strong-box, or hidden closet compartment), and upon the size, weight, and number of the items to be stolen.

We believe that traditional thieves—other than the professionals described above—differ substantially, depending on whether or not they are addicted to drugs. In general, addict thieves, due to their habit, tend to steal greater quantities, steal more frequently, and when drug need is great, steal less carefully than thieves who are not addicted. For these reasons and because of the incidence of drug-related arrests, addict thieves tend to have much more extensive records than do thieves who are not addicts. Another interesting general observation is that, in contrast to the professional thieves described above, thieves in other categories tend to engage in extensive crime-switching.[15, 18]

Consider first the category that Gibbons labels "professional 'heavy' criminals and semiprofessionals" and that Petersilia *et al.* label "intensives." Gibbons describes these types of property offenders as follows:[19]

> *Professional heavy criminals engage in armed robbery, burglary, and other direct assaults upon property. They are highly skilled at crime, so although the element of coercion and threat of violence is involved, actual force is rarely employed. The modus operandi of professional 'heavy' criminals involves a relatively lengthy period of detailed planning prior to the execution of the criminal offense. The semiprofessional property criminal also engages in strong-arm robberies, holdups, burglaries, larcenies and similar direct assaults upon personal or private property. They employ crime skills which are relatively simple and uncomplicated. For example, strong-arm robbery does not involve much detailed planning and careful execution of the crime, but rather application of crude physical force in order to relieve a victim of his money. This is referred to as semiprofessional crime, because even though technical skill is not characteristic of these offenders, most of them attempt to carry out crime as an occupation.* (p. 273)

We could find no estimates of annual income for this type of offender, but Table 4-3 contains estimates of the average monetary

Table 4-3 Estimated Monetary Gains From Burglary by Two Types of Thieves at Various Career Periods

	Juvenile		Young Adult		Adult	
	Intensive (N = 11)	Intermittent (N = 16)	Intensive (N = 14)	Intermittent (N = 15)	Intensive (N = 5)	Intermittent (N = 4)
Median gain per burglary	$100	$15	$200	$300	$300	$50
Median gain per burglar	$6,000	$140	$10,000	$3,000	$7,500	$100

SOURCE: Petersilia, J., *et al.*, *Criminal Careers of Habitual Felons* (Santa Monica, Cal.: Rand, 1977), p. 108.

gain for burglary at various career stages. Judging from Petersilia's description, intensives' annual incomes range from part-time supplements of a few thousand dollars a year to incomes approaching those for professional burglars. In contrast to professional thieves, those in the intensive category usually have rather extensive records and have spent a good deal of time in jail. Considering the relative ease of entry and the high risks, this area of thievery appears to be quite competitive.

The final group of blue-collar thieves is the occasionals or intermittents. Consider the description of this group in Petersilia *et al.*:[15]

> *Most did not view themselves as professional criminals. Their criminal activity seemed to have a more irregular and opportunistic character, and it often produced minimal gains. Their responses suggest that they were frequently oblivious to the risks and consequences of their criminal acts; this seeming indifference, compared with the posture of the intensive type, disposed them to a higher rate of arrest. In a sense, they were 'losers.'* (p. 28)

Table 4-3 contains estimates for the average gains from burglary for this type of offender. This type of thief appears to belong to a highly competitive world. With few skills and little serious commitment, occasional or intermittent thieves are probably most like the casual, unskilled workers of the legitimate world.

Nontraditional Theft. We define this category to include those individuals who steal in the course of their legitimate employment. We know much less about this type of offender but the scant information available seems to indicate that there are two basic types of employee thieves: those with a commitment to legitimate pursuits who are stealing on the side, and those who are more extensively involved in and committed to illegal activities.

Klockars' fence was particularly attracted to the first kind of thief because of the low risks involved. Indeed, he was careful to school them in the least risky methods of stealing merchandise.[20]

> *See, I school my drivers. I mean, if they got an overload, that's a free thing, a gift. They can bring it to me just like it's legitimate. But stealin' I tell 'em they just gotta use their heads. You pick a day when it's rainy an' cold an' the shipper's rushed. That's when you want to throw on an extra carton. Or the same goes when you're deliverin'. If the guy's got five trucks waitin' he ain't gonna count what you got. It don't make sense to steal from your own truck either, if you can just as easy pick up a couple of cartons where somebody else unloaded 'em. Oh, I school my drivers; show 'em how to go about doin' things, you know.* (p. 125)

Judging from the Bureau of Domestic Commerce's survey of the literature in trade publications,[21] this type of employee thief is most likely to be in transportation, warehousing, shipping, receiving, and sales, although even office employees are involved, judging by the increasing amount of office supplies and equipment which disappear each year. A recent study[7] found engineers in electronics manufacturing firms and nurses in hospitals to be involved in employee theft.

British researchers have suggested that employee theft is so common as to have become a standard part of the work milieu. They see much of this activity as socially, rather than economically, oriented. Pilfering, fiddling, and dealing on the job are, according to this school of thought, merely one method employees have of dealing with the depersonalization and the routine jobs associated with large-scale bureaucratic organizations.[22]

Employees engaged in cargo theft are often examples of the second type of employee thief. Consider the description of such a theft contained in a publication by Walsh:[23]

> *A truckload of color television sets leaves a secured railway yard for a regional distribution warehouse. The number of the truck, its cargo, and the time of departure are known because individuals inside the railway yard have access to and have provided this information. Their reasons for doing this are that they owe their jobs to the corruptive influence of others and expect to continue to be rewarded for such activities. The driver of the truck, who may also owe his employment to others, is given a chance to earn extra money if he follows certain directions. In this case, he is told to collect his cargo and proceed on his way, stopping at a certain truck stop for coffee. He is also told to have a long coffee break. (p. 18)*

It has been alleged that at times this type of organized employee theft is controlled by organized crime or corrupt union leaders. Unions of truckers and longshoremen in the New York City area are believed to have been quite extensively involved in the early 1970s.[24]

The first type of employee thief is rarely caught and, if caught, is often not prosecuted.* This type of employee thief appears to see

---

* In England, employee theft is reported to police in only one in four cases.[38] In the United States, employees are prosecuted in only one fifth of the occasions when offenses have been detected (Smigel and Ross,[39] p. 121). The usual punishment is dismissal from work, often without documents which indicate the true cause for dismissal.[7]

his or her actions as not really illegal but rather as a method of supplementing income, striking out at the organization, or making the workday more bearable. Such income supplementation is often rationalized on the basis of low income or other grievance. Wage guidelines, which can contribute to dissatisfaction with income by limiting raises, may lead to increased employee theft. Rewards can be quite high for the time, risk, and effort involved. The need for a legitimate job to carry out this type of theft presents a moderate barrier to entry. Rewards in areas where large numbers of individuals have access appear to be competitive, while rewards in areas with limited access are higher. We would guess that general merchandise employee theft is a competitive industry, while more specialized theft is largely oligopolistic.

The second type of employee is much better organized and rewards appear to be quite substantial. We would guess that this area is either monopolistic or oligopolistic, judging by the large sums and extensive organizations involved.

The Fencing Industry

Most of our knowledge of the fencing industry comes from ethnographic and autobiographical accounts, although Walsh[2] has recently completed a study which makes extensive use of police and other criminal justice records. The earliest examples of this type of research are Defoe's[25] and Fielding's[26] biographies of the great London fence and thief taker, Jonathan Wild. The classic work in the United States is Jerome Hall's *Theft, Law and Society.*[27] Five more recent works will form the basis for most of what is reported below.[1, 2, 20, 28, 29]

A number of typologies of fences have been offered, starting with Hall,[27] who suggested that fences be divided into three categories: (1) the lay receiver, (2) the occasional receiver, and (3) the professional receiver. Judging by the greater complexity of more recent typologies, the fencing industry has become considerably more complex in recent years. These more recent typologies find a number of types of professional fences. Klockars suggests that we must at least divide professional receivers into specialist fences and general merchandise fences.[30] Blakey and Goldsmith and Walsh suggest more complicated typologies based on degree of sophistication, appearance of legitimacy, and degree of organization.[2, 23, 28] Since professional fences of all types are faced with many of the same problems and employ many of the same techniques, we will describe the industry generally.

Professional fences of all types must deal with many of the same problems as do legitimate wholesalers and retailers: capital, supply, demand, and distribution.[30] In addition, the professional fence is faced with the problem of avoiding arrest and conviction. We will consider solutions to each problem in turn.

There seem to be three basic ways in which capital is built up: (1) theft, (2) legitimate business, and (3) deals with organized crime. Most "local" fences appear to obtain capital from either the first or second source. ("Local" is the standard term used for fences who operate in relatively restricted geographic areas.) The second source is particularly attractive since it also decreases the likelihood of discovery when stolen and legitimate merchandise can be mixed in inventory. Professional fences who deal in used stolen property are most frequently in the second-hand business or own pawnshops or antique shops. Professional fences who deal in new merchandise, such as that which comes from much employee theft, may be in any number of legitimate wholesale and retail businesses such as drug-stores, appliance stores, and general merchandise wholesale dis-tribution. Fences who receive their capital from and are associated with organized crime are quite a distinct type and are more like legitimate brokers than wholesalers or retailers. Both Walsh and Blakey and Goldsmith have separate categories for this type of fence. The unique feature of this type of fence is the degree to which he or she is able to insulate himself or herself from the actual theft and redistribution process. Continuing Walsh's cargo theft example, cited above, one obtains an excellent example of the way in which this type of fence operates.[31] While the driver is taking his coffee break:

> *Another individual of a very marginal type is given the chance to make $50.00 cash. He is told to proceed to the above noted truck stop, given a description of the truck, and told to drive it away to another location and disappear. When he has gone, several individuals arrive with smaller trucks and unload part of the cargo into each. They then proceed to destinations given them. In this case the destinations are three different television and appliance stores some 200 miles from the event. The owners of these stores expect the shipments and on arrival the trucks are unloaded and the television sets placed in the store. A predetermined amount of cash is given to the driver who then leaves. It is likely that this will have occurred before the original truck has been located, and in some cases before the crime has been reported.*
> (p. 190)

In this example, the broker fence organizes in the background. The "legitimate" businessman acts as the retailer.

A fence develops a supply of goods by developing contacts with thieves and obtaining their confidence. Fences may often recruit thieves and, as noted above, provide substantial training. Once established, a fence's network of thieves seems to develop mainly by word of mouth.

Demand for stolen goods comes both from legitimate purchasers and from those who consciously purchase stolen goods. Those purchasing from stores that appear legitimate may have no idea they are purchasing stolen goods, although low prices are often a tip-off. At least some people who purchase from second-hand and other used goods outlets that handle stolen goods are aware that they are purchasing stolen goods. At the other end of the spectrum, those who purchase from fences without legitimate fronts are obviously aware of the fact that the goods they buy are stolen. Purchasers run the gamut of society, although Klockars' fences' best customers were those connected with law enforcement, either as enforcers or offenders. Known purchase of stolen merchandise seems to be most common in lower-income neighborhoods of large cities.[24]

Wholesale demand requires that a set of trusted relationships be developed or that a convincing legitimate front be established. Apparently many legitimate business persons are quite willing to purchase stolen goods knowingly in order to increase profit margins. Professional buyers are believed to buy stolen goods to give their legitimate employers unusually low prices, but also to pocket a sizeable "commission."

The most unusual aspect of the distribution of stolen goods is caused by attempts to avoid arrest and conviction. Thus, fences will often not deal directly with thieves (particularly addict thieves), but rather have them "drop" goods at designated places. Goods that can be turned over quickly are highly desired, as a quick turnover lessens the chance of discovery. Fences are quite happy to act as brokers, never actually receiving delivery of stolen goods themselves.

Fences have developed a number of methods of avoiding arrest and conviction other than those noted above. To understand the nature of these techniques, one must understand that under most existing statutes a conviction requires proof of three things: first, that the goods under consideration are indeed stolen; second, that the accused fence indeed had the goods in his or her possession; third, that the accused receiver had reasonable cause to know that the goods were stolen. Fences hide the identity of stolen goods by removing labels and other identifying materials, and by mixing stolen goods with other goods. The fence tries to avoid having goods in his or her possession to the greatest extent possible by having anonymous warehouses and by keeping goods in direct possession for the shortest time possible. In addition, fences will often produce documents of sale which would allow them to reasonably claim that they were unaware of the fact that the goods were stolen. The false bill–cancelled check procedure is particularly popular.[32] Perhaps the major way of avoiding arrest is to have a good front. In her most recent work, Walsh suggests that three types of fronts are often used: (1) the integrative front, (2) the functional facilitating front, and (3) the dissonant front.[33] The most common front, the integrative front, is a legitimate business through which stolen property can be distributed directly to customers. Both wholesale (e.g., salvage company) and retail (e.g., furniture and appliance stores) fronts of this type are used. The functional facilitating front is less common, but is often used to handle large volumes of goods. Such fronts either ease the acquisition of stolen goods (e.g., the "fancy" restaurant owner who tells thieves what people have made reservations); the transportation of stolen goods (e.g., hauling and storage companies) or the sale of stolen goods (e.g., barber, beautician). Dissonant fronts are most often used by those handling low volume, high value goods (such as objets d'art, jewelry) and serves to camouflage extensive (often international) travel and high incomes.

Like the theft industry, the fencing industry's industrial structure varies depending on the type of fence under consideration. On the average, however, there are at least some barriers to entry at all levels so that fences appear to earn higher incomes and suffer from less competition than thieves of similar skill. The fence/thief whom Emerson studied worked only part time with no legitimate cover and was able to clear $9,000 a year. Specialized fences with organized crime connections earn much more. Plate estimates that such a fence who specialized in jewelry on the West Side of Manhattan cleared $300,000 in a single year.[34] The typical fence is probably between these two extremes and often mixes a moderate return from legitimate business with much more substantial returns earned by dealing in stolen goods. Overall the fencing industry seems to include all industrial structures from the monopolistically competitive to virtual monopoly in some specialized areas and in broker fencing. However, an oligopolistic structure with tacit collusion appears most common in professional fencing activities. As Walsh characterizes the situation: "Overt links between fences remain a minor feature of the industry, but a sense of 'groupness' does nevertheless characterize much of the behavior of the individual criminal receiver."[35]

The Cost and Benefits to Individuals and Organizations Directly Involved

The major benefit to buyers in the stolen goods industry is the lower prices available. As noted in the appendix to this chapter, price discounts are substantial, with both retail and wholesale buyers receiving discounts as high as 80 percent of the corresponding legitimate price. The lower prices available on stolen goods markets mean that reported measures of the level of prices such as the Consumer Price Index overstate the true level of prices to the degree to which they do not not reflect the price of stolen goods. Given the rapid growth of stolen goods markets in the 1960s, we may have overstated our rates of inflation during that perod. However, the tapering off of growth in the size of the stolen goods markets in the 1970s means that this source of overstatement has not been present in more recent years.

Risk to buyers in stolen goods markets appears minimal; thus the price discounts available in these markets are not subject to an extensive risk premium. At least some buyers appear to be attracted to the stolen goods dealers to participate vicariously in "the illegitimate."[36]

Professional thieves and fences appear attracted to the industry because the real incomes (both monetary and nonmonetary) in these professions are higher than incomes in legitimate alternatives available to them. Interestingly, the stolen goods industry (thievery and fencing) offers one of the more dynamic opportunities in our economy for individual entrepreneurship. While most legitimate enterpreneurship requires relatively substantial human and financial capital, entrepreneurship of the old "blood and guts" kind still seems possible in the stolen goods sector of the economy.

Intermittent or occasional thieves who commit traditional offenses seem driven to theft by financial or personal necessity. For this group rewards are small and participation seems to come from dire financial need, problems of addiction (drugs, gambling, alcohol), or a need to strike out.

Part-time employee thieves and fences, on the contrary, appear to be easily supplementing their incomes and/or making a "dull" life more interesting. The identification of such individuals with legitimate life styles means that much rationalization of illegitimate activities takes place. (See Clark *et al.*,[7] Chapter 3, for examples.)

Government at all levels incurs extensive enforcement costs as a result of the stolen goods markets. Federal, state, and local police have extensive antitheft and less extensive antifencing programs. Courts and corrections deal with large numbers of property offenders each year. Overall criminal justice expenditures to combat property crime exceeded $10 billion in the mid 1970s. In addition, all levels of government lose taxes as a result of untaxed illegal transactions and incomes. For example, assuming a 17 percent tax rate (the rate assumed for unreported income by IRS in its recent report), federal income tax receipts were $1 to $1.7 billion less than they should have been in 1975 because of the stolen goods industry.

Social costs of the stolen goods industry are substantially greater. While, as noted above, the actual theft of goods has no social costs but represents, from an economic perspective, an equity problem, the external economic effect of such forced transfers is substantial. Business feels the costs in increased insurance premiums, inventory costs, and increased expenditures on prevention. Business prevention expenditures alone amounted to almost $6 billion in 1976.[37] We as consumers feel these increased business costs in higher prices. In addition, we incur prevention expenditures ourselves (such as locks and guards) and alter our daily living habits. Our lives are generally less rich due to fear of property crime. As a society, we lose further from the work disincentive generated by our society's inability to enforce property rights.

Endnotes

1. Roselius, T., and D. Benton. 1973. "Marketing Theory and the Fencing of Stolen Goods," *Denver Law Journal* 50 (2):177–205.
2. Walsh, Marilyn E. 1977. *The Fence: A New Look at the World of Property Theft*. Westport, Conn.: Greenwood Press.
3. Henry, James. 1976. "Calling in the Big Bills," *Washington Monthly* (May), pp. 27–33.

4. Becker, G. 1968. "Crime and Punishment: An Economic Approach," *Journal of Political Economy* 76 (March/April):169–217.
5. Long, Sharon K., and Ann D. Witte. 1980. "Current Economic Trends: Implications for Crime and Criminal Justice," in Kevin N. Wright (ed.), *Crime and Criminal Justice in a Declining Economy*. Cambridge, Mass.: Oelgeschlager, Gunn & Hain.
6. Levenson, I. 1976. *The Growth of Crime*. Croton-on-Hudson, N.Y.: Hudson Institute.
7. Clark, John P., *et al.* 1980. "Theft by Employees in Work Organizations: A Preliminary Final Report," report to the National Institute of Law Enforcement and Criminal Justice, U.S. Department of Justice.
8. Trepel, Jeffrey M. (ed.) 1979. *Organized Auto Theft*. Raleigh, N.C.: National Association of Attorneys General.
9. U.S. Congress, Senate, Permanent Subcommittee on Government Operations. 1971. *Hearings on Organized Crime: Stolen Securities*. 92d Cong., 1st Sess.
10. Bossard, A. 1974. "Theft of Cultural Property," *International Criminal Police Review* 276 (March):58–74.
11. Clamen, M. 1975. "Museums and the Theft of Works of Art," *International Criminal Police Review* 285 (February):51–58.
12. Mason, D.L. 1977. "Art Theft and the Need for a Central Archive for Stolen Art," *The Police Chief* (June), pp. 42–43.
13. Sutherland, E.H. 1937. *The Professional Thief*. Chicago: University of Chicago Press.
14. Gibbons, Don C. 1977. *Society, Crime, and Criminal Careers: An Introduction to Criminology*. Englewood Cliffs, N.J.: Prentice-Hall.
15. Petersilia, J., *et al.* 1977. *Criminal Careers of Habitual Felons*. Santa Monica, Calif.: Rand.
16. Gibbons, *Society, Crime, and Criminal Careers*.
17. Pennsylvania Crime Commission. 1972. *1971–1972 Report*. Saint David, Penn.: Office of the Attorney General, pp. 115–314.
18. Wolfgang, M., *et al.* 1972. *Delinquency in a Birth Cohort*. Chicago: University of Chicago Press.
19. Gibbons, D. 1965. *Changing the Lawbreaker*. Englewood Cliffs, N.J.: Prentice-Hall.
20. Klockars, Carl B. 1974. *The Professional Fence*. New York: Free Press.
21. U.S. Department of Commerce, Bureau of Domestic Commerce. 1976. *The Cost of Crimes Against Business*. Washington, D.C.: U.S. Government Printing Office.
22. Henry, Stuart. 1978. *Hidden Economy—The Context and Control of Borderline Crime*. London: Martin Robertson & Co.
23. Walsh, Marilyn E. 1976. *Strategies for Combatting the Criminal Receiver (Fence) of Stolen Goods*. Washington, D.C.: U.S. Government Printing Office.
24. Emerson, F.E. 1971. "They Can Get It for You Better than Wholesale," *New York* 22 (November):34–37.
25. Defoe, Daniel, 1901. *The King of the Pirates, Including the Life and Actions of Jonathan Wild*. New York: The Jenson Society.

26. Fielding, Henry. 1926. *The Life of Mr. Jonathan Wild the Great.* Oxford: Basil Blackwell.
27. Hall, Jerome. 1952. *Theft, Law and Society.* Indianapolis: Bobbs-Merrill Co.
28. Blakey, G. R., and M. Goldsmith. 1976. "Criminal Redistribution of Stolen Property," *Michigan Law Review* 74 (August):1512–1626.
29. Roumasset, J., and J. Hadreas. 1977. "Addicts, Fences, and the Market for Stolen Goods," *Public Finance Quarterly* 5 (April):247–272.
30. Klockars, *Professional Fence,* p. 180.
31. Walsh, *Strategies for Combatting the Criminal Receiver.*
32. Klockars, *Professional Fence,* p. 91.
33. Walsh, *The Fence.*
34. Plate, Thomas. 1975. *Crime Pays: An Inside Look at Burglars, Car Thieves, Loan Sharks, Hit Men, Fences and Other Professionals in Crime.* New York: Simon and Schuster, p. 88.
35. Walsh, *The Fence,* p. 138.
36. Klockars, *Professional Fence.*
37. U.S. Department of Commerce, *Cost of Crimes Against Business,* p. 7.
38. Martin, J.P. 1962. *Offenders as Employees.* London: Macmillan, p. 90.
39. Robin, G.D. 1970. "The Corporate and Judicial Disposition of Employee Thieves," in E. Smigel and H.L. Ross (eds.), *Crimes Against Bureaucracy.* New York: Van Nostrand Reinhold, pp. 214–246.

ESTIMATING THE NATIONAL INCOME OF THE STOLEN GOODS MARKET

In this appendix, we estimate the national income of the stolen goods market. First, however, we must decide what the factors of production in this market are, what activities in the stolen goods market should be considered in our attempts to use national income accounting methods to compute its national income, and, finally, how we value the results of various "productive" activities in this market. Some authors (for example, Henry[1]) would consider thievery a transfer, albeit an involuntary one, and not include any of it in the national income of the underground economy under the usual accounting methods. However, the activity of a fence in buying stolen goods from a thief and selling them to other customers within and outside the underground economy is clearly analogous to that of the owner of a legitimate wholesale or retail store. Accordingly, it should be included in underground national income. Similarly, it is almost as natural to include the economic activity that a thief performs when he sells his stolen goods to a fence. We will include both of these activities in our computations of the national income of the stolen goods market. However, we will not include the total value of the goods that a thief steals and keeps for his own consumption. Nor will we include the total dollar value of the money which thieves steal. The major portions of these latter two seem more analogous to involuntary transfers, and therefore are not contributions to current output—that is, are not a component of national income. For those who would like to include the total value of these two activities, we compute such a value at the end of this appendix.

Our approach will be to first determine the number of property offenses of each type and then to estimate the average value of items stolen. We will multiply these numbers together to determine a value for certain goods and money stolen in 1975. We will make separate calculations, using different sources for property crimes against businesses and for property crimes against individuals and their residences. Finally, we will try to estimate what proportion of these stolen goods are sold to fences, what percentage of market value fences pay thieves for these goods, and at what percentage of market value fences sell these goods to their customers. Finally, we estimate the costs of doing business for both thieves and fences.

The most generally available information on the number of property offenses is the information obtained from the Federal Bureau of Investigation's Uniform Crime Report (UCR). While this information is extremely valuable and provides the only national information available for an extended time period, the UCR has been criticized on a number of grounds. Perhaps most important for present purposes is the belief that UCR information seriously underestimates the amount of property crime due to nonreporting of offenses.

The crime rate as measured by UCR data increased by 8 percent a year in the 1960–1972 period. Property offenses of robbery and larceny over $50 increased most rapidly during this period, by approximately 10 percent per year. Thus, based on UCR information alone, one would estimate that this sector of the underground economy grew rapidly during the 1960–1972 period.

Beginning in 1973, the results of national victimization surveys became available. These surveys allow one to estimate the actual amount of certain crimes, not just reported crime. Results of these surveys for the 1973–1975 period indicate that the rate of increase in robbery has declined markedly. At the same time, the rate of increase for larceny remained high (22 percent increase for the two-year period) and business burglaries increased at a moderate rate (by 9.6 percent during the two-year period). Thus, the growth rate of traditional sources of stolen goods may actually have decreased in the early 1970s.

The word traditional is important. Victimization surveys cover only robbery and burglary in their data on commercial establishments. However, by far the majority of business losses come in other areas, such as cargo theft, employee theft, and shoplifting. Since 1971 the Bureau of Domestic Commerce (BDC) of the U.S. Department of Commerce has made estimates of the cost of "ordinary" crime to business for certain sectors. Table A4-1 contains these estimates for the 1971–1976 period. As can be seen in this table, the estimated loss to business sectors studied grew from $12.2 billion in 1971 to $25 billion in 1976, an annual average rate of growth of over 15 percent per annum. These figures seem to indicate that property crime against business may be one of the more dynamic sectors of the underground economy in recent years. The BDC figures exclude construction and agriculture. While no dollar figure is available for construction, a 1972 survey indicated that between 21 and 24 percent of building contractors suffered losses due to theft in 1971.[2] As far as we are aware, there exists no estimate of theft loss by governments. However, recent work on employee theft from hospitals indicates that such theft from public and other nonprofit institutions may be substantial. (Clark *et al.*[3] indicate that 37 percent of the hospital workers surveyed admitted to taking hospital supplies, 10 percent admitted to taking or using medication, and 8 percent admitted to taking tools and equipment.)

Table A4–1 indicates that the relative theft loss is highest in retailing and wholesaling and lowest in manufacturing. In recent years, the *rate* of growth in theft loss has been the highest in the service and wholesaling industries. It is interesting that loss in the transportation industry has tapered off in recent years.

There is one final source of information which reflects trends in the stolen goods market: FBI reports on stolen and recovered property. Table A4-2 presents this data for the 1960–1975 period. As can be seen in this table, the overall rate of increase in property *reported* stolen has been very large, although it has tapered off somewhat in recent years. The largest increase has been in the area of miscellaneous goods, which are believed to make up a large portion of the merchandise on the stolen goods market.

Let us now put some of this information together to estimate the size of the stolen goods market. We need to know the volume of goods entering this market and the value of these goods at all levels of the distribution chain. We will use estimates of: (1) the total number of certain property crimes from the victimization survey, (2) the dollar loss to certain business sectors from the BDC study, and (3) the value of property stolen and reported to the police. For the offenses that it covers, we believe that the victimization survey

Table A4-1 Estimated Loss Due to Property Offenses Against Business, by Sector ($ billions)

Business Sector	1971	1973	1974	1975	1976	Percentage Increase 1971–1976	1974 Loss as a Percent of 1974 Industry GNP
Retailing	$4.8	$5.2	$5.8	$6.5	$8.1	69%	{4%
Wholesaling	1.4	1.8	2.1	2.4	3.4	143	
Manufacturing	1.8	2.6	2.8	3.2	4.3	139	1
Services	2.7	3.2	3.5	4.3	6.7	148	2
Transportation	1.5	1.7	1.9	2.3	2.5	67	2
Total	12.2	14.5	16.1	18.7	25.0	104%	

SOURCES: U.S. Department of Commerce, Bureau of Domestic Commerce, 1976, p. 7 and Economic Report of the President, 1977, p. 193.

100

Beating the System

Table A4-2   Stolen Property in Dollars per 100 People (in current dollars)

Year	Total	Auto	Misc.[a]	All other[b]
1960	$502	$246	$112	$144
1961	508	249	112	147
1962	535	267	124	144
1963	679	346	159	174
1964	824	445	190	189
1965	840	445	190	205
1966	831	457	190	184
1967	991	535	276	180
1968	1152	588	305	259
1969	1287	656	375	256
1970	1356	637	445	275
1971	1483	653	525	305
1972	1349	588	490	271
1973	1375	558	549	268
1974	1587	579	664	344
1975	1979	737	812	428
Annual rate of growth:				
1960–1969	11.3%	11.5%	14.4%	6.6%
1970–1975	7.8%	3.0%	12.8%	9.2%

SOURCE: Blakey, G. R., and M. Goldsmith, "Criminal Redistribution of Stolen Property," *Michigan Law Review* 74 (August 1976): 1617.

[a] Includes all property not included in other categories, such as office equipment, firearms, household goods, consumable goods, and livestock.
[b] Includes clothing, furs, currency, and jewelry.

provides the most complete information. However, this data gives only the number of offenses, not the value of goods stolen. Fortunately, the FBI in its Uniform Crime Report gives estimates of the average loss incurred in various types of property offenses. If we multiply these figures by the estimated number of offenses from victimization surveys, we obtain estimates of loss for each offense covered. Summing these, we obtain an estimate of approximately $6 billion property loss in 1975 for the offenses covered by the victimization survey. (See Table A4-3.) Since this survey excludes white-collar crimes, employee theft, and shoplifting against businesses, we will use the victimization surveys to estimate only the number of crimes against individuals and their residences. We will then use the BDC data to estimate the losses of business because of property crimes.

To exclude the amount and value of robberies and burglaries against businesses from the victimization study data in Table A4-3

Table A4-3   Estimated Value of Stolen Goods in 1975

Offense	Estimated Number	Average Loss ($)	Estimated Loss ($)
Robbery	1,383,099	133	189,952,167
Burglary	8,207,303	422	3,463,481,866
Larceny (except motor vehicles)	9,670,663	166	1,605,330,058
Motor vehicle theft	508,472	1,457	740,843,704
Total			5,993,607,795

SOURCE: Gottfredson, M. R., *et al.*, *Sourcebook of Criminal Justice Statistics, 1977* (Washington, D.C.: U.S. Government Printing Office, 1978), pp. 303, 463.

we assume that individuals and residences accounted for 77 percent of the victimizations for these two offenses and 60 percent of the value lost. Multiplying the figures in the first two rows of the last column of Table A4-3 by .6 and adding this result to items 3 and 4 in the last column yields an estimate of $4.5 billion in property theft against individuals in 1975. Adding this to BDC estimates of business loss due to property theft for five industries in Table A4-1 ($18.7 billion), we obtain a conservative estimate of $23.2 billion for the value of property stolen. Assuming further that government loses the same proportion of its GNP to theft as the service industry (2 percent), that construction loses the same proportion of its GNP to theft as the wholesale and retail sector (4 percent), and that agriculture loses the same proportion of its GNP as manufacturing (1 percent), we obtain an estimated loss for these three industries of $5.6 billion in 1975. Adding this to our previous figures, we obtain an estimate of $28.8 billion worth of property stolen in 1975.

We now have an estimate, however rough, of the value of goods stolen in 1975; however, we want an estimate of the value of goods changing hands on the stolen goods markets. To obtain this estimate, four adjustments are necessary. First, we must adjust for the loss of value that goods suffer when being traded in illegal markets. Second, we must adjust for the amount of stolen goods retained for personal use and thus not entering the illegal market. Third, we must adjust for the proportion of loss from property crime in the form of money rather than goods. Finally, we must adjust for the proportion of goods which do not enter stolen goods markets because they are recovered.

The President's Commission on Law Enforcement and the Administration of Justice[4] estimates the amount received by thieves for stolen goods may be between 20 and 33 percent of market value. This seems quite consistent with the thieves' proverb: "When you take something to a fence you should try to get a third of the value of the goods."[5] More recent work by Walsh, who studied a sample of over 100 fences in a northeastern city, suggests that the price received by the thief can vary rather substantially. She suggests that the most important factors affecting this price are: (1) the type of thief involved, (2) the fence's desire to guide the stealing behavior of thieves by providing appropriate monetary incentives, and (3) the degree of competition in the fencing industry. She suggests that prices will be lowest (perhaps 10 percent of the retail price) for thieves who are addicted to drugs and who steal objects not desired by fences when the fence occupies a monopolistic position, and highest (perhaps 50 percent of wholesale price) for the professional burglar who steals goods badly wanted by fences who operate in a relatively competitive environment.[6] Considering all of the above, we estimate that thieves on the average receive 25 percent of the retail value of the goods they steal.

Fences mark up the price of the goods they purchase from thieves by varying amounts depending on: (1) the type of good, (2) the volume of good to be purchased, (3) market conditions, (4) the relevant (wholesale or retail) legitimate market price, (5) the "legitimacy" of the goods, and (6) the "legitimacy" of the fencing outlet. Thus, we would expect the mark-up to be lowest for nondurable goods of questionable origin in ample supply that are sold by the thief or a part-time fence without a legitimate front, and to be highest for durable goods that give all appearances of being legitimate and that are in great demand or are sold by a "legitimate" retailer. Table A4-4 contains prices charged by a small, part-time New York thief/fence in 1971. Another fence, studied by Klockars, used a second-hand merchandise store as a front and charged approximately 50 percent of retail price to retail clothing customers and 34 percent of retail price to wholesale customers for the same merchandise.[7] Walsh found jewelers and antique dealers to mark up goods purchased from thieves by as much as 100 to 200 percent.[8] Clothing fences generally sold stolen clothing for two-thirds of the retail price. Considering all of the above, we estimate that small-time fences with no cover resell these goods for approximately 30 percent of the retail price, and that "professional fences" charge approximately 50 to 70 percent of retail to retail customers and 30

Table A4-4   Selected Prices Charged by a Thief/Fence, New York City, 1971

Item	Legitimate Retail Price	Stolen Market Price	Stolen Market Price as a Percent of Legitimate Price
Mack tractor-trailer	$35,000	$9,000	26%
1971 Cadillac Fleetwood	9,500–9,700	2,500	26
Black Diamond mink coat	3,000	900–1,300	37[a]
1.85-carat diamond ring	975	200	21
RCA color TV (23-inch screen)	497	100	20
Minolta SRT 101 single-lens reflex camera	265–385	65	20
Man's wool overcoat	200	60–75	34
Man's wool suit	185	50	27
Man's suede overcoat	165	60	37
Olivetti Lettera 36 portable electric typewriter	180	40–50	25
Woman's suede midi coat	115	45	40
Bulova "Accutron" watches	110–195	45–60	34
Man's leather jacket	110	45	41
Singer sewing machine (Touch and Sew)	349	65	19
Woman's fur-trimmed coat	175	60	34
Whirlpool 13,500-BTU air conditioner	319	100	31
6′ × 9′ Rya rug	159	45	28
Johnnie Walker Red (case)	79.92 plus tax	40	50
American Tourister 3-suiter	63	20	32
Sunbeam Mixmaster electric mixer	60	15	25
Jonathan Logan dresses	24–34	7–10	29

SOURCE: Emerson, F. E., "They Can Get It for You Better than Wholesale," *New York* 22 (November 1971): 39.

[a] When ranges are given, the midpoint is used.

percent of retail to wholesale customers. We could find no information on prices further down the stolen redistribution system, but given that most individuals who bought wholesale from Klockars' fence were "legitimate" wholesalers and retailers, it seems likely that prices quite like the prevailing legitimate price were charged by these individuals. Overall, we assume that the average stolen good is finally sold to the ultimate consumer for between 50 and 75 percent of the prevailing retail price.

To continue our calculations on the national income of the stolen goods market, we want to estimate what proportion of the $28.8 billion of goods and currency stolen in 1975 actually reached the level of the fence. Using FBI data, Walsh estimates that in 1974 16 percent of all property stolen was currency.[9] Applying this percentage to our 1975 data leads us to believe that $24.2 billion in goods and $4.6 billion in currency was stolen in 1975. Again using FBI data, the classification system of Table A4-2, Blakey and Goldsmith estimate that 37 percent of all stolen autos, 41 percent of miscellaneous goods, and 22 percent of all other goods were recovered in 1975.[10] We could find no estimates of the proportion of stolen property kept by thieves for their personal use; however, 10 to 25 percent does not appear an unreasonable estimate.

Based on the literature cited above, we will now make some heroic assumptions to obtain estimates of incomes to thieves and fences who participate in the stolen goods market. First, we estimate aggregate 1975 income for thieves. Recall that we estimated that $28.8 billion in property was stolen in 1975. Assuming that 16 percent of this was currency, we arrive at an estimate of $24.2 billion in goods stolen in 1975. Assuming that thieves kept 10 to 25 percent of this for personal use, that 30 to 35 percent of goods are recovered, and that 90 percent of the goods recovered have not passed through the stolen goods market, we estimate that $13 to $15 billion worth of goods entered the stolen goods market in 1975. Assuming that thieves receive 25 percent of the value of the goods they steal, we would estimate that thieves had a gross income of $3.25 to $3.75 billion dollars from the stolen goods market in 1975. To obtain net income, we must subtract the thieves' costs of doing business, which we assume to be approximately 10 percent. This gives thieves an estimated net income of $3 to $3.4 billion in 1975.

Next, we estimate the income that fences receive from stolen goods sales. Assuming that on the average stolen goods are eventually sold to consumers for between 50 and 75 percent of retail price, we obtain an estimate of total gross fence income of $3.25 to $7.5 billion in 1975. Assuming that business expenses are equal to 25 percent of gross income, we obtain an estimate of net fencing income of $2.4 to $5.6 billion in 1975. Adding this to the income of thieves as estimated above, we obtain an estimate of national income for this portion of the stolen goods sector of the underground economy of between $5.6 and $9.4 billion in 1975.

As noted above, we have not included in the above estimate either the amount of currency stolen or a value for the goods stolen by thieves and kept for their personal use. The above calculations estimate that 16 percent of all property stolen in 1975 was currency. We also estimated that thieves kept 10 to 25 percent of all property stolen for their own use. This would amount to $2.4 to $6.0 billion worth of stolen goods in 1975. Such goods should not be given their market value, however, but should be valued somewhere between their market value and the price that fences would pay for these goods. If we value these items at 50 percent of their market value—twice the amount which we've assumed a fence would pay for them—we are led to value such goods between $1.2 and $3.0 billion in 1975. Thus, we estimate the total value of the money and goods kept by thieves in 1975 to be between $5.8 and $7.6 billion. Finally, we assume that 10 percent of this total value is payment for productive services—$.57 to $.76 billion. Adding this amount to our estimate of the income of thieves from fenced goods and our estimate of fencing income, we obtain an estimate of $6.0 to $9.8 billion for the national income of the stolen goods industry in 1975. Moving this 1975 figure backward in time and using the consumer price index as a deflator, we obtain an estimated 1974 national income for the stolen goods industry of between $5.4 and $8.9 billion.

Endnotes

1. Henry, James. 1976. "Calling in the Big Bills," *Washington Monthly* (May), pp. 27–33.
2. U.S. Department of Commerce, Bureau of Domestic Commerce. 1976. *The Cost of Crimes Against Business*. Washington, D.C.:U.S. Government Printing Office.
3. Clark, John P., *et al.* 1980. "Theft by Employees in Work Organizations: A Preliminary Final Report," report to the National Institute of Law Enforcement and Criminal Justice, U.S. Department of Justice, p. 25.

4. President's Commission on Law Enforcement and Administration of Justice. 1967. *Task Force Report: Crime and Its Impact—An Assessment.* Washington, D.C.: U.S. Government Printing Office.

5. Klockars, Carl B. 1974. *The Professional Fence.* New York: Free Press, p. 114.

6. Walsh, Marilyn E. 1977. *The Fence: A New Look at the World of Property Theft.* Westport, Conn.: Greenwood Press, pp. 71–76.

7. Klockars, *Professional Fence.*

8. Walsh, *The Fence.*

9. Walsh, Marilyn E. 1976. *Strategies for Combatting the Criminal Receiver (Fence) of Stolen Goods.* Washington, D.C.: U.S. Government Printing Office, p. 123.

10. Blakey, G.R., and M. Goldsmith. 1976. "Criminal Redistribution of Stolen Property," *Michigan Law Review* 74 (August):1512–1626.

Chapter 5

POLICY ALTERNATIVES FOR CONTROL OF TAX EVASION AND ILLEGAL TRANSFERS

Our discussion thus far has amply demonstrated the diversity of those sectors of the underground economy that generally deal with legal goods and services. Activities in this portion of the underground economy range from illegal transfers of money and goods by strong-arm tactics to complex and sophisticated tax evasion schemes. The illegal alien sector is unusual in a number of aspects. From a policy perspective, perhaps its most unique characteristic is the need to take international as well as domestic politics into consideration.

There are large gaps in our knowledge concerning all sectors. While this is not too surprising given that it is only during the last five years or so that we have attempted to analyze these areas as sectors of an economy, it means that in many cases policy suggestions are based on very limited knowledge. In the sections that follow we also make suggestions concerning areas in which we feel research is badly needed, especially policy oriented research.

Unreported Income and Tax Evasion

One is struck by the dearth of good, empirically based, policy oriented research on unreported income and tax evasion in the United States other than that done by the IRS. We were able to find only two such studies in our literature review—Schwartz and

Orleans[1] and Groves.[2] The first of these studies was conducted in cooperation with the IRS, and the second was conducted in cooperation with the Wisconsin Department of Revenue. The lack of such empirical work in recent years is probably due to the increased stringency of privacy statutes and increased sensitivities of taxing agencies. While the secrecy of individual returns must be maintained, we feel strongly that much additional research could be usefully carried out. This research could be based on aggregate data or on individual data from which all personal identifiers had been deleted. We believe it is important that such research be possible for independent researchers as well as for the IRS and its contractors. Current efforts by the IRS to develop research about the factors affecting compliance are certainly a step in the right direction, but we believe that a broader-based effort than that which resulted from recent IRS efforts would be desirable.

We would like to voice our support for two GAO suggestions. The first suggestion is that IRS "expand and accelerate its research into factors which influence compliance."[3] This research should carefully assess the rather extensive theoretical (psychological, sociological, and economic) literature and be careful to specify models that include social, psychological, and economic factors as well as factors more directly under the control of the IRS, such as audit rates. This will require integration of census and other data sources, including sample surveys. (A survey of taxpayer opinion done in 1980 for IRS by CSR, Inc., is a useful step forward in the effort to obtain attitudinal data.[4]) Recent proposals to IRS for research on the factors affecting individual compliance consider a much narrower set of factors than would seem desirable if we are to thoroughly understand the causes of tax evasion.

The second suggestion is that IRS "initiate action to periodically estimate the size and analyze the characteristics of the nonfiler population."[5] IRS data-matching programs with the Social Security Administration and state and local government agencies would be one potential source of data. Alternatively, IRS could attempt an estimate tax evasion for a "typical area," using the total population lists compiled by the Bureau of Census in connection with the 1980 census. The recently constructed Exact Match File for tax year 1977 will allow new, updated estimates of the nonfiler population.

We would like to suggest that future IRS research work be subject to extensive external review and comment. In the past, IRS research has been circulated only to a limited extent, although it generally contains no individual data. We feel that increased external review could improve both the quality and breadth of IRS research.

Existing theoretical research on tax evasion has tended to be quite narrow in perspective and could be usefully broadened. Integration of insights from more traditional deterrence work and sociological and psychological theories could prove most useful. The work by Spicer and Lundstedt, which we discussed in Chapter 1, is interesting in this regard.

Much of the research cited in Chapter 1 has potential policy implications. Perhaps most importantly this material seems to suggest that a broader range of policy instruments be used to encourage tax compliance. Education and moral appeal may have as great if not a greater effect than high audit rates and penalties. The negative effect of audits on taxpayers' attitudes toward taxes is particularly interesting in this regard. Improving the public image of government may also prove a relatively cheap method of improving compliance. Finally, tax law and tax form simplification could substantially increase reporting by low-income groups. Since a HEW-funded "reading power" study of 1971 individual income tax forms and instructions found that taxpayers would have to read at the college graduate level to be able to comprehend the tax instructions without assistance, IRS has actively and beneficially sought to simplify its forms.[6] Currently IRS believes that further simplification will depend on simplifying the tax laws themselves.[7] Given the broad range of policy instruments available, optimal enforcement policies should be broadly and carefully assessed.

Another set of policies with great potential is the expansion of withholding and reporting at source (that is, by the payors of the income). When reporting at source for incomes and dividends was begun in 1964, reported income from these sources increased by 45 percent. The marked jump in unreported interest income noted in Chapter 1 may make this an area ripe for withholding or at least closer computer checking of reported information on interest income. Before recommending such increased withholding, the government should consider both the costs (such as increased record-keeping) and benefits involved. A good example of the type of study needed is a recent Joint Committee on Taxation report on independent contractors.[8] This report concluded that "it is doubtful whether additional tax revenues obtained from nonfilers would justify the administrative complexity and expense which withholding on self-employment earnings would entail."[9]

Another intriguing policy alternative is novel sentencing practices. For example, part of the sentence imposed in a recent anti-trust case against firms and individuals involved in price fixing in the paper label industry was that individuals involved make speeches to public bodies concerning the nature of their offenses. Similar sentences are imposed on persons convicted in tax fraud cases in Germany. When one considers the "respectability" of many tax evaders, this type of sentence may have significant deterrent effects.

The policy suggestions made above have a rather limited range and are designed to work within the existing institutional structure. More effective policies may be possible if the existing institutional structure is altered. The most effective step we can take to decrease the amount of unreported income is to decrease the incentives not to report. This may be done most simply by decreasing marginal tax rates and other costs (for example, regulations and paper work) imposed by government on individuals and businesses. However, such reductions will not be painless. Reductions in taxes will require either cuts in government expenditures, larger budget deficits, or both. The question is how large these cuts or deficits must be. Supply-side economists suggest that their size will be less than expected since incentives to work and invest will be increased. Our work suggests an additional factor which may serve to decrease the size of necessary expenditure cuts. Cuts in marginal tax rates may cause at least some "underground" activity to resurface. Unfortunately, we do not know how much the incentive effects and resurfacing of underground activity will be able to offset the tax reductions that would nominally occur. Our own best *guess* is that they will offset them rather substantially (by perhaps as much as 25 percent), but that large cuts in government expenditures will be needed if larger deficits are to be avoided.

Cigarette Smuggling

Since the mid-1970s government policies on cigarette smuggling have been carefully revised. Cigarette smuggling is now a federal offense with stiff penalties. Agents of the U.S. Bureau of Alcohol, Tobacco, and Firearms have now joined state tax and law enforcement personnel in the fight against smuggling. While this increased law enforcement effort has slowed the growth of cigarette smuggling, and may even have slightly decreased the number of cigarettes smuggled, it has not and is not likely to remove the problem as long as cigarette smuggling remains as lucrative as it is at present. Further inroads into the smuggling problem can probably be more effectively made by direct efforts to decrease the profitability of cigarette smuggling rather than by further increases in law enforcement efforts against smugglers.

ACIR made an interesting proposal that would serve to decrease the profitability of cigarette smuggling. They suggested a federal incentive plan to encourage all states to adopt a cigarette tax in the range of 8 to 15 cents within five years. During the first year of this plan, states with low taxes would be given a one-cent rebate for each two-cent increase in state taxes; states with high taxes would be given a one-cent rebate for each one-cent decrease in state taxes; and states with tax rates between 8 and 15 percent would be given a two-cent rebate for each pack sold. Rebates would be paid for by increases in the federal excise tax on cigarettes. If this plan were successful, it would substantially decrease the profitability of smuggling. However, even if enacted, which it has not been, the plan would seem unlikely to convince low-tax, tobacco-producing states to increase their tax rate on cigarettes. Major interest groups in these states are concerned about the effect of higher prices on overall cigarette consumption, and feel that cigarette smuggling is a "high-tax state problem."

Another possible way of decreasing the profitability of cigarette smuggling would be to attempt to decrease demand for untaxed cigarettes. A two-pronged attack combining a major public education effort with the enactment and enforcement of *reasonable* penalties for the possession of even small amounts of untaxed cigarettes might cut demand substantially. Penalities should be relatively small so that they would be enforced. Fines as low as $25 to $50 might well be effective given the low financial benefits to the consumer of purchasing untaxed cigarettes. Such fines would be much more likely to be enforced than would more stringent laws such as those of Pennsylvania.

Finally, we might make cigarette smuggling more costly and difficult by shifting state and local taxation from the wholesale and retail level to manufacturers. If manufacturers were not required to affix stamps but, rather, to just note on the invoice the amount of tax paid, increases in manufacturers' costs should not be too great. Any increase in manufacturers' costs could be reimbursed by the states from current "distribution discounts" for affixing tax stamps. These discounts amounted to approximately $87 million in 1975.

As might be expected, given the relatively recent emergence of the problem, there has not been a great amount of research on cigarette smuggling. What research there is has been done mainly by economists and has been concerned primarily with: (1) estimating demand equations for cigarettes, (2) estimating interstate flows, and (3) estimating state revenue losses.[10–12] This research has been very useful, but has improved our understanding of the nature of the cigarette smuggling industry only to a limited extent. Research using police records that detail the way in which the industry operates could prove very useful. This research should indicate at what level (manufacturer, wholesaler, retailer) cigarettes are purchased, how they are transported, how they are distributed, and who the ultimate consumers are. In addition to this "industry structure" research, investigation on the relative deterrent effect of various policies could prove to be a great aid in law enforcement efforts.

Illegal Aliens

Factors affecting U.S. policy toward illegal aliens go well beyond economics. Foreign policy and human rights concerns must be given major importance. The deportation of the current illegal population (assuming that they could be found) and the closing of the border between the U.S. and Mexico (assuming that this could be done) would contribute markedly to unrest in Mexico. Indeed, many believe that the high level of agrarian revolt in Mexico during the mid-1970s was in part due to a tightening of U.S. immigration policy and increased patrols along the U.S.-Mexican border at that time.

Trying to take all of these factors into account, we recommend a policy which would: (1) improve the lot of workers in countries from which large numbers of illegals come, (2) make legal immigration a more feasible alternative, and (3) decrease the likely benefits of illegal immigration. Most research to date suggests that people usually immigrate for economic reasons. Most of the current illegal alien population, including Cubans, came to the United States to improve their financial position. The United States could usefully direct its economic aid toward the development of labor-intensive industry and agriculture in these countries (Mexico and Caribbean countries). Much U.S. aid to date has served to lower the price of capital goods relative to labor and thus encouraged more capital-intensive projects than would otherwise have been undertaken.[13]

This is obviously a policy that will have beneficial effects only after a substantial period of time. Further, given current and probably future levels of U.S. aid, even the long-term beneficial effects cannot be expected to be great.

Recent changes in U.S. immigration law and policy have served to decrease the possibility of legal immigration to the U.S. For example, the number of immigrant visas available to Mexican nationals decreased from 62,205 in FY 1975 to 57,863 in FY 1976 and 44,079 in FY 1977. In addition, the average waiting time for such visas appears to now exceed the average of two and one-half years established in the early 1970s. We recommend that U.S. immigration laws and policies be changed to allow for increased and easier legal immigration from Mexico and the Caribbean countries. Preference in immigration should then be given to those who have no recent history of illegal entry into the United States (that is, illegal entry after the recommended policies are adopted). The extent of liberalization of immigration laws possible seems likely to be small relative to the size of the illegal alien population. Thus, we believe that it will be desirable to establish a carefully documented and monitored system of temporary immigration. The U.S. has done this in the past under the Bracerio program, which allowed Mexican nationals to work in the United States on a temporary basis during the 1950s. Most northern European countries currently have guest worker programs that allow the citizens of other countries, mainly southern European countries, to work in their countries on a temporary basis. An effective temporary immigration policy could be formulated by carefully examining European experiences with such programs.

The rewards for illegal immigration to the U.S. can be decreased in a number of ways. First, INS can step up its efforts to apprehend and deport illegal aliens. Second, higher fines can be imposed on those apprehended and jail terms given to repeat offenders. Third, current laws against "professional people smugglers" could be more strictly enforced. Finally, efforts by the IRS and others aimed at uncovering and punishing employers who operate "off the books" could be increased. The effectiveness of such efforts in curtailing the growth of the illegal alien population could be greatly improved if a federal law against the hiring of workers known to be illegal aliens were passed. The burden of *reasonable* checking on status could usefully be put on employers.

If the above policies or others are successful in stemming the flow of illegal immigrants, the United States still has the problem of what to do about the 4 to 6 million illegal aliens currently in the country. Given the alternatives (increased unrest in Mexico and the Caribbean, major infringements of civil rights), we support recent proposals to legitimize the long-term resident, illegal alien population in this country. Both President Reagan and former President Carter have made this proposal. Thus, it would appear possible to develop broadly based political support for such a policy. However, the manner in which these proposals were received by Congress seems to indicate that it may still be a number of years before such proposals are actually adopted.

Reviewing the literature on illegal aliens, one is struck by its comparatively recent vintage. Most work has been done in the last decade and has been concerned with estimating the size and impact of the illegal alien population. However, there is still much that we don't know about this population. Future research should include efforts to do a representative study of the illegal alien population. The study, by identifying regional motivations for migration, would allow the government to more effectively control illegal immigration. Furthermore, the methods for estimating the size of the illegal population developed by Heer, Lancaster and Scheuren, Korns, and Robinson should be updated now that 1980 census data are available. The purpose of this research would be twofold. First, it will give new insights on the size and trends of illegal immigration. Second, it will allow us to assess the relative merits of these alternative techniques.

Research should be done on migration which explicitly incorporates the possibility of illegal immigration. Existing migration models, which implicitly assume legal immigration, could be usefully married to the models of the decision to migrate illegally. Such models would have to take into account changes in immigration policy. Also, intense effort should be undertaken to develop labor-intensive methods of industrialization for developing countries. Finally, in order to improve our knowledge of the labor market effects of illegal immigration, there should be a more geographically detailed source of labor market data. Thus, the illegal alien problem provides yet one more reason for developing good small-area statistics.

We feel that the illegal immigration issue is going to be a public concern for many years. The above policy suggestions should ease the flow of illegal immigration, while future research on the topic undoubtedly will help us understand more about the dynamics of illegal immigration and how to formulate more effective policy.

Stolen Goods Markets

Traditionally, law enforcement efforts have focused on the traditional thief when attempting to control property crime. As has been pointed out by a number of authors, this may be a short-sighted approach since replacement in these occupations appears to occur quite rapidly. An alternative approach would be to focus property crime abatement efforts on the fencing industry. Walsh[14] provides a long list of potential strategies. However, even most of these strategies focus on the traditional portion of the industry. The dynamic growth of loss to white collar and employee thieves and, thus, presumably to fences who sell predominantly stolen goods from such thieves, would seem to make this area ripe for some innovative law enforcement efforts.

As has been pointed out in some detail by Blakey and Goldsmith,[15] successful large-scale prosecution of fences requires changes in existing law. Blakey and Goldsmith provide a model theft and fencing law in their paper; thus we feel it unnecessary to go into needed legal changes here.

One potential long-run policy is to use and record identifying insignia on products. This marking combined with computerized lists of stolen goods could be quite helpful in increasing the recovery rate for stolen property. Currently, only approximately one third of all stolen goods are recovered. Some researchers suggest that we develop a computerized "telecrook" system modeled after existing systems for detecting bad checks.[16] A Vehicle Identification Numbering (VIN) system has been used by automobile manufacturers for some time and, in combination with improved ignition locking systems, appears to have been at least partially responsible for a leveling off of auto theft in recent years. However, one should not underestimate the innovativeness of thieves and fences. In response to the VIN system, those in the auto theft profession have turned increasingly to selling unmarked parts (produced by "chop shops"), forging documents (such as the "salvage switch"), and stealing buses, trucks, and construction equipment. Those specializing in the fencing of entire autos now frequently export their wares, with Mexico, South America, and the Middle East being particularly popular destinations. Barter also appears to be common in this area of the stolen goods industry, with automobiles and other transport equipment being traded for drugs along the Mexican border.

In the area of employee theft, a two-pronged approach would seem to have potential for success. First, business needs to increase security through more careful inventory control and preemployment screening. Recent research suggests that a multifaceted approach indicating serious and continual employer concern with the problem is likely to be most effective. Second, business must be willing to punish employee thieves when they are caught. Recent evidence suggests that retail businesses at least could shift some enforcement resources to employee theft. Consider the following findings of the Bureau of Domestic Commerce:[17]

> *In discount stores, it is estimated that for every dollar lost to a shoplifter, three are lost to employees. Although apprehensions of shoplifters outnumber those of employees by 10 to 1, one company reports that dollar losses from employee pilferage are more than seven times as great as shoplifting losses.*

As far as we are aware, there have been no previous attempts to estimate the overall size of stolen goods markets in this country. We feel that additional research in this area could be very beneficial. One intriguing possibility would be for the relevant agencies of the Departments of Justice and Commerce to cooperate in expanding the victimization surveys to include a much wider spectrum of property crime against business. The Bureau of Domestic Commerce could then try to reconcile its figures for business loss due to property crime obtained from the trade literature with estimates obtained from victimization surveys.

The Bureau of Domestic Commerce or an alternative agency (for example, Department of Housing and Urban Development, Department of Agriculture) should be encouraged to obtain estimates of property crime loss for construction and agriculture. More importantly, we need estimates of property crime loss for all levels of government. Data for such estimates could be obtained in connection with existing surveys such as the Census of Governments.

There has been a good deal of research on traditional thieves; however, this research is poorly integrated at present and could be usefully synthesized. Our knowledge of employee thieves is much sparser. Research in this area using criminal justice and business records could be very informative. In addition, surveys using nontraditional questioning methods (such as random reponse) could provide valuable insights into the methods used in this sector. Ethnographic work on white-collar thieves of the type recently carried out by Henry[18] in Britain could prove extremely useful, as has such information regarding traditional thieves.

A good deal of research has been done recently on fencing, but most of it concentrates on relatively small-time dealers. In addition, this research has generally taken a legal or sociological approach. Further research on "legitimate" fences and broker/fences could prove valuable. In addition, it seems likely that substantial insights could be obtained from a business or economic approach to the fencing industry. Roselius and Benton[19] produced some interesting insights using a marketing approach.

Conclusions

In this chapter we have suggested policies and research for each portion of the "legal" sector of the underground economy. In reading these sections one is struck by the uniqueness of each sector. The policies recommended for each type of activity are quite different and range from rewriting of immigration and fencing statutes to increasing "withholding at source." The common thread running through these policy suggestions is that if one wishes to decrease the amount of an activity, one should increase the costs and decrease the benefits of that activity. In contrast to the situation in some of the illegal sectors of the underground economy, one hears few calls for abolition of taxes (as nice as that might be), unrestricted immigration, or the legalization of stolen goods. We as a society appear convinced that we should be taxed, that immigration should be restricted, and that stealing and fencing money and goods should be illegal. Given the acceptance of laws in these areas and limited law enforcement resources, we must rely to a large degree on voluntary compliance. That is, we must rely on convincing people that either they don't want to or won't benefit from breaking these laws. The first method of control is morally or psychologically based and has been most important in the tax area, where we rely heavily on voluntary compliance. The second method, at least the law enforcement portion of it, is usually referred to as "general deterrence." Under this form of control, we seek to convince people that they are likely to be caught quickly and to be given penalties that largely wipe out the gains achieved by their illegal activity. In fact, in none of the areas discussed in this chapter have we been doing this very effectively. Policies designed to increase both the rapidity with which laws are enforced and the likelihood that they are enforced could be quite helpful. Also, the level of penalties needs to be carefully assessed. If penalties are too large (as is the case in some states for cigarette smuggling), they are unlikely to be imposed. If they are too small, they will not effectively deter.

Turning from policy to research, we again see diversity, but also a common thread. Research strategies range from analysis of audit results to extensive matching of different data sets. In each area, however, we are attempting to understand activities that the perpetrators have every incentive to hide. Rigorous techniques for estimating and understanding these types of activities have for the most part only been developed in recent years. Where an identifiable victim exists, as one clearly does for stolen goods, much valuable information can be obtained from this victim, who usually has substantial incentives to report. Creative use of police, insurance, and victimization data in such areas could be extremely valuable. In areas like tax evasion and illegal immigration, a victim is difficult to identify; and most information will have to be obtained as a byproduct of enforcement efforts and by creative use of multiple data sets. Statistical techniques for creatively using these multiple data sets have been developed in the illegal aliens area and could usefully be developed for other areas as well.

Endnotes

1. Schwartz, R. D., and S. Orleans. 1967. "On Legal Sanctions," *University of Chicago Law Review* 34 (Winter):274–300. There have also been a number of surveys which attempt to elicit self reports of tax evasion.
2. Groves, H. M. 1958. "Empirical Studies of Income Tax Compliance," *National Tax Journal* 11 (December):291–301.
3. Comptroller General of the United States. 1976. *How the Internal Revenue Service Selects Individual Income Tax Returns for Audit*. Report to the Joint Committee on Internal Revenue Taxation. Washington, D.C., p. 56.
4. CSR, Incorporated. 1980. *A General Taxpayer Opinion Survey*. Report prepared for the Office of Planning and Research, Internal Revenue Service.
5. Comptroller General, *How IRS Selects Individual Returns*, p. 56.
6. See Comptroller General of the United States. 1976. *IRS Assistance to Taxpayers in Filing Federal Income Tax Returns*. Washington, D.C.: General Accounting Office.
7. U.S. House of Representatives, Subcommittee on Oversight, Committee on

Ways and Means. 1980. *Hearings on the Underground Economy.* Washington, D.C.: U.S. Government Printing Office, p. 27.

8. Joint Committee on Taxation. 1979. *Issues in the Classification of Individuals as Employees or Independent Contractors.* Washington, D.C.: U.S. Government Printing Office.

9. *Ibid.*, p. 38.

10. Manchester, Paul B. 1976. "Interstate Cigarette Smuggling," *Public Finance Quarterly* 4 (April):225–238.

11. Wertz, Kenneth L. 1971. "Cigarette Taxation by American States," *National Tax Journal* 24 (December):487–492.

12. Wiseman, A. C. 1968. "The Demand for Cigarettes in the United States," unpublished Ph.D. dissertation, University of Washington.

13. For example, see Alba, Francisco. 1978. "Mexico's International Migration as a Manifestation of Its Development Pattern," *International Migration Review* 12 (Winter):502–513; and Witte, Ann D. 1973. "Employment in the Manufacturing Sector of Developing Economies: A Study of Mexico and Peru," Journal of Development Studies 10(October):33:49.

14. See Walsh (1976).

15. See Blakey and Goldsmith (1976, pp. 1620–1626).

16. See Roumasset and Hadreas (1977).

17. See U.S. Department of Commerce, Bureau of Domestic Commerce (1976), p. 19.

18. Henry, S. 1978. *Hidden Economy—The Context and Control of Borderline Crime.* London: Martin Robertson & Co.

19. Roselium, T., and D. Benton. 1973. "Marketing Theory and the Fencing of Stolen Goods." *Denver Law Journal* 50(2):177–205.

Part III

PRODUCTION AND DISTRIBUTION OF DRUGS

Parts I and II of this book have examined the production of goods and services that are legal but are not properly reported. Parts III and IV will deal with the production and distribution of illegal goods and services—the illicit sector of the underground economy.

We begin in Part III with a description of the segment which derives its profits from the sale and distribution of illegal goods, in particular, illegal drugs. The government has outlawed the use and sale of these goods on the belief that they can cause severe mental and physical damage to their consumers, resulting in a decrease in general health, happiness, and productivity. This ban on drugs has also drawn support from an ethic which frowns on the seeking of pleasure for its own sake. Because of these laws, the production and distribution of these drugs take place in the underground economy where their black market status leads to large price mark-ups, and untaxed profits.

In the three chapters of Part III, we discuss the three principal illegal drugs: heroin, cocaine, and marihuana. We begin with the heroin industry because it has generated more research interest and federal enforcement expenditure than any other sector of the underground economy. As a result, we know more about the heroin distribution system than we do about any other sector, and the campaign against heroin use has been one of the most successful attacks on the underground economy. In addition, careful cost-benefit analyses have been carried out for some of the current approaches to the heroin problem. These studies are models of what could be done for other segments to increase significantly both our under-

standing of the underground economy and our success in decreasing its negative effects.

Chapters 7 and 8 deal with the cocaine and marihuana industries. These industries have structures similar to that of the heroin distribution industry, though somewhat less formal and organized. We estimate that over half a million Americans profit from the sale of illegal drugs. The national income of the illegal drug industry was over $10 billion in 1974.

In Part IV, we study the sectors of the underground economy that produce illegal services, concentrating on fraud arson, illegal gambling, loan sharking, and prostitution. The production of these "services" is part of the underground economy because our society feels that they are moral offenses against the common good. Furthermore, they are attempts to get around the regulations which society has placed on the legal production of services such as gambling and lending. These regulations are based on the belief that the provider of these services can easily take advantage of the consumer and on the fear that organized criminal organizations are profiting from the provision of these services.

As we did in Parts I and II, we describe the size and organization of each of these sectors. We also discuss the costs and benefits for the individuals directly involved in the transactions and for society as a whole. Later, we will consider some policy implications which our analysis suggests.

Chapter 6

HEROIN

The heroin industry has been the most thoroughly studied segment of the underground economy. The drug problem attracted national attention in the early 1970s, especially as narcotic use reached the high school population. This notoriety resulted in increased support for research on the causes and consequences of drug abuse, with an emphasis on the study of heroin. Criminologists, sociologists, psychologists, physicians, economists, and epidemiologists painted a fairly complete picture of the heroin market. They described its monopolistic structure and vertical organization and studied its production, distribution, and consumption costs. Some have estimated the size of the population of heroin users, both in selected cities and nationwide; others have detailed the economic costs of the use of heroin and other narcotics to our society and have performed cost-benefit analyses for various proposed solutions to the drug-abuse problem.

Heroin: Its Nature and Production

Heroin, usually found in the form of a crystalline powder, is produced by a chemical treatment of morphine with acetic acid. The acetic acid often gives heroin—especially Mexican brown heroin —a strong vinegarlike odor. Morphine is an opiate, a product of the opium which is produced from the poppy plant, *Papaver somniferum* (literally, "the sleep-bearing poppy"). This poppy is an annual plant, having a thin, main stalk (sometimes three to four feet tall) with several egg-shaped pods on top. During summer, the poppy blooms into large colorful flowers, three to five inches in diameter. After the blossoms lose their petals, workers carefully slit their unripe seed pods, allowing a milky white sap or latex to gradually ooze out onto the surface of the pod. The next morning, after the latex has congealed into a brown, sticky substance that is the raw opium, the workers scrape the opium from the poppy plant. Fuqua has reported: "An acre of poppies can be expected to yield about 10 kilos of opium. On the average, it takes a worker 40 hours or more to collect each pound. For their labors, farmers can expect to receive, depending on the state of the world market, somewhere between $25 and $100 per kilo."[1]

A little less than one half of the opium produced is sent to pharmaceutical firms to manufacture pain killers such as morphine and codeine. According to Fuqua, "We still cannot synthetically produce a painkiller that is as effective and free from unwanted side effects as the product of the opium poppy. . . . At the present time eight countries—Bulgaria, India, Iran, Japan, Pakistan, Turkey, the U.S.S.R., and Yugoslavia—produce almost all of the world's supply of licit opium."[2] India, the largest producer, produced a harvest of nearly one million kilograms in 1972.

The Bureau of Narcotics and Dangerous Drugs (BNDD) estimated in 1970 that the total licit production of opium was 1,060 to 1,085 metric tons annually, while the world's illicit production was 1,250 to 1,400 metric tons.[3] The Burma-Laos-Thailand "Golden Triangle" produces most of the world's illicit opium. However, these countries consume most of their own opium. According to BNDD estimates, 80 percent of the opium used by the heroin market in the United States in 1970 came from Turkey, 15 percent from Mexico, and 5 percent from the Far East. The BNDD estimated that 10,000 to 12,000 pounds of heroin were sufficient to supply the entire U.S. heroin market for one year.[4] This requires roughly 100,000 to 120,000 pounds of opium, about 2 percent of the estimated world production of illicit opium. This amount could easily be grown on an area of 12 square miles and transported in a single medium-sized airplane.[1, 5]

The conversion of the raw opium gum into morphine is a rather simple process. First, the raw opium is added to a large vat of heated water. Lime is added to force the impurities to settle to the bottom. After this solution is filtered and reheated, ammonia is added to precipitate out the morphine. After the morphine base has dried, it usually constitutes about 10 percent of the volume of the opium from which it was extracted.

The conversion of the morphine base to heroin is a more complicated process, requiring some skillful chemistry techniques. The first and most important step in this procedure is the mixture of equal quantities of morphine base and acetic anhydride.

Until the mid-1970s, most heroin that reached the U.S. market was produced from poppies grown in Turkey. Syndicates in or near Istanbul transformed the raw opium to the morphine base, which was then shipped—by boat or overland through Bulgaria and Yugoslavia—to covert laboratories in southern France. These laboratories refined the morphine into heroin, which was then smuggled into the United States through New York, Montreal, or some large port.[6]

During the early 1970s, a series of events combined to effectively smash the Turkish-French connection. As a result of intense international enforcement efforts, a large number of French and Corsican drug traffickers were jailed and key drug figures throughout the western hemisphere were successfully put out of business. At the same time, in reaction to intense international diplomatic pressure, the government of Turkey banned all cultivation of the opium poppy. This ban effectively dried up illicit opium supplies.[7]

To take up this slack, Mexico became the main supplier of the heroin used in the United States. This transition was quickly and easily made for a number of reasons. First, for years the opium poppy had been cultivated on a small scale in Mexico, especially by Chinese immigrants. Second, Mexico had been for a while a major transshipment point for European heroin bound for the United States, and third, there already was an active marihuana smuggling trade from Mexican fields to American cities. While Mexico produced 10 to 15 percent of the U.S. heroin supply in 1971, the Office of Drug Abuse Policy estimated that Mexico provided 65.9 percent of the U.S. heroin supply in 1976, with the Burma-Laos-Thailand triangle providing 32.5 percent, and Near Eastern countries (Pakistan, Afghanistan, India) the remaining 1.6 percent.[8] The signature program for heroin seized in the United States in 1977 found that 87-88 percent of the seized heroin originated in Mexico, 11 percent in Southeast Asia, and 1 percent in the Near East.[9]

During the late 1970s, heroin from the Burma-Laos-Thailand triangle began supplanting Mexican heroin in the United States market. First of all, this region had a bumper crop of the opium poppy during this period. Second, the region was beset by increased political turmoil, making the cultivation, refinement, and shipment of heroin much simpler than it had been. Finally, the heroin for this region is of a much higher quality than Mexican heroin; its arrival was greeted enthusiastically by heroin users. Its high quality and quantity appears to be leading to dramatic increases in heroin use in American cities. Most of the shipment of heroin from the Golden Triangle to the United States appears to be taking place along the old routes of the Turkish-French connection.

The Structure of the Heroin Distribution Industry

In this section, we will discuss the structure of the heroin distribution system in the United States and consider such questions as: Is the industry competitive, monopolistic, or somewhere in between? What is its horizontal and vertical structure? What are the characteristics of the different levels within the industry?

A number of researchers have provided rather careful descriptions of the heroin distribution industry. In an early study of the structures of clandestine industries, Rottenberg presented economic arguments for the structure that was apparent in the heroin industry.[10] Preble and Casey used interviews with 150 heroin users in New York City to describe the various structured levels in this industry.[11] Using this study and his own work with addicts and policemen in New York City, Mark Moore extended and refined these descriptions of the heroin hierarchy and the economic motivations for the structure in the industry.[12, 13] Holahan summarized and further refined Moore's description.[14] Our account is a synthesis of these four descriptions of the structure of the heroin industry in New York City in the early seventies. Although most of this economic analysis probably still applies to the new heroin industry of the late 1970s, there is clearly a need for a new study of the present structure and its price system.

The first question researchers consider is: What basic goals are motivating the decisions and activities of those at the upper levels of this industry? All the studies argue that the top suppliers are not simply profit-maximizers, but are also deeply concerned with minimizing their risks of arrest and imprisonment. In response to this threat of arrest and imprisonment, dealers make two adjustments: "They invest time and money in strategies to reduce the risk, and they demand more money to compensate themselves for the increased risk of staying in business."[15]

They also structure the heroin distribution network so that it can most efficiently achieve these goals of high profit and low risk. In particular, such distribution network must:[16]

1. restrict the total supply of heroin in the U.S. market to maintain high market prices;
2. meet demand fairly closely in order to keep customers content and inventories low;*
3. manipulate supply conditions above them covertly yet accurately;
4. develop an information network that computes and broadcasts supply and demand fairly, accurately, and covertly.

Clearly, a monopolistic framework would be more suitable for meeting these objectives than a competitive organization. In a competitive market "with many suppliers at the top, there are more transactions, more explicit negotiations, more occasions of short supply or large inventories, more information circulating freely— and thus a greater probability of arrest. A monopoly, therefore, is logically the most efficient type of organizational structure at high levels."[17]

Furthermore, the heroin industry possesses some natural barriers to entry to enforce a monopolistic framework. To become a high-level dealer of heroin, one must develop substantial capital, arms, and allies sufficient to protect this capital and the resulting supply of heroin, and an information network tight enough to offset the high level of risk in the trade. In addition, one must find and convince a connection, who will be wary of powerful groups with no track-record or references. Furthermore, established distribution systems can exclude newcomers by using violence against the aspiring entrant or by alerting the police to the activities of a newly-formed illegal organization.

"The combinations of formidable barriers to entry, significant economies of scale, and a small market imply that a relatively small number of firms will be active at high levels."[18] However, since the connection is probably the strongest barrier to entry, since there are a number of different countries with which connections are possible, and since the foreign morphine-producing syndicates will find it profitable to sell to a number of importers—forcing them to bid against each other and thus raise the price of heroin—one can

---

* The most persistent and pervasive threat is that they will be discovered while possessing or exchanging heroin (Moore, p. 23).

expect more than just two or three distribution networks to be established. In 1972, the Bureau of Narcotics and Dangerous Drugs estimated that ten or twelve wholesale heroin operations existed in the United States.[19, 20] However, Moore estimated that an assumption of 25 importers in New York City was most consistent with the structure of his carefully constructed model of the New York City distribution system.[21]

In any case, "the system has probably developed into an oligopoly or cartel, with each firm maintaining a type of monopoly control of firms below it in the lower distribution levels. It is not clear what agreements, if any, exist among these firms with respect to prices or market areas, but the risk of detection may limit the mobility of distributors between top-level suppliers, thus allowing firms to maintain vertically integrated supply systems."[22]

The same goals and objectives that encourage this monopolistic framework lead to the existence of small, relatively isolated distribution units and a rather long vertical organizational system. Small distribution units of 5 to 20 customers have advantages: they require just a small number of transactions, they discourage information leaks, they facilitate supervision and discipline of customers, and they allow for quick and efficient adjustments in behavior. Furthermore, these distributional units will be well isolated from one another so that each dealer can limit information on his activities to just a few trusted customers, both for his own protection and to exploit some of his monopoly advantages.

Because heroin is produced in relatively large batches and no dealer wants to handle more than a few customers, many levels are added between production and sales. Different levels deal in different quantities of heroin, have different capital requirements, and face different levels of risk. Thus, not only are there many different levels, but the levels choose different pricing and security strategies. The valuable characteristic is that the aggregate system is very difficult for the police to successfully attack. Police making an arrest at one level will find it difficult to expand the case, and a very small part of the overall organization will be disrupted.[23]

Preble and Casey, Moore, Holahan, and Fuqua provide a more detailed picture of how this vertical organization existed in New York in the early 1970s.[24-28] At each level, profits include: (1) the excess of the actual financial return over the return which can be realized in that segment's next best alternative career, (2) returns to compensate for any risks of arrest and imprisonment which are faced, and (3) returns to monopoly power. At the top of this vertical system are the major heroin importers upon whose orders large shipments of heroin enter the United States. The importers buy bulk quantities of 80 percent pure heroin for about $5,000 per kilo. These operators have high operating costs since they must hire skilled smugglers and must have large quantities of cash available. They are fairly difficult to identify since they probably never see or touch the heroin they import. Thus their risks are rather low, compared to other levels. Opportunity costs are also low, since once an importer sets up his smuggling and information network, he can probably do better in the heroin trade than in any other comparable undertaking. Each importer sells his shipment of heroin, uncut and undiluted, to a trusted customer, called a "kilo-connection," at a price of $15,000 to $20,000 a kilo. Part of the profit here is a consequence of the monopolist position attached to the one-on-one personal dealing.

The kilo-connection is probably the most powerful component in the system. While the probability of arrest is low, high profits exist at this level through a combination of monopoly power and high opportunity costs (illegal gambling and loan sharking are profitable alternatives). However, costs are fairly high too, because of the need to develop an intricate exchange and information system, discipline lower-level suppliers, and maintain and protect inventories of heroin.

If one follows Moore's model of the distribution system,[29] then one finds each kilo-connection cutting his heroin and selling it to five trusted wholesalers, called "connections," for $38,000 a kilo. The connections begin the process of diluting the purity of the drug and of cutting it into more manageable pieces. The most commonly-used dilutants are quinine, mannite, and lactose. The quinine heightens the sensation of the "rush" when the injectable solution reaches the user's nervous system. The mannite inflates or "fluffs up" the volume, and the lactose, a milk sugar used in baby formulas, inflates the volume. Each connection uses this process to double the volume and weight of the heroin mixture in his possession, thus cutting the purity of the mixture to 40 percent. He then packages this mixture into parcels that weigh about one-sixteenth of a kilo each and sells these parcels (called "eighths") to about six trusted customers, called "weight-dealers," for $4,500 an eighth.

Connections have reasonably high production costs since they must hire agents to develop markets, to discipline customers, to dilute and repackage the heroin, and to make deliveries. They may also have to buy protection from other criminal organizations. The increased handling of the heroin and resultant increased visibility of the connection mean that connections face much higher risks than those at levels above them. They derive some monopoly power by restricting access to information. They have moderately low opportunity costs, once they set up a reasonably elaborate organization.

A typical weight-dealer buys heroin from his connection in units, each of roughly 40 percent purity. He dilutes it again, so that its purity is reduced to 25 percent and cuts it into "street-ounce" size portions, each of which is a bit short of a full ounce. He then sells his heroin to about eight reliable customers, called "street dealers," for somewhere around $1,200 a "street ounce."

A typical street dealer dilutes and cuts his purchase so that its purity is reduced by half to somewhere between 10 and 15 percent. He packages the diluted heroin in "half-ounces" and "bundles." He sells the bundles directly to six or seven users for $150 a bundle. He sells the "half-ounces" to three or four "jugglers" for $450 per half-ounce. Each juggler dilutes each bundle of heroin again and cuts it up into ten bags. He sells his bags directly to users, for $5 a bag, although he uses about one third of the heroin he purchased for his own consumption. In addition, a number of the street dealers may be users too.

The weight dealers, street dealers, and jugglers form the bottom half of the distribution system. They have few operating costs since they have no employees and they try to turn over their inventory as quickly as possible. Their major costs are sometimes bribes to policemen and extortion or protection payments to criminal groups. They are all highly visible in their dealings and thus most of their profit is probably compensation for the high risks they must take. Because they lack skills for other enterprises, they have low opportunity costs. They have some monopoly power because they control access to information. However, because users are always looking for a better deal and a purer heroin, the competition at the lowest levels is fairly intense. At best, one can view the economic situation of weight dealers and street dealers as that of monopolistic competition.

The following table and figure from Moore, *Buy and Bust*, summarize the vertical structure of the heroin distribution system and the cuts, dilutions, and value added at each level, assuming that 100,000 heroin users consume 940 kilos of pure heroin a year in

Table 6-1   Estimated Levels of Activity for Various Levels of Distribution Systems

Level of Distribution System	Number of Dealers	Number of Transactions per Dealer per Year	Purchase Price	Dilution Process	Sales Price	Value Added per Dealer per Kilo	Total Value Added ($ millions)
Importers	25	2–10	$5,000/kilo	None	$15,000/kilo	$10,000	$12
Kilo Connections	25	6–28	$15,000/kilo	None	$38,000/kilo	$23,000	$27
Connections	125	45–173	$38,000/kilo	1:1	$4,500/eighth	$34,000	$40
Weight-dealers	750	110–220	$4,500/eighth	4:3	$1,200/ounce	$96,000	$113
Street-dealers	6,000	180–520	$1,200/ounce	2:1	$450/half-ounce	$96,000	$113
Jugglers	18,000	320–2000	$450/half-ounce	1:1	$150/bundle and $5/bag	$16,000	$19

SOURCE: Adapted from Mark Moore. *Buy and Bust* (Lexington, Mass.: Lexington Books, 1977), pp. 110–111. Used by permission.

Note: These levels assume consumption of 1,175 kilos of heroin in New York City.

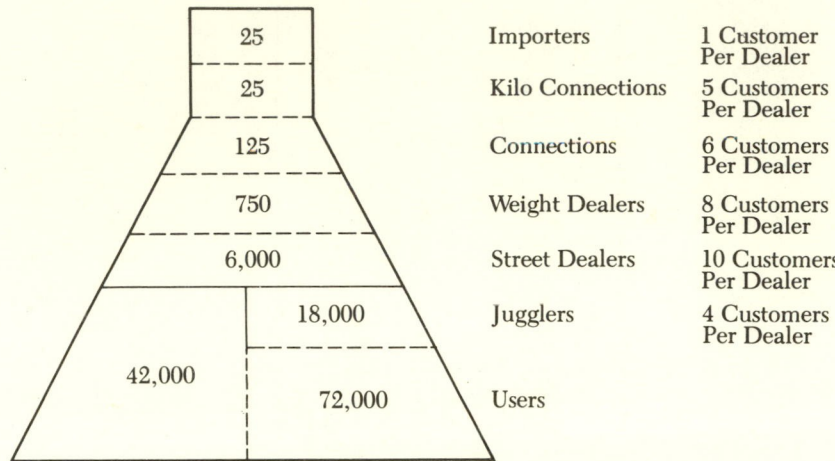

Importers	1 Customer Per Dealer
Kilo Connections	5 Customers Per Dealer
Connections	6 Customers Per Dealer
Weight Dealers	8 Customers Per Dealer
Street Dealers	10 Customers Per Dealer
Jugglers	4 Customers Per Dealer
Users	

Figure 6-1 One Possible Model of the New York City Distribution System (100,000–150,000). *(Source: Mark Moore,* Buy and Bust, *Lexington, Mass.: Lexington Books, 1977, p. 100. Used by permission.)*

New York City. Note that the total value added for annual consumption is $324 million.

For a description of the heroin-using community in a Chicago neighborhood, see Hughes et al.[30] This article gives an example of how the vertical structure in the heroin system works. For a description of the names, personalities, and activities of persons at all levels of the heroin economy, see the exposé in *Newsday*.[31]

The Heroin User

Because of the high cost and low purity of the heroin available to them, American users of heroin usually inject the drug directly into their bodies to assure themselves of the strongest possible sensation. (In other countries, higher-grade heroin is often smoked or inhaled.) Novices and experimenters often inject the drug just under the skin, a practice called "skin popping." More serious heroin users inject the drug directly into their veins, a practice called "mainlining."

Moore developed a systematic typology of users in his study of the variations in habit size, durations of use, levels of multiple-drug abuse, and levels of criminal activity of drug abusers. In his development of this typology he tried to ensure that "characteristics are consistent with anecdotal information about the behavior of users with known correlations of single variables, and with the findings of other researchers who have developed typologies of users for different purposes."[32] (See, for example, Fiddle[33] and Larner and Tefferteller.[34]) We summarize Moore's typology by presenting two tables from *Buy and Bust*. (See Tables 6-2 and 6-3.) The first presents the characteristics of users in each type; the second describes the distribution and level of heroin consumption of each type of user. Moore's Table 2-8 in *Buy and Bust* (pp. 86–87) lists the 17 sources that he used to construct and amplify his typology.

In summary, Moore estimated that there were 100,000 to 150,000 heroin users in New York City at any one time in the early 1970s, consuming a total of 940 kilograms of pure heroin. He estimated that the "average user" consumed four and one-half $5 bags of heroin a day, derived 44 percent of his income from thefts and 32 percent from narcotics dealing, and was on the street (that is, not in jail or in a treatment center) 78 percent of the year.

Note that about three-fourths of the heroin users in Moore's typology are daily users who consume 4 to 7 bags of heroin per day.

In another interesting study which sheds light on the life of a heroin user, Silverman and Spruill used a time series analysis to estimate the price elasticity of demand for heroin and the cross-elasticity of crime with respect to the price of heroin in Detroit in the early 1970s.[35] They found that when the price of heroin increases by 10 percent, demand for heroin decreases, but to a lesser degree, -2.7 percent. This relative unresponsiveness of heroin demand to price increases means that as prices rise total heroin expenditures rise too. This long-run price elasticity of $-.27$ for the average heroin habit places heroin in the class of moderately inelastic consumer goods. It is a little less inelastic than gas and oil ($-.16$), hospital services ($-.16$), and physicians' services ($-.22$), but a bit more inelastic than auto maintenance ($-.36$). Of course, this is an aggregate elasticity; however, it does point to the difficulty in assuming that the aggregate demand for heroin is completely inelastic, as some policy studies have suggested.

Silverman and Spruill also found that a 10 percent increase in heroin leads to a 3.1 percent increase in total property crime against the poor nonwhite population. The largest effect was an increase in nonresidential burglary. Armed robbery was the only category of crime that was affected in rich white neighborhoods. Silverman and Spruill also state, "Heroic extrapolation of our estimated elastic-

Table 6-2   A Typology of Users

Types of Users	Characteristics of Users						
	Characteristics Defining Types of Users				Characteristics Imputed To Types of Users		
	Duration of Use	Habit Size	Level of Multiple-Drug Use	Level of Criminality	Health of User	Level of Legitimate Employment	Motivation to Seek Treatment
Joy poppers	Short	Small-medium	Low	Moderate-high	Moderate	Low	Low
Drug dabblers	Short	Small-medium	Moderate-high	Low-moderate	Moderate	Low	Low-moderate
Addicts	Moderate	Medium-high	Medium-high	Medium-high	Poor	Low	Low
Hustlers	Moderate	Small-medium	Low	High	Moderate	Low	Low
Drug dependents	Moderate	Medium-high	High	Low	Poor	Low	Low
Conformists	Moderate	Small-medium	Low	Low	Moderate	Medium-high	Medium-low
Maturing-out users	Long	Varies	Low	Low	Moderate	Moderate	High
Burned-out users	Long	Varies	High	Low-medium	Poor	Low	Low

SOURCE: Mark Moore. *Buy and Bust* (Lexington, Mass.: Lexington Books, 1977) p. 83. Used by permission.

Table 6-3 Estimated Annual Aggregate Consumption of Heroin (100,000 Users)

Types of Users	(1) Estimated Number of Users[a]	(2) Estimated Habit Size[b]	(3) Estimated Fraction of Habit Consumed Each "Day on Street"[c]	(4) Estimated Fraction of "Days on Street"[d]	Levels of Heroin Consumption — Implied Consumption of Heroin			
					(5) Bags per Year (millions)	(6) Pure Heroin per Year (kilograms)[e]	(7) Dollars per Year (millions)[f]	(8) Fraction of Total Consumption (percent)
Joy poppers (8%)	8,000	1.2	0.30	1.00	1.0	1.0	5.0	1.1
Drug dabblers (8%)	8,000	1.0	0.30	0.80	0.7	7	3.5	0.7
Addicts (32%)	32,000	5.6	0.95	0.75	46.6	466	233.0	49.6
Hustlers (16%)	16,000	3.8	0.70	0.70	10.9	109	54.5	11.6
Drug dependents (25%)	25,000	6.5	0.60	0.80	28.5	285	142.5	30.3
Conformists (6%)	6,000	1.5	0.95	1.00	3.0	31	15.5	3.3
Maturing-out users (3%)	3,000	4.6	0.80	0.50	2.0	20	10.0	2.1
Burned-out users (1%)	1,000	5.1	0.60	1.00	1.1	11	5.5	1.2
Total	99,000	4.6	0.70	0.78	94.0	940	470	100

SOURCE: Mark Moore. *Buy and Bust* (Lexington, Mass.: Lexington Books, 1977) p. 90. Used by permission.

a Assumes 100,000 users. Total of 99,000 comes from rounding errors.
b Assume: μ of small habits = 0.75 bag per day; μ of moderate habits = 3.5 bags per day; μ of large habits = 10 bags per day.
c Based on combination of habit size, willingness to substitute other drugs, capacity to finance.
d Based on combination of desire for treatment and vulnerability to arrest.
e Based on an estimate of 10 milligrams pure heroin per bag. This is consistent with dilution process to be described later, and with observed quantities of material and purity of drugs.
f Based on $5 per bag.

ity (which is not justified, either mathematically or scientifically)
would suggest that 30 percent of Detroit property crime is committed to support the consumption of heroin."[36]

In viewing the heroin user, it is important to determine the
factors that brought about the initial use of heroin. Unlike marihuana and other drugs, first use of heroin follows a distinctive
pattern in that it typically occurs between the ages of fifteen and
twenty-one and it appears to be unaffected by other potential
substitutes.[37]

In the conventional scenario, a drug-pusher, usually a stranger,
possibly even a nonuser, approaches the susceptible youth and tries
to coax him into joining the pusher's heroin customers. However,
epidemiologist Mark Greene[38] argues:

> *The conventional notion of the "pusher" as the vector is effectively
> dispelled by a careful review of those studies in which an effort was
> made to trace the spread of heroin use from person to person. In these
> studies, it is clear that, in the vast majority of instances, an addict was
> introduced to the use of heroin by a well-meaning friend, usually in
> the setting of a previously established peer group activity. Brown and
> his coworkers (1971) have shown that 66 percent of male juveniles
> studied reported "influence of friends" as the main reason for first
> using heroin. In most instances, the "initiator" was himself relatively
> new to the use of heroin, perhaps not yet addicted. Initiators are often
> long-standing friends of the people they introduce to heroin, and their
> homes are frequently the place in which introduction to heroin takes
> place. . . . Hunt (1973) has shown that 80% of new users are created
> within a year of their initiator's onset of heroin abuse. . . . It is the
> new user of heroin who probably contributes most significantly to
> heroin use incidence. It is possible that the most effective way to
> intervene in any ongoing heroin epidemic is to identify users who have
> only recently become involved with heroin and to develop treatment
> alternatives that will attract them away from the use of heroin. (pp.
> 4–5)*

For descriptions of the everyday lives and dealings of heroin users,
the reader is encouraged to read the accounts in *Newsday*,[31]
Fiddle,[33] and Larner and Tefferteller.[34] For descriptions of the
heroin-using community, see Hughes et al.[30]

The Number of Heroin Users: Size and Trends

Researchers have used different techniques to estimate the number
of heroin users. Joseph Greenwood, who has been estimating the

size of the population of heroin users every year since 1969 for the Bureau of Narcotics and Dangerous Drugs, made the following estimates for the years 1969 to 1974.

Table 6-4   Greenwood's Estimate of the U.S. Heroin User Population

Year	Number of Users
1969	315,000
1970	524,000
1971	559,000
1972	626,000
1973	602,000
1974	725,000

SOURCE: Reprinted with permission from Table 2, p. 112, Chapter 8 in *The Heroin Epidemics* by Leon G. Hunt and Carl D. Chambers. Copyright 1976 by Spectrum Publications, Inc. New York.

Greenwood used the arrest and rearrest figures of the BNDD register to compute his estimates. In a given period he knew how many heroin users were on the register. He used the rearrest data of these "marked" users to estimate the size of the user population. This method is analogous to counting balls in an urn by marking a sample of balls in the urn (say m balls), mixing them completely back into the urn, and drawing out a new *random* sample of balls from the urn. The fraction of marked balls to total number of balls in the second sample should approximately equal m divided by the total number of balls in the urn.

In his study of heroin use in New York City, Moore used arrest-rearrest data for New York City in a similar way, along with a comparison of the number of heroin users in New York City's "Narcotics Register" with a count of deaths among all heroin users in the city.[39, 40] Let

A = the set of heroin users in New York City,

B = the subset of A consisting of all those users on the Register's list,

C = the subset of A consisting of all those users that died during the year,

$B \cap C$ = users on the list that died during the year.

The size of the last three subsets is computable. Therefore, if the list is representative, one can compute the size of A, $\#(A)$, by the formula:

$$\frac{\#(B \cap C)}{\#(B)} = \frac{\#(C)}{\#(A)}.$$

(The success of this method of estimation depends on a number of factors, including the reliability and representativeness of the agency's count and a consistent and reasonably thorough diagnostic drug screening of all autopsied deaths. One could not have used this technique with confidence in the District of Columbia before July 1970, since only 6.3 percent of the bodies autopsied were checked for drug use in that period. This percentage increased to 51 percent after July 1970.)

In cities with active drug treatment centers, one can estimate the size of the heroin user population by using sampling techniques or urn-counting techniques to estimate what percentage of the user population is seeking treatment. Robins and Murphy and others have shown that an extremely high percentage of heroin *addicts* come to the attention of legal authorities or treatment programs. [41, 42]

Another estimating method is based on the widely-held belief that 25 to 50 percent of all property crime (excluding automobile theft) in metropolitan areas is caused by heroin addicts seeking funds to continue their habits. Grizzle used this method to estimate the number of heroin users in Charlotte, North Carolina in 1971. [43] In her calculations, she had to take into consideration such data as victimization rates, the street price of heroin, and the fencing discount on stolen goods.

Some epidemiologists, such as Leon Hunt, employ careful comparisons of the data on heroin users that each of the different agencies and institutions in a given urban area have compiled. [44] This method becomes especially powerful when it is combined with sophisticated statistical sampling techniques and theories. "Each new set [of data] extends our range of local drug use, sometimes providing a description of an entirely new group of users and sometimes defining the conjunction between two formerly unrelated groups. . . . The uniqueness of each source guarantees the identification of a bona fide group of users with distinct characteristics." [45]

Hunt and Chambers use this technique to argue that Greenwood's arrest-rearrest method grossly underestimates the size of the heroin-user population. [46] In the first place, they argue that the second sample that Greenwood counted (the rearrest group) was far from random; a person who has been arrested once has a higher probability of being rearrested than others in the user population. To reinforce this argument, Hunt and Chambers point out that later data indicate that 9,030 heroin users reported for treatment in the Washington, D.C. Narcotics Treatment Administration clinics in 1969, and 7,500 heroin users were treated at San Francisco's Haight-Ashbury Clinic in 1969. These figures are nearly double the estimates of 4,600 users in Washington and 4,200 users in San Francisco that were components of Greenwood's estimate of 315,000 U.S. heroin users in 1969. Hunt and Chambers further argue that their careful statistical marking process indicates that only one third of the active users in Washington, Los Angeles, Detroit, and Phoenix were known to their local treatment centers at any given time. They conclude that one can conservatively multiply Greenwood's estimates by six to achieve more realistic estimates of the heroin user population. They back up this claim by indicating that their own independent general population estimates are roughly six times those of Greenwood.

The difference, they claim, lies in a distinction between heroin users and heroin addicts. They feel that the techniques of Greenwood and others are fairly accurate estimators of the population of heroin addicts—those who use the drug daily and who have developed a strong dependence on it. On the other hand, they argue that there are at least three million Americans who use heroin only occasionally while they "hold steady jobs, live in stable families in conventional communities, and manifest none of the outward signs of social distress associated with the 'junkie' addict."[47]

We will use Greenwood's estimates in Table 6-4 as measures of the size of the population of heroin addicts in the United States—725,000 in 1974. We will also assume that there were another one to three million noncompulsive, irregular users. As this table indicates, the number of users increased in the period between 1969 and 1974. However, all studies indicate the number of those who begin their use of heroin in any given year peaked in 1969 and has been declining rapidly since then. Epidemiologists who study the incidence of heroin use all draw graphs similar to the one in Figure 6-2, relating each year to the number of persons who first used heroin in that year. (For examples, see Endnotes 4, 37, 38, 44, 48, 49, and 50). We have not labeled the vertical axis in units because different researchers considered different populations and different measurement techniques in describing the incidence of heroin abuse.

As noted earlier, it is the new user who probably contributes

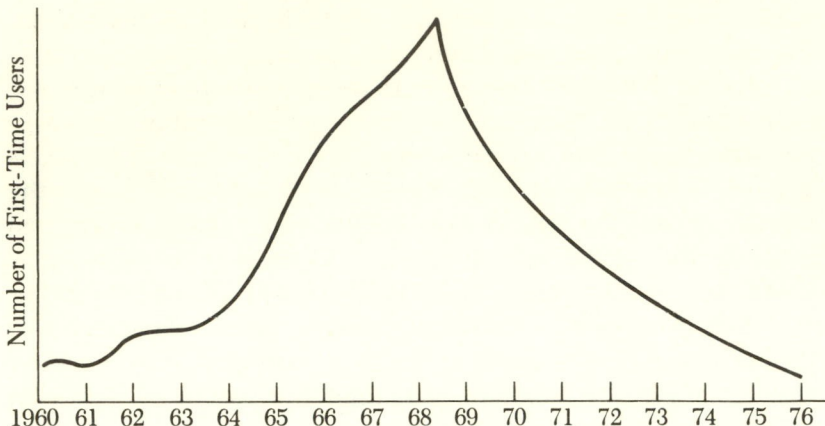

Figure 6-2 Year of First-Incidence Use of Heroin.

most significantly to the spread of the heroin epidemic. Thus, Figure 6-2 certainly leaves the clear impression that the war on heroin has met with success, at least between the years 1969 and 1975, and that the uncontrolled increase of the heroin epidemic of the late 1960s has been overcome. One can take some hope in the fact that the number of narcotic overdose deaths, the hepatitis rate, the number of addicts seeking treatment, and the crime rate for property crimes associated with heroin addiction all decreased between 1971 and 1973.[51]

However, Hunt and Chambers[52] and Hunt[53, 54] found that incidence of first use was still peaking *in 1974* in cities with populations under 400,000. They argue, however, that the heroin epidemic has not recurred in any of the populations or geographic areas which saw an earlier incidence peak: "These new epidemics, if indeed they continue to such a point, are occurring in demographically or geographically distinct segments of cities, unlike those that supported earlier outbreaks of use."[55] Hunt states: "In the next five years [1975–1979], one might estimate that no more than 200,000 new users are likely to appear in places where heroin use has not yet become widespread. These estimated results suggest the need for continuous reallocation of drug treatment funds to smaller and smaller cities as peak use shifts and treatment demand declines in areas of older heroin use."[56]

A few caveats are in order here. First of all, in the mid-1970s, the "Mexican connection" took over as the chief supplier of heroin in the United States. The incidence graph for Los Angeles, a major center in the new distribution system, is quite different from the shape of the previous graph. The total number of reported voluntary admissions to treatment centers was 50 percent higher for Los Angeles than it was for New York City in 1976.[57] Articles in the *Washington Post* in August of 1979 point to a sudden marked increase in heroin use in our nation's capital.

As we mentioned earlier, this increase is probably due to the arrival of large supplies of high-quality heroin from the Burma-Laos-Thailand region. American health officials fear that this new supply of heroin has started sending the incidence curve (Figure 6-2) abruptly higher in the late 1970s.

The National Income of the Heroin Distribution Industry

To estimate the national income of the heroin distribution industry in 1974, we will use a couple of approaches. First, we will extrapolate Moore's figures for New York City to arrive at national figures. Moore's estimate of 100,000 heroin users in New York included some irregular users ("joy poppers," "drug dabblers," and "conformists"). As Table 6-3 indicated, there were 78,000 New Yorkers in the other five classes of heroin users—each of which had a habit of over four bags a day. This figure is roughly one tenth of Greenwood's estimate for the national population of heroin addicts in 1974. If we assume that the national income of the U.S. heroin distribution industry is a corresponding ten times that of the New York City figure of $324 million, we are led to an estimate of $3.24 billion for the value-added of the U.S. industry.

A second source of information is the *1978 Annual Report* of the Office of Drug Abuse Policy, which made estimates both of the value of heroin imported into the United States and of the value of the heroin consumed in the United States in 1976. The ODAP estimated that there were 500,000 daily users and 1,500,000 less-than-daily users in the United States in 1976, figures consistent with our discussion in the previous section. Under the assumption that each daily user required an average of 50 mg a day for 365 days a year, ODAP estimated that daily users consumed 9.1 metric tons in 1976. Combining this estimate with one that less-than-daily users consumed .9 metric tons in 1976, ODAP suggested that 10 metric tons were consumed. Assuming a cost of $1.43 per milligram of pure heroin, the ODAP estimated that $14.3 billion of heroin was consumed in 1976.

However ODAP's estimate of the total supply of heroin available to the U.S. market was 6.16 metric tons—well below their estimate of the 10.0 metric tons consumed. Believing that (1) the supply figures are more reliable, (2) most heroin addicts used less than 50 mg a day and could consume heroin only 80 percent of the year, and (3) the average addict spent less than $1.43 per mg, we will multiply the above total cost figure by (6.16/10.0) to arrive at an adjusted estimate of $8.6 billion. This adjusted estimate derives further support from the fact that the National Narcotics Intelligence Consumers Committee estimated that $8.8 billion of heroin was consumed in 1977. Finally, to change this total cost estimate to a national income estimate, we multiply it by the ratio of value-added to total cost (324/470) that Moore found in his detailed study to arrive at a national income of $6.5 billion for the heroin industry in 1976. Finally, we move this figure to 1974 by multiplying it by the appropriate price ratio (100/130)—the supply and addict populations were rather steady in this period—to obtain an estimate of $5 billion for the national income of the heroin industry in 1974.

Costs to Society of Heroin Abuse

In order to understand the magnitude of the problem of heroin abuse, to compare its impact with that of other problems facing society, and to evaluate alternative courses of action for dealing with the heroin problem, society needs a careful estimate of the total economic costs of heroin abuse. Since 1970, a number of researchers have attempted to measure these costs. Holahan, as part of a cost-benefit analysis of Washington, D.C.'s Narcotic Treatment Administration Program, estimated the social costs of the heroin problem in the District of Columbia for 1969.[58] Leslie,[59] Fujii,[60] McGlothlin et al.[61] and the Arthur D. Little Company[62] were among those estimating some or all of the costs of heroin abuse to society. Lemkau et al.[63] published a comprehensive report based on a study conducted at Johns Hopkins University.

One of the most recent and most careful reports in this direction is that of Rufener, Rachal, and Cruze, researchers at North Carolina's Research Triangle Institute, as part of a cost-benefit evaluation of the drug abuse treatment programs sponsored by the National

Institute of Drug Abuse.[64, 65] Despite the significant differences in their techniques, the three most recent studies arrive at figures that are surprisingly similar. The A. D. Little[62] study estimated that the economic cost to society of drug abuse for the calendar year 1973 was $9.7 billion, while the Hopkins study[63] arrived at a figure of $10.9 billion for the same period. The Rufener, Rachal, and Cruze report (Vol. II) estimated the costs as $10.3 billion for the fiscal year 1975 (July 1, 1974 through June 30, 1975).[65] Gillespie[66] summarizes the estimates of these three reports item by item in his Table 1. He also describes some conceptual errors in all three reports—errors which lead to some substantial overestimations. We have incorporated Gillespie's suggestions in our discussion of heroin's costs to society. Because the Rufener, Rachal, and Cruze report used the most careful estimation procedures and the most recent data available, we will summarize its results.

The Rufener-Rachal-Cruze report estimates the total economic costs to society of *all* drug abuse for the fiscal year 1975.[67] Later, in their Appendix A, they estimate the costs due to heroin abuse alone. We present both sets of figures in our summary.

The researchers first enumerate the tangible costs borne by society because of drug abuse. For convenience, these costs are divided into two groups: direct costs and indirect costs.[68]

> *An explicit or direct cost is one in which resources are used and a formal payment is made in cash or in kind (that is, through the direct provision of some commodity or service). When resources are used to treat the medical consequences of drug abuse, the labor is paid for in wages, the materials used are paid for, and the capital used receives a return. On the other hand, an indirect or implicit cost occurs whenever resources are used for which no formal payment is made; that is, these resources are not priced by any market mechanism. When a drug abuser is treated in a hospital, his time is being used, but no formal payment is made for its use. In order to place a value on this indirect cost, one looks at the value of what the individual gave up, or the opportunity cost. To the extent that the resources are used because of drug abuse (the extent is measured by the cost estimate), the resources are unavailable for producing other goods for increasing societal welfare and thus a cost is incurred.*

For two rather important reasons, the actual total costs to society of drug abuse are much larger than the figures computed. First of all, Rufener, Rachal, and Cruze compute only tangible costs, that is, costs that can be valued with a reasonable use of resources. As a result, they omit costs of inconvenience and human suffering associated with drug abuse. These costs include the pain and suffering experienced by the addicts, "the displeasure people feel when viewing abusers and the conditions abuse creates, the costs of disruptions of neighborhoods, the destruction of families, and corruption of law officials. . . . The current state of the art with respect to measuring and pricing these costs is not sufficiently advanced to permit their estimation."[69]

In addition, the authors "estimate the economic costs to society of drug abuse for only one year. Some costs, however, extend for more than one year. For example, if a drug abuser dies in fiscal year 1975, not only is an economic cost present in that year but it extends into the future as well. The cost would be the loss of goods and services the abuser would have produced throughout his or her working lifetime."[70]

Table 6-5 summarizes the costs to society of drug abuse. It differs from the tables in Volume II of Rufener, Rachal, and Cruze only in that it does not include their direct cost for "nondrug crime." This adjustment is made to avoid a double-counting pointed out by Gillespie.[66] Following is a detailed description of each of the costs shown in Table 6-5.

Direct Costs

Medical Treatment.   Some drug abusers will experience medical problems that require treatment involving medical personnel, equipment, buildings, and supplies of various types.

Law Enforcement Costs.   Society has decided that possession or sale of certain drugs is a crime and has passed laws against drug abuse. Enforcement of these laws requires expenditures for personnel, buildings, equipment, and supplies—all of which represent a cost to society. Drug abuse is also related to violation of nondrug laws. For example, it is usually estimated that a large percentage of property crimes are committed to support heroin habits. New York City Police Commissioner Pat Murphy estimated in 1972 that 25 percent of that city's crimes are committed by heroin addicts. (See Markham,[71] p. 6, and Grizzle,[43] p. 5.) Silverman and Spruill make a rough estimate that "30% of Detroit's property crime is committed to support the consumption of heroin."[72] Moore estimates rather carefully that the roughly 100,000 heroin users in New York City in one year in the early 1970s bought $470 million of heroin, $206 million of which was purchased with funds obtained through

Table 6-5 Economic Costs of Drug Abuse (Fiscal Year 1975, Assuming 750,000 Addicts, in $ Million)

	All Drugs	Heroin
Direct Cost Component		
Medical Treatment	$494	$111.2
Emergency room visits	12	1.2
Inpatient care	314	72
Mental hospital inpatient care	35	8
Miscellaneous medical costs	133	30
Law Enforcement Costs	1,342	780
Drug laws	667	105
Nondrug laws; public expenditures	419	419
Nondrug laws; private expenditures	256	256
Judicial System Costs	296	151
Drug laws	172	27
Nondrug laws	124	124
Correction Costs	294	161
Drug laws	158	25
Nondrug laws	136	136
Drug Traffic Control	93	46.5
Drug Abuse Prevention	995	535
Housing Stock Loss	84	84
Total Direct Costs	$3,598.0	$1,868.7
Indirect Cost Component		
Unemployability	3,716.0	3,716.0
Emergency Room Treatment	0.4	0.04
Inpatient Hospitalization	20.0	4.6
Mental Hospitalization	8.0	1.8
Drug-related deaths	12.5	2.3
Absenteeism	1,595.0	161.0
Incarceration	1,205.0	494.0
Drug laws	845.0	134.0
Nondrug laws	360.0	360.0
Work Loss Due to Treatment	88.0	47.0
Total Indirect Costs	6,643.9	4,426.74
Total Direct Costs	3,598.0	1,868.70
Total Costs	$10,241.9	$6,295.44

SOURCE: Adapted from Rufener, Rachal, and Cruze, *Management Effectiveness Measures for NIDA Drug Abuse Treatment Programs, Vol. II: Costs to Society of Drug Abuse* (1976), p. 13.

thefts.[73] By way of comparison, Singer estimates that total thievery from homes, from persons, and by shoplifting in New York City in 1970 amounted to a total of $330 million.[74] The close relationship between property crime and heroin use is especially evident if one compares year-*vs.*-number graphs of these two phenomena. (For example, compare figures 2 and 10 in DuPont and Greene.[48])

Judicial System Costs.   During fiscal year 1975, many drug users were arrested and processed through the criminal justice system as a result of law violations brought on by their drug use. As a result, society had to pay the costs for the use of such resources as personnel to staff courts and to prosecute and defend those in trial, and for the corresponding buildings, equipment, and supplies that were used.

Corrections Costs.   "Some of those convicted of violation of drug laws and nondrug laws will be incarcerated, and others will be placed on probation. Obviously, for those convicted of violations of drug laws the resource costs for correction are related to drug abuse; for violators of nondrug laws we again must assume a relationship between criminal behavior and drug abuse."[65] (p. 8)

Drug Traffic Control Costs.   A number of federal agencies outside of the Justice Department (Justice Department costs were included in the Enforcement component) use labor, equipment, buildings, and supplies in the course of their attempt to control drug trafficking.

Drug Abuse Prevention Costs.   "Society uses its resources to treat drug abusers, to educate the population, to train drug abuse personnel, to conduct research and evaluation, and to provide management and support."[65] (p. 9)

Housing Stock Loss.   Addicts often occupy vacant buildings as havens for heroin use, and sometimes they inadvertently start fires. This destruction of housing is a cost to society.

Indirect Costs

Unemployability.   Rufener, Rachal, and Cruze assume that heroin abuse results in higher levels of unemployment than would be the case in the absence of drug abuse. Assuming that there are 500,000 addicts in the United States in fiscal year 1975, these researchers estimate that heroin addicts forego $2,478 million in earnings because of their habit.

Emergency Room Treatment.   "Some medical emergencies

Table 6-6   Summary of Heroin Usage for 1974

Number of heroin users	
Addicts	725,000
Nonaddicted users	3,000,000
Amount of pure heroin consumed	6 to 8 metric tons
Total cost of heroin consumed	$4.9 to $7.3 billion
National income of heroin distribution industry	$3.2 to $5.0 billion
Cost to society	
Heroin	$6.3 billion
All drugs	$10.2 billion

occur while the abuser is at work, necessitating that the abuser leave work to receive treatment."[75]

Indirect Inpatient Hospitalization Costs. "Drug abuse often results in injury or illness that must be treated on an inpatient basis in a hospital. Were it not for these injuries and illnesses, some of the time spent by abusers would have been spent working."[76]

Indirect Mental Hospitalization Costs. Rufener, Rachal, and Cruze estimate that work loss due to mental hospitalization of drug addicts was $8 million in fiscal year 1975, with $1.8 million of this attributable to heroin addicts.

Drug-Related Deaths. Because of the premature drug-related deaths of some drug abusers, society had to forego the goods and services that could have been produced.

Absenteeism. Drug abuse can result in higher levels of absenteeism from the job.

Incarceration. Abusers who are incarcerated as a result of activities related to their drug use are not available for work, and total societal production is decreased.

Work Lost Due to Treatment. Drug abusers being treated in a residential or inpatient environment are unavailable for employment. Rufener, Rachal, and Cruze estimate that the indirect treatment costs for fiscal year 1975 were $88 million, with $47 million of this total attributable to heroin use.

Table 6-6 summarizes the estimates we have made in this chapter regarding heroin usage and the heroin distribution industry in 1974.

Endnotes

1. Fuqua, Paul. 1978. *Drug Abuse: Investigation and Control.* New York: McGraw-Hill, p. 51.
2. *Ibid.*

3. Bureau of Narcotics and Dangerous Drugs. 1970. "The World Opium Situation." Unpublished paper.
4. *Ibid.*
5. Holahan, John. 1972. "The Economics of Heroin," in P. M. Wald, and P. B. Hutt (eds.) *Dealing with Drug Abuse.* New York: Praeger Publishers, pp. 255–299.
6. *Ibid.*, p. 269.
7. Fuqua, *Drug Abuse,* p. 58.
8. Office of Drug Abuse Policy. 1978. *1978 Annual Report.* Washington, D.C.: U.S. Government Printing Office.
9. *Ibid.*, p. 63.
10. Rottenberg, Simon. 1968. "The Clandestine Distribution of Heroin, Its Discovery and Suppression," *The Journal of Political Economy,* p. 76.
11. Preble, E., and J. Casey. 1969. "Taking Care of Business: The Heroin User's Life on the Street," *International Journal of Addictions,* p. 4.
12. Moore, Mark H. 1970. *Policy Concerning Drug Abuse in New York State, Vol. III: Economics of Heroin Distribution.* Croton-on-Hudson, New York: Hudson Institute.
13. Moore, Mark. 1977. *Buy and Bust.* Lexington, Mass.: Lexington Books.
14. Holahan, "The Economics of Heroin."
15. Moore, *Buy and Bust,* p. 11.
16. Holahan, "The Economics of Heroin," p. 272.
17. *Ibid.*, p. 273.
18. Moore, *Buy and Bust,* p. 55.
19. Holahan, "The Economics of Heroin," p. 275.
20. Bureau of Narcotics and Dangerous Drugs, "The World Opium Situation."
21. Moore, *Buy and Bust,* p. 100.
22. Holahan, "The Economics of Heroin," p. 275.
23. Moore, *Buy and Bust,* p. 53.
24. Preble and Casey, "Taking Care of Business."
25. Moore, "Policy Concerning Drug Abuse in N.Y.C."
26. Moore, *Buy and Bust.*
27. Holahan, "The Economics of Heroin."
28. Fuqua, *Drug Abuse.*
29. Moore, *Buy and Bust.*
30. Hughes, Patrick H., G. A. Crawford, N. W. Barker, S. Schumann, and J. H. Jaffe. 1971. "The Social Structure of a Heroin Copping Community," *American Journal of Psychiatry* 118 (Nov.):551–558.
31. *Newsday* staff and editors. 1973. *The Heroin Trail.* (Long Island, N.Y.: Newsday, Inc.)
32. Moore, *Buy and Bust,* p. 82.
33. Fiddle, Seymour. 1967. *Portraits from a Shooting Gallery.* New York: Harper and Row.
34. Larner, Jeremy, and Ralph Tefferteller. 1964. *The Addict in the Street.* New York: Grove Press.
35. Silverman, Lester P. and Nancy Spruill. 1977. "Urban Crime and the Price of Heroin," *Journal of Urban Economics* 4:80–103.

36. *Ibid.*, p. 102.
37. Hunt, L., and C. Chambers. 1976. *The Heroin Epidemics*. New York: Spectrum Publications, p. 79.
38. Greene, Mark. 1974. "An Epidemiological Assessment of Heroin Use," *American Journal of Public Health* 64 (December):1–10.
39. Moore, *Buy and Bust*.
40. Newman, Robert, and Margot Cates. 1974. "The New York City Narcotics Register: A Case Study," *American Journal of Public Health* 64 (December):24–28.
41. Robins, L. N., and G. E. Murphy. 1967. "Drug Use in a Normal Population of Young Negro Men," *American Journal of Public Health* 57:1580–1597.
42. Hunt, Leon, and N. E. Zinberg. 1976. *Heroin Use: A New Look*. Washington, D.C.: Drug Abuse Council, Inc.
43. Grizzle, Gloria A. 1972. "How Many Heroin Addicts in Charlotte-Mechlenburg?" Discussion paper for community Drug Action Committee, Charlotte-Mecklenburg, North Carolina.
44. Hunt, Leon G. 1977. *Assessment of Local Drug Abuse*. Lexington, Mass.: D.C. Heath and Company.
45. *Ibid.*, p. 23.
46. Hunt and Chambers, *The Heroin Epidemics*.
47. Hunt and Zinberg, *Heroin Use: A New Look*.
48. Dupont, Robert L., and Mark H. Greene. 1973. "The Dynamics of a Heroin Addiction Epidemic," *Science* 181 (August):716–722.
49. Hunt, Leon G. 1974. "Recent Spread of Heroin Use in the United States," *American Journal of Public Health*, 64 (December):16–23.
50. Kaskowitz, David H., Charles Norwood, and Eduardo Siguel. 1978. "Estimation of Changes in Incidence of Heroin Abuse Using Admissions Data." Menlo Park, California: S.R.I. International preprint.
51. Office of Drug Abuse Policy. 1973.
52. Hunt and Chambers, *The Heroin Epidemics*.
53. Hunt, "Recent Spread of Heroin Use."
54. Hunt, *Assessment of Local Drug Abuse*.
55. Reprinted by permission from p. 72, Chapter 3 in *The Heroin Epidemics* by Leon G. Hunt and Carl D. Chambers. Copyright 1976, Spectrum Publications, Inc., New York.
56. Hunt, "Recent Spread of Heroin Use," p. 16.
57. Kaskowitz *et al.*, "Estimation of Changes in Incidence," p. 9.
58. Holahan, John. 1970. "The Economics of Drug Addiction and Control in Washington, D.C.: A Model for Estimation of Costs and Benefits of Rehabilitation." Washington, D.C.: District of Columbia Department of Corrections Report.
59. Leslie, Alan C. 1972. *A Benefit/Cost Analysis of New York City's Heroin Addiction Problem and Programs—1971*. New York: Office of Program Analysis, Health Services Administration, City of New York.
60. Fujii, Edwin T. 1974. "Public Investment in the Rehabilitation of Heroin Addicts," *Social Science Quarterly* 55:39–51.
61. McGlothlin, W. H., V. A. Tabbush, C. D. Chambers, and K. Jamison. 1972.

Alternative Approaches to Opiate Addiction Control: Costs, Benefits, and Potential. Washington, D.C.: U.S. Department of Justice, Bureau of Narcotics and Dangerous Drugs.

62. Arthur D. Little Company. 1975. *Social Costs of Drug Abuse.* Cambridge, Mass.: A. D. Little Company.
63. Lemkau, P. V., Z. Amsel, B. Sanders, J. Amsel, and T. Seifl. 1975. *Social and Economic Costs of Drug Abuse.* Baltimore, Md.: Johns Hopkins University School of Hygiene and Public Health.
64. Rufener, Brent L., J. V. Rachal, and A. M. Cruze. 1976. *Management Effectiveness Measures for NIDA Drug Abuse Treatment Programs, Vol. I: Cost-Benefit Analysis.* Rockville, Md.: National Institute of Drug Abuse, 1976.
65. Rufener, Brent L., J. V. Rachal, and A. M. Cruze. 1976. *Management Effectiveness Measures for NIDA Drug Abuse Treatment Programs, Vol. II: Costs to Society of Drug Abuse.* Rockville, Md.: National Institute of Drug Abuse, 1976.
66. Gillespie, Robert W. 1978. "Heroin Addiction, Crime and Economic Cost," *Journal of Criminal Justice*, 6:305–313.
67. Rufener, Rachal, and Cruze, "Costs to Society," Vol. II.
68. *Ibid.*, pp. 2, 3, 7.
69. *Ibid.*, pp. 3, 4.
70. *Ibid.*, p. 5.
71. Markham, James. 1972. "What's All This Talk of Heroin Maintenance?" *The New York Times Magazine* (July 2), pp. 6–9, 29–32.
72. Silverman and Spruill, "Urban Crime and Price of Heroin," p. 102.
73. Moore, *Buy and Bust.*
74. Singer, Max. 1971. "Addict Crime: The Vitality of Mythical Numbers," *Public Interest*, p. 23.
75. Rufener, Rachal, and Cruze, "Costs to Society," Vol. II, p. 10.
76. *Ibid.*, pp. 10–11.

Additional References

Abuse Strategy Council. 1975. *Federal Strategy for Drug Abuse and Drug Traffic Prevention, 1975.* Washington, D.C.: U.S. Government Printing Office.

DE ALARCON, R. 1969. "The Spread of Heroin Abuse in a Community," *Bulletin on Narcotics* 21 (July-September):17–22.

BROWN, B.S., S.K. GAUNEY, and S.D. STARK. 1971. "In Their Own Words— Addicts' Reasons for Initiating and Withdrawing from Heroin," *International Journal of Addictions* 6:635–645.

BROWN, GEORGE F. and L.P. SILVERMAN. 1974. "The Retail Price of Heroin: Estimation and Applications," *Journal of the American Statistical Society* 69:595–606.

CLAGUE, CHRISTOPHER. 1973. "Legal Strategies for Dealing with Heroin Addictions," *American Economic Review* 63 (May):263–269.

DE LONG, JAMES V. 1972. "The Drugs and Their Effects," in Patricia Wald and Peter B. Hutt (eds). *Dealing with Drug Abuse.* New York: Praeger Publishers.

Domestic Council on Drug Abuse Task Force. 1975. *White Paper on Drug Abuse.* Washington, D.C.: U.S. Government Printing Office.

DUPONT, ROBERT L. 1974. Testimony before Health and Environment Subcommittee, House Interstate and Foreign Commerce Committee, October 7, 1974.

FERNANDEZ, RAUL A. 1963. "The Problem of Heroin Addiction and the Radical Political Economy," *American Economic Review* 63 (May):257–262.

HUGHES, PATRICK H., N. W. BARKER, G. CRAWFORD, and J. H. JAFFE. 1972. "The Natural History of a Heroin Epidemic," *American Journal of Public Health* 62 (July):995–1001.

HUGHES, PATRICK H., and G. A. CRAWFORD. 1972. "A Contagious Disease Model for Researching and Intervening in Heroin Epidemics," *Archives of General Psychiatry* 27 (August):149–155.

HUGHES, PATRICK H., and J. H. JAFFE. 1971. "The Heroin Copping Area," *Archives of General Psychiatry* 24 (May):394–400.

HUNT, LEON G. 1973. *Heroin Epidemics—A Quantitative Study of Empirical Data.* Washington, D.C.: Drug Abuse Council Monograph.

MOORE, MARK H. 1971. "Economics of Heroin Distribution." Teaching and Research Materials of Public Policy Programs, Kennedy School of Government, Harvard University.

MOORE, MARK H. 1973. "Policies to Achieve Discrimination on the Effective Price of Heroin," *American Economic Review* 63 (May):270–277.

MOORE, MARK H. 1976. "Anatomy of the Heroin Problem: An Exercise in Problem Definition," *Public Analysis* (Fall), pp. 639–662.

O'DONNELL, JOHN A., H. L. VOSS, R. R. CLAYTON, G. T. SLATIN, and R. C. ROOM. 1976. *Young Men and Drugs—A Nationwide Survey*, National Institute on Drug Abuse Research Monograph Series, No. 5. Washington, D.C.: U.S. Government Printing Office.

VOTEY, HAROLD L., JR. "Detention of Heroin Addicts, Job Opportunities and Deterrence: An Econometric Systems Evaluation of Options for Property Crime Control." University of California, Santa Barbara, Preprint.

VOTEY, HAROLD L., JR. and LLAD PHILLIPS. 1976. "Minimizing the Social Cost of Drug Abuse: Economic Analysis of Alternatives for Policy," *Policy Sciences* 7:315–336.

WALD, PATRICIA M., and PETER B. HUTT, eds. 1972. *Dealing with Drug Abuse.* New York: Praeger Publishers.

WALD, PATRICIA M., and PETER B. HUTT. 1972. "The Drug Abuse Survey Project," in P. M. Wald and P. B. Hutt, (eds.), *Dealing with Drug Abuse.* New York: Praeger Publishers.

WILSON, JAMES Q., M. H. MOORE, and I. D. WHEAT, JR. 1972. "The Problem of Heroin," *The Public Interest* 29 (Fall):3–28.

Chapter 7

COCAINE

In the mid-1800s Sigmund Freud was a struggling young neurologist suffering from depression, chronic fatigue, and other neurotic symptoms. Desperate to cure his depression and lethargy, he injected into his veins some cocaine—a white crystalline powder extracted from the leaf of the coca bushes of South America. Freud found that cocaine was "a magical drug" that lifted his depression, cured his indigestion, and gave him a feeling of "exhilaration and lasting euphoria, which in no way differs from the euphoria of a healthy person. . . . You perceive an increase in self-control and possess more vitality and capacity for work. . . . In other words, you are simply normal, and it is soon hard to believe that you are under the influence of any drug."[1]

Freud was soon prescribing cocaine for his patients and writing papers in praise of its powers. His close friend Dr. Carl Koller discovered that cocaine was also highly effective as a local anesthetic in eye operations, thus ushering in a period of over 50 years in which cocaine was a major medical anesthetic. Freud's enthusiasm for the drug was dampened when a close friend who had been taking massive doses of cocaine on Freud's advice, to ease a chronic excruciating pain, developed a severe cocaine-induced psychosis with a feeling of "white snakes creeping over his skin." By 1890, after a few other cocaine users developed similar psychoses after long or heavy use, Freud's enthusiasm for cocaine and that of Europe's medical profession diminished considerably.

Cocaine was highly popular in the United States in the 1800s, too. It became the officially recommended remedy of the Hay Fever Association. Mixed with an extract of the kola nut, it was an important ingredient in the popular drink Coca-Cola. (In 1903,

Coca-Cola manufacturers were forced to switch to decocainized coca leaves. These sanitized coca leaves are still used as a flavoring agent in Coca-Cola.[2, 3]) However, after the turn of the century, public attitude turned against cocaine. In 1906, the Food and Drug Administration curtailed the use of cocaine in over-the-counter medicines. In 1914, the U.S. Congress passed the Harrison Narcotics Act, which made illegal the use or sale of such drugs as opium, morphine, heroin, and cocaine, thereby giving black market status to the U.S. cocaine market.

In 1932, scientists developed a group of powerful *synthetic* stimulants—the amphetamines. These drugs had a kick similar to that of cocaine but the effect lasted much longer, and the new drugs were much cheaper. As a result, the smuggling and use of cocaine diminished dramatically in the United States. But, in the late 1960s, law enforcement efforts and rigid production quotas severely limited the black market supply of amphetamines. To fill this gap, a new interest and enthusiasm for cocaine appeared, so that by the 1970s cocaine was a highly fashionable drug—"the ultimate status symbol in the drug scene."[4]

Cocaine is an extract of the leaf of the coca bush (*Erythroxylon coca*), a medium-sized bush that grows abundantly on the slopes of the Andes mountains of Peru, Bolivia, Ecuador, Chile, and Colombia. (See Brecher, pp. 269–271, Grinspoon and Bakalar, pp. 71–75, and Fuqua, pp. 101–103 for a more detailed description of the material in this section.) The Spanish conquistadors used coca leaves to exploit their Inca subjects around 1550, just as southern plantation overseers in the United States used cocaine to get more work out of their black laborers around 1900. These Spaniards were, of course, responsible for introducing cocaine to Europe. An estimated 90 percent of the adult males that live in the Peruvian Andes consume cocaine by chewing the coca leaf without any sign of physical harm or addiction. The potent stimulation and appetite suppression of cocaine may help these Andean leaf-chewers survive the rigors of their harsh climate.

Today, cultivation of the coca plant is legal only in Peru and Bolivia, although it is still grown illegally in abundance in Chile, Colombia, and Ecuador. The Peruvian and Bolivian governments regard the coca leaves, which they export as a medicine and as a soft drink flavoring, as an important component of their foreign exchange. Nevertheless, because the black market price of coca leaves is so much higher than the official market price, as much as 80 percent of Peru's and Bolivia's coca leaf crops ends up in the black market.[5]

Cocaine Production

The extraction of cocaine from the coca leaves is a fairly simple process. The Indians who harvest the coca leaves dry them carefully and take them to a nearby primitive laboratory set up and operated by the local trafficking organization. There the leaves are soaked in a mixture of water, kerosene, and calcium carbonate until the raw cocaine precipitates out of the solution in the form of an off-white paste. Once carefully dried, this paste is shipped to a secret finishing laboratory, possibly in a nearby country such as Brazil or Paraguay. There the paste is treated with a dilute solution of hydrochloric acid, and then with potassium permanganate and sodium carbonate. The end result, precipitated out of this solution and collected by filtration, is 70 to 86 percent pure cocaine, a pulverized rock called cocaine hydrochloride.

Smuggling and Distribution

The next step is to smuggle the processed cocaine into the United States. This operation is coordinated by two organizations—one in South America, the other in the United States (especially in Miami, New York, or Los Angeles).* The Latin American syndicate "buys coca leaves, sets up the laboratories, maintains contacts with local officials, arranges for payoffs, and dispatches local couriers to the United States. The Miami boss, like the head of a large commercial corporation, has deputies in charge of travel, transportation, personnel, security, accounting, and quality control."[6] Before Castro's revolution, much of the cocaine-smuggling organization was run by Cubans. Since the revolution, many of these Cuban businessmen and former politicians have moved their drug operations to Miami.[7] The *Wall Street Journal* quotes the southeast regional director of the DEA, Frederick Rody, Jr., as estimating that "90 percent of all

---

* Brecher (pp. 302–304), Grinspoon and Bakalar (pp. 50–58), and Fuqua (pp. 111–115) provide some details of the smuggling and distribution operation. Brecher bases much of his account on articles by *New York Times* correspondent George Volsky.

wholesale marihuana and cocaine transactions in the U.S. . . . . involve Miami."[8]

The syndicates coordinate two methods of smuggling. In one method, they recruit South American citizens to smuggle two to three kilos of cocaine into the United States. The couriers may be housewives, students, or tourists, and usually know very little about the smuggling organization. They are given simple, precise instructions about where to pick up the cocaine (possibly already well concealed in some innocent-looking merchandise) and where to drop it off in the United States. They are paid $500 to $1,000 per kilo. If caught, they're usually given a suspended sentence and deported to their homeland where their earnings will bring them a good life and prestige. Alternatively, the syndicates may use a private plane or boat to try to smuggle a much larger shipment of cocaine, via a complex, well-planned route, into the United States.

The cocaine distribution system resembles the successful heroin distribution system. The system has a long vertical organization, with each distribution unit servicing only five to twenty customers. For greater protection and insulation from law enforcement agencies, and to exploit some monopoly advantages, these distributional units are well insulated from units below them. Just as in the heroin distribution system, each participant in the cocaine distribution system dilutes or "cuts" the cocaine in his possession to increase its volume and substantially raise its price. Common adulterants— besides the lactose and quinine used in heroin dilution—include dextrose, lidocaine, procaine, mannitol, and inositol. "By the time the drug reaches the user, it is rarely over 5 to 10 percent pure. That means that the same kilo that cost $4,000 to $5,000 in Latin America, or $20,000 delivered stateside, will yield 80 or more kilos of cut cocaine. By the time that this is sold in gram or spoon lots, its value will have risen to well over $300,000."[9]

There are a few significant ways in which the cocaine distribution system differs from the heroin distribution system. First of all, it is far more informal and less organized. It is not uncommon for an individual not yet in the distribution system to buy cocaine on the streets of Colombia or Chile, smuggle it into the United States himself, and sell it for a hefty mark-up on the streets or to his acquaintances. The young and independent smugglers of Colombian marihuana often find it profitable to sneak in a few kilos of "coke" with their bales of marihuana.[10, 11, 12] Because complete control of the cocaine market is so difficult, criminal organizations appear to have a much smaller impact on the cocaine distribution industry than they do on the heroin industry.[13] Finally, unlike in the heroin industry where the upper echelons are reluctant to sample the drug they sell, more people who deal in cocaine are regular cocaine users.[14]

Size, Trends, and National Income

We next estimate the size and national income of the cocaine market. Table 7-1 summarizes the results of five surveys on the extent of cocaine use in the 1970s among youth and adults in the United States. The results of these surveys exhibit a clear increase in the number of regular cocaine users between 1972 and 1976.

The Office of Drug Abuse Policy in conjunction with the Departments of Health, Education and Welfare, State, and Justice, and the CIA used the last survey listed in Table 7-1 to develop an estimate of the amount of cocaine hydrochloride that was imported into and used in the United States in 1976. First, ODAP used their survey results to estimate that 4,075,000 Americans used cocaine in 1976. Then they broke down these users by frequency of use, as indicated in Table 7-2, and suggested that in a typical session the user administers the drug to himself at least three times, with an average amount of 50 mg for each of these administrations.

The ODAP study next described a Drug Enforcement Administration estimate that the purity of street level cocaine was 13 percent in 1976. However, since many regular users may have access to much purer forms of cocaine, ODAP used an average purity of 30 percent in their calculations. This implied that a user consumed 45 mg of pure cocaine (.30 × 150) in an average three-dose session. To estimate the total amount of pure cocaine consumed in 1976, ODAP multiplied the entries in column 2 of Table 7-2 by the corresponding entries in column 4 and then multiplied that result by 45 (45 mg/session) to arrive at an estimate of 13,185 kg of cocaine consumed in the United States in 1976. More than half of this amount (6,693 kg) was consumed by the daily users. If one uses the DEA estimate of 53 cents per mg for the street price of heroin, one arrives at an estimate of $7 billion for the total cost of consuming these 13.2 metric tons. (See also p. 473 of the *1977 Sourcebook of Criminal Justice Statistics*. For some unspecified reason, ODAP used the 1974 price of 49 cents per mg instead of the 1976 price of

Table 7-1   Extent of Cocaine Use[a]

Year of Survey	Population Surveyed	Percentage Who Had Ever Used Cocaine	Percentage Who Had Used Cocaine in Past Year	Regular Number of Users as Projected by Survey
1972[b]	Youth (ages 12–17)	1.5	1.1	270,000
	Adults (ages ≥ 18)	3.2	1.6	2,230,000
1974[c]	Youth (ages 12–17)	3.6	2.7	680,000
	Adults (ages ≥ 18)	3.4	2.0	2,880,000
1976[d]	Youth (ages 12–17)	3.4	2.3	570,000
	Adults (ages ≥ 18)	4.1	2.0	2,990,000
1974–75[e]	Young Men (ages 20–30)	14.0	7.0	1,310,000
1976[f]	Youth (ages 12–17)		2.3	575,000
	Adults (ages ≥ 18)		6.9	3,500,000
	Adults (ages 18–25)		7.0	2,500,000
	Adults (ages ≥ 25)		0.9	1,000,000

[a] See Glenn and Richards (1974) for a compendium of surveys.
[b] National Commission on Marihuana and Drug Abuse (1973).
[c] Abelson and Atkinson (1975).
[d] Abelson and Fishburne (1976).
[e] O'Donnell et al. (1976), as summarized in the 1977 *Sourcebook of Criminal Justice Statistics*, pp. 768–770.
[f] Office of Drug Abuse Policy. *1978 Annual Report*. Washington, D.C.: U.S. Government Printing Office. ODAP added 400,000 to the survey results for the 18 to 25-year bracket "to allow for underreporting."

Table 7-2 Breakdown of Cocaine Use

Frequency of Use	Annual Number of 3-Administration Sessions	Percentage of Users	Number of Users
Daily	365	10	407,500
Every weekend	156	10	407,500
Two weekends/month	72	10	407,500
One weekend/month	36	10	407,500
Twice/month	24	30	1,222,500
Once/2 months	6	30	1,222,500

SOURCE: Office of Drug Abuse Policy. *1978 Annual Report*. Washington, D.C.: U.S. Government Printing Office, p. 68.

Table 7-3 Estimate of Cocaine Entering U.S. Annually

Estimated maximum possible cocaine hydrochloride available for world use	63 tons
Less cocaine hydrochloride not converted because of inefficient production methods, spoilage, waste, loss in transit, pilferage	32–42 tons
Subtotal	21–31 tons
Less cocaine hydrochloride used outside U.S.	5–10 tons
Less 2 tons seized worldwide	2 tons
Subtotal = Range of cocaine hydrochloride estimated to enter the U.S. market each year	14–19 tons

SOURCE: Office of Drug Abuse Policy. *1978 Annual Report*. Washington, D.C.: U.S. Government Printing Office, p. 70.

53 cents per mg in their computations.) If the price per mg is set at 25 cents, to take into account peculiarities in the distribution system, the corresponding cost would be $3.3 billion.

The ODAP complemented their demand-side estimate with a supply-side estimate. They began with an estimate of the coca leaf production in Peru and Bolivia, the main growers of the leaf. Taking into consideration the amount lost to spoilage, waste, pilferage, and production and transportation inefficiencies, and subtracting the cocaine consumed outside the United States or seized by worldwide drug trafficking authorities, ODAP estimated that 14 to 19 metric tons of cocaine hydrochloride enter the United States market each year. This estimate is not inconsistent with their demand-side estimate of 13.2 metric tons. Table 7-3 summarizes ODAP's supply-side computations.

If we assume that 19 metric tons entered the United States in 1976 and that this cocaine was sold at the street price of 53 cents per mg, then we arrive at an upper estimate of $10.1 billion for the total retail value of cocaine in 1976. Our lower estimate just cited was $3.3 billion. Since the median of these estimates is close to our "most likely" estimate of $7 billion, we will continue to use the latter figure as a point estimate for the total retail value of cocaine sold in 1976.

One could argue that this estimate is a little high, since the survey results used by ODAP gave much higher estimates than the other surveys described in Table 7-1. On the other hand, one could argue that our estimate is a bit low after comparing it with the $10.8 billion estimate suggested by the Internal Revenue Service's 1979 report,[13] which used figures supplied by the National Narcotics Intelligence Consumers Committee. Balancing all these considerations, we will stick to our point estimate of $7 billion.

To estimate the national income of the cocaine distribution industry, we need to subtract from our total expenditure estimates the dollar outlays to foreign cocaine exporters. As indicated by Fuqua, the importer pays $4,000 to $5,000 a kilo if he obtains the cocaine in South America and $20,000 for each kilo delivered stateside.[15] These figures are 1.3, 1.7, and 6.7 percent, respectively, of the $300,000 that this kilo will eventually bring on the street. In its estimates on the cocaine distribution industry, the Internal Revenue Service quoted estimates by the National Narcotics Intelligence Consumers Committee that outlays to foreign drug exporters formed 1.8 percent of the total retail value in 1976, with expenditures on legal activities adding another 3.0 percent.[16] Taking all these estimates into consideration, we will subtract 4.5 percent from the estimated total retail value in 1976 to obtain an estimate of $6.7 billion for the national income estimate of the cocaine distribution industry.

Finally, we need to move these figures back to 1974 so that they can be compared with our estimates for other sectors of the underground economy. Such an adjustment would need to take into consideration the change in price and the change in quantity consumed between 1974 and 1976. Comparing the second, third, and fifth surveys summarized in Table 7-1, we can assume that the total amount consumed did not rise significantly in this two-year period. The DEA reported a street price of 49 cents per mg of cut cocaine in 1974, and a corresponding price of 53 cents per mg in 1976. Taking this price change into consideration, our adjusted national income for 1974 would be $6.2 billion. If the number of regular users rose

Table 7-4 Summary of Estimates of the Cocaine Distribution Industry in 1976

Number of current users	4,075,000
Percentage of adults who are current users	2.0 to 6.9
Percentage of youth who are current users	2.3
Number of pure kilos of cocaine hydrochloride consumed in the U.S.	13 to 19 metric tons
Cost per mg on the street	53 cents
Total retail value of cocaine consumption	$7.0 billion
National income of the cocaine distribution industry in 1976	$6.7 billion
National income of the cocaine distribution industry in 1974	$5.6 to $6.2 billion

by 10 percent between 1974 and 1976, we would need to adjust our estimate further to $5.6 billion. Allowing for this latter possibility, we arrive at our final estimate of $5.6 to $6.2 billion for the national income of the cocaine distribution industry in 1974. Table 7-4 summarizes the estimates used in this section.

Benefits and Costs to the User and Seller

As is often the case with heroin, a cocaine user will usually have his or her first introduction to the drug at an informal gathering at a friend's home. Unlike most other drugs except alcohol, cocaine appears to be primarily a party drug.[17] Most users[18] prefer to inhale cocaine by sniffing or "snorting" it off a 50 mg spoon. First the user grinds up the cocaine granules with a razor blade or similar instrument to make sure that none of it will block his nasal passages. Then "he pinches one nostril shut and inhales the powder deeply through the other. Within moments, the drug will have passed through the lining of the nasal passages into the bloodstream and be on its way to the brain."[19] A few more serious users prefer to inject the drug directly into the bloodstream with a hypodermic needle.

The usual effects of cocaine are "wakefulness, alertness, a decreased sense of fatigue, elevation of mood with increased initiative, confidence, and ability to concentrate, elation and euphoria, and an increase in motor and speech activity."[20] (For first-hand reports by cocaine users, see Malcolm X[21] and the quotes of Freud from Jones, as discussed in Brecher, pp. 273–274.) These effects are similar to the effects of the synthetic amphetamines, except that they last only a few minutes as compared to several hours for amphetamine users.

As the liver breaks down the cocaine, these effects soon diminish. Sometimes, especially for frequent users, the elation brought on by the drug is replaced by anxiety, depression, and fatigue as the drug wears off. (See Fuqua, p. 117, Brecher, p. 276, and DeLong, p. 105.) This fact often leads the user to snort another dose. A few users have found that a combination of cocaine and heroin (generally called a "speedball") can modify post-cocaine depression.

Chronic cocaine usage over an extended period of time can increase the drug's harmful effects. One common physical sign of cocaine abuse is erosion of the nasal mucosa as a result of the snorting process. The major long-term effect of cocaine (and amphetamine) abuse is a paranoid psychosis that is often indistinguishable from a schizophrenic reaction.[22] The victim of such a psychosis can become severely agitated and overwrought—even violent. He may also experience audible and visual hallucinations like the ants or snakes crawling under the skin that Freud's patient described. However, if he seeks treatment in time, the abuser can usually recover from his psychosis within 6 to 12 months.[23, 24] It would certainly be important in choosing a cocaine policy to know more about what use patterns can lead to this psychosis and with what probability. DeLong hints that the development of this psychosis is a "fairly predictable" event, especially for amphetamine users.[25] Grinspoon and Bakalar call the danger "remote," certainly much less probable than the corresponding effect of amphetamines.[26] The Drug Abuse Council believes that most experienced users can regulate their dose levels to avoid toxic psychosis and that most cases of this adverse reaction result "from deliberate attempts to see how large a dose the user can tolerate, rather than from any normal reaction to amounts of the drug ordinarily used."[27]

There are two other unresolved but basic questions about cocaine use: First, is it addictive, and second, does one develop a tolerance toward cocaine so that higher doses are required to achieve the same effects?[28] Cocaine users do not suffer strong physical withdrawal symptoms when deprived of their drug like heroin users do. They are more likely to feel psychological withdrawal symptoms, like people who are trying to give up tobacco.[29-31] Although there have been cases in which individuals developed a massive tolerance toward cocaine, researchers are still in basic disagreement about the general tolerance pattern. (See Fuqua, p. 276, Brecher, p. 276, and DeLong, p. 108.)

The possibility of drug abuse led the U.S. Congress in 1914 to ban the use and sale of cocaine. As a result, those who desire to experience cocaine's stimulating effects have been forced to buy their drug on the black market. The costs to the user because of the black market status of cocaine include the risk of arrest, fine, or imprisonment if he or she is caught using or even possessing the drug, the high unit price (which is also a result of the long vertical distribution system),[32] the lack of information about the quality of the drug, and the possibility that tainted additives will be cut into the drug before it reaches the street.

The members of the cocaine distribution network experience the same costs and benefits as members of the heroin distribution network do. In fact, these networks probably overlap. The major costs are the risk of arrest, fine, and imprisonment; the major benefit is the high profit margin resulting from the drug's black market status. Part of this high profit is a compensation for the risks involved. To reduce these risks, members of the cocaine distribution industry establish a long vertical organizational structure with each unit well insulated from the units below it, and bribe law enforcement officers whenever the opportunity to do so would reduce the risk of arrest or harassment.

Costs and Benefits to Society

The major benefits to society of the cocaine distribution industry are the availability of the drug to those who use it carefully, and the aggregation of the sense of stimulation and euphoria which these individual users experience. The major cost is the aggregation of the psychological and physical suffering that individual drug *abusers* undergo, and the resulting effects on their welfare, family life, and productivity. In addition, because of the illegal status of cocaine use, society suffers all the costs listed in the last section of our chapter on heroin, including law enforcement, judicial, correctional, and medical costs—both direct and indirect.

There is universal agreement that the social costs resulting from cocaine consumption are much less than those of other drugs of abuse, especially heroin. In 1975, the Domestic Council Drug Abuse Task Force described to President Ford "the apparently low current social cost" of cocaine use. In 1978, the Office of Drug Abuse Policy reported to President Carter that cocaine "produces few overdose deaths or emergency room episodes, when used infrequently, and by sniffing or 'snorting' it up the nose. Cocaine-related deaths number only about 20 a year, contrasted with over 2,000 heroin-related deaths . . . . Clearly, a federal policy must differentiate between cocaine as a high-priced commodity in the international economic distribution system, and cocaine as a drug of abuse in the United States with its currently low probability of causing serious health and social consequences."[33]

Endnotes

1. Jones, Ernest, as quoted in Brecher, Edward M., and editors of *Consumer Reports*. 1972. *Licit and Illicit Drugs*. Boston: Little, Brown & Co., p. 273.
2. Grinspoon, Lester, and James B. Bakalar, 1976. *Cocaine: A Drug and Its Social Evolution*, pp. 27–28.
3. Fuqua, Paul Q. 1978. *Drug Abuse: Investigation and Control*. New York: McGraw-Hill, pp. 106–107.
4. *Ibid.*, p. 108.
5. *Ibid.*, p. 109.
6. *New York Times*, Feb. 1, 1970.
7. Grinspoon and Bakalar, *Cocaine*, p. 53.
8. *The Wall Street Journal*, 1979. "Miami Is Prospering, Aided by Latin Money, Illegal-Drug Business" (November 28).
9. Fuqua, *Drug Abuse*, p. 115.
10. Brecher, *Drug Abuse*, p. 304.
11. Grinspoon and Bakalar, *Cocaine*, pp. 52–54.
12. Goldman, Albert. 1979. *Grass Roots: Marihuana in America Today*. New York: Harper & Row, p. 158.
13. U.S. Department of the Treasury, Internal Revenue Service. 1979. *Estimates of Income Unreported on Individual Income Tax Returns*. Washington, D.C.: U.S. Government Printing Office, p. 139.
14. Grinspoon and Bakalar, *Cocaine*, p. 54.
15. Fuqua, *Drug Abuse*, p. 115.
16. IRS, *Estimates of Income*, p. 139.
17. Grinspoon and Bakalar, *Cocaine*, pp. 58–67.
18. Office of Drug Abuse Policy. *1978 Annual Report*. Washington: U.S. Government Printing Office.
19. Fuqua, *Drug Abuse*, p. 116.
20. DeLong, James V. 1972. "The Drugs and Their Effects," in *Dealing With Drug Abuse*, Wald and Hutt (eds.). New York: Praeger Publishing.
21. X, Malcolm. 1965. *The Autobiography of Malcolm X*. New York: Grove Press, p. 134.
22. DeLong, in *Dealing With Drug Abuse*, p. 106.
23. *Ibid.*, p. 107.
24. Grinspoon and Bakalar, *Cocaine*, p. 144.
25. DeLong, in *Dealing With Drug Abuse*, p. 107.

26. Grinspoon and Bakalar, *Cocaine*, p. 144.
27. Drug Abuse Council. 1980. *The Facts About "Drug Abuse."* New York: The Free Press, p. 180.
28. Fuqua, *Drug Abuse*, p. 118.
29. Brecher, *Licit and Illicit Drugs*, p. 276.
30. DeLong, in *Dealing With Drug Abuse*, pp. 108–109.
31. Grinspoon and Bakalar, *Cocaine*, p. 144.
32. Office of Drug Abuse Policy, *Annual Report*, p. 70.
33. Office of Drug Abuse Policy, *1978 Annual Report*, pp. 29–30.

Additional References

ABELSON, HERBERT, and RONALD B. ATKINSON. 1975. *Public Experience with Psychoactive Substances*. Rockville, Md.: National Institute of Drug Abuse.

ABELSON, HERBERT, and PATRICIA M. FISHBURNE. 1976. *Nonmedical Use of Psychoactive Substances: 1975/76 Nationwide Survey Among Youth and Adults*. Princeton, N.J.: Reponse Analysis Corp.

GLENN, WILLIAM A. and LOUISE G. RICHARDS. 1974. *Recent Surveys of Nonmedical Drug Use: A Compendium of Abstracts*. Rockville, Md.: National Institute of Drug Abuse.

JONES, ERNEST. 1953. *The Life and Work of Sigmund Freud*, 3 vols. New York: Basic Books.

National Commission on Marihuana and Drug Abuse. 1973. *Drug Abuse in America: Problem in Perspective*. Washington, D.C.: U.S. Government Printing Office.

O'DONNELL, JOHN A., HOWARD L. VOSS, RICHARD R. CLAYTON, GERALD T. SLATIN, and ROBIN G. W. ROOM. 1976. *Young Men and Drugs—A Nationwide Survey*. Rockville, Md.: National Institute of Drug Abuse.

U.S. Department of Justice. Law Enforcement Assistance Administration. 1977. *Sourcebook of Criminal Justice Statistics*. Washington, D.C.: U.S. Government Printing Office.

Chapter 8

MARIHUANA

The hemp plant, *Cannabis sativa*, has been cultivated for thousands of years. It is a tall, slender plant—sometimes reaching 18 feet in the wild—whose leaves are clusters of five to eleven thin, serrated, hair-covered leaflets. Before the invention of the cotton gin and of machinery for mass-producing wool, the fibers in the woody stem of the cannabis plant were woven into hemp. This hemp was the principal fiber in the rigging rope and canvas sails of all the world's sailing ships.

From its introduction to North America by the Jamestown settlers in 1611 until the Civil War, the hemp, or marihuana, plant was a major crop in North America. Thomas Jefferson and George Washington grew it on their Virginia plantations—presumably for the hemp fiber—although Washington indicated in his diary that he separated male plants from female plants, a practice which increases the potency of the marihuana drug without much effect on its fiber capabilities.[1, 2] "By the nineteenth century, large hemp plantations were to be found in Kentucky, Mississippi, Georgia, California, South Carolina, Nebraska, and elsewhere, including Staten Island, New York. For a period of many years only tobacco and cotton ranked above hemp as America's leading cash crop."[3]

Even though the mass production of wool and cotton had decreased the world's reliance on hemp, there were still over 10,000 acres of hemp farms in Kentucky, Illinois, and Wisconsin in the 1930s. Production was increased during World War II, at the encouragement of the Department of Agriculture, because of a scarcity of rope. Even though hemp cultivation has been discontinued, the fact that cannabis is such a prolific and easy-growing weed has resulted in the existence of tens of thousands of acres of *wild* cannabis plants throughout the Midwest.

169

Of course, while many valued the stalks of the cannabis plant for the hemp fibers they produced, others preferred the small stems, leaves, flowers, and resin for the medicine and intoxicant they yielded. Once these latter parts are separated from the plant and dried by the sun or in an oven, they are chopped into a tobacco-like mixture (marihuana) which is usually smoked as a cigarette or in a pipe. A marihuana smoker in the proper frame of mind and physical setting experiences an increased sense of well-being, an enhanced sensitivity to colors, patterns, textures, and tastes, a feeling that time and space have expanded, a relaxation of inhibitions, and a dreamy carefree state of relaxation.[4-7]

In the early 1900s, marihuana smokers in the United States were primarily sailors and Mexican workers. Jazz and marihuana arrived in New Orleans at about the same time, and the two became intertwined. As the jazz scene spread to New York, Chicago, Detroit, and other northern cities, so did the use of marihuana. (See Brecher, pp. 410–411; Fuqua, p. 129; and especially DeLong, pp. 66–82.) With the post-War "Beat" movement of Kerouac, Ginsberg, and others, marihuana came out of the underground world of jazz and into the mainstream of American counterculture. When millions of Americans protesting the Vietnam War joined this counterculture in the 1960s, the use of marihuana exploded. By 1977, over 60 percent of Americans between the ages of 18 and 25 had smoked a marihuana cigarette and nearly 30 percent of this age group was smoking marihuana regularly.

The marihuana smoked by American users comes from all over the world, including Colombia, Mexico, Panama, Jamaica, India, Thailand, Vietnam, Hawaii, California, Indiana, and even New York City. Before 1970, Mexico was the chief source of marihuana used in the United States. After international efforts closed the Turkish-French heroin connection, the Mexican marihuana smuggling routes began supplying heroin to the black market. By the mid-seventies, most of the heroin on American streets originated in Mexico. In reaction to this new Mexican heroin connection, President Nixon aggressively battled the flow of all drugs from Mexico. Quickly and easily, Colombia stepped in to supply the American marihuana market. Aided by the fact that Colombian marihuana was superior to its Mexican counterpart, Colombia now supplies nearly 70 percent of the American market.[8]

Because of uncertainties in the foreign marihuana supply and the hardiness and abundance of the cannabis weed, it was natural that Americans would start cultivating their own marihuana again.

Although there are large marihuana farms throughout the United States, the center of the American marihuana production is the northwestern part of California, especially Humboldt and Mendocino counties. In its 1979 crop-report summary, Mendocino County's agricultural department estimated that the county's marihuana crop generated $90 million in revenues—second only to the county's timber revenues.[9, 10]

The Marihuana Distribution Industry

The marihuana distribution industry shares a number of similar characteristics with the heroin and cocaine industries. For example, all three networks have a long vertical organizational framework, with members of each level dealing with a small number of people at the level below and achieving a measure of insulation from those in all other levels.

There are, however, three major differences between the distributional system for heroin and cocaine and that for marihuana. First of all, unlike heroin and cocaine, marihuana is rarely diluted as it passes from one level to the next, although each level does repackage the marihuana in its possession into smaller parcels. Secondly, as mentioned above, marihuana can easily be grown domestically. As a result, American marihuana users are not completely dependent on the ability of a well-organized importing syndicate's ability to smuggle in their drug from some well-specified corner of the world. Finally, although criminal organizations play a major role in the complex heroin distribution system, the typical operators in the marihuana business:[11]

> *are loosely knit teams of young men who have no prior experience in crime and who are in most respects indistinguishable from thousands of other young men fresh out of college. The banality of these boys, apart from a handful of specially endowed leaders, is perhaps their most striking characteristic. Being in so many ways just like everybody else, they suggest what a thin line divides the ordinary citizen today from the successful criminal. Apart from courage, the only thing required to become a dope smuggler is a certain amount of capital. Even that is easily acquired, thanks to the extraordinarily favorable economics of the Game. . . . The typical smuggling family . . . is a bunch of guys who have been pals since they were in high school. They have known each other for years, played games together, drunk together, partied together, all close bonding relationships. Then, bit by bit, they drift into the Dope Game.*

To describe the marihuana distribution industry, we will follow the typical path that marihuana takes from the fields of Colombia to the streets of the United States. Most Colombian marihuana is grown in the isolated Guajira Peninsula on Colombia's north coast. A small number of Colombian families direct the export operation. Members of these organizations inspect the marihuana crops grown in their region, try to select a crop of high quality, organize the shipment of the crop from the farm to the place of exportation, bribe police and government officials, and oversee the loading of the marihuana onto the boat or plane that will carry it to the United States.

Three different methods are used to smuggle large quantities of marihuana from Colombia into the United States. In the first case, the American smuggler may rent or buy an airplane and fly the marihuana directly from improvised landing strips near the coast of Guajira to a small private airport somewhere in the United States. One trade magazine—*Trade-a-Plane* magazine, as quoted by Goldman[12]—estimates that there are 5,000 airstrips in Texas and 150,000 private planes in Florida, numbers which imply that smuggling by plane is difficult to control by law enforcement agencies. The main hazard of airplane smuggling is landing—undetected— on the improvised air strips in Colombia. In 1976, about 60 smuggling planes crashed.[13] In 1979, the Colombian army captured more than 80 planes, while another 34 crashed at the landing strips.[14]

The second smuggling method is to rent or buy a ship and operate it directly between an obscure marina in the southern United States and the coast of Guajira, where it will be loaded by Colombian natives under the direction of the Colombian middleman. Boat smuggling is much cheaper than plane smuggling, since both the basic equipment and the skilled pilots are much less expensive. Furthermore, boats can handle much larger cargoes. The slower speed of the boats does make them more conspicuous and thus more liable for arrest by coast guard patrols or southern sheriffs. Some professional boat smugglers register their boats under foreign flags to discourage coast guard probes.

Whether he uses a boat or plane, the smuggler will usually fly to Colombia before the smuggling operation to work out the details with his Colombian connection. There he may select the marihuana crop he will carry, work out the intricate details of the loading operation, and take care of the financial arrangements. He will have to pay his connection about $40 a pound for the marihuana and the loading services. Roughly 10 percent of this amount will eventually reach the farmer who grows the marihuana.

In the third method for smuggling marihuana into the United States from Colombia, the Colombian syndicate loads a large South American freighter ship with about fifty tons of marihuana and sends this boat to the waters off the southeastern coast of the United States. There this mother ship will rendezvous with five to ten cabin cruisers—often at night. The lighter boats will unload their marihuana at hidden docks or marinas near the inland waterway. The American smuggler in this situation will have many fewer equipment expenses and risks than in operations which involve clandestine trips to Colombia. He will have to fly to Colombia only once to formalize his relationship with his Colombian connection. Arrangements for future shipments can be made by coded letter or telegram. The fee to the middleman for this offshore delivery service is $80 to $100 per pound.

Once he has successfully smuggled his shipment of marihuana into this country, the American smuggler will divide his shipment into four or five parcels and sell each parcel to a distributor for $350 per pound.* (He may first ship it by truck to a metropolitan area well inland.) The high price mark-up is justified by the expenses and high risks that the smuggler faces in sneaking the marihuana into this country, for most of the current federal antimarihuana program is directed at the smuggling end of the distribution chain. As Table 8-1 illustrates, the amount of marihuana seized by Customs and Drug Enforcement Administration (DEA) agents has in-

Table 8-1   Marihuana Arrests and Seizures

Year	Arrests for State Drug Law Violations	Drug Seizures at Ports and Borders by U.S. Customs Service and Immigration and Naturalization (in pounds)	Drug Removals from Domestic Market by DEA (in pounds)
1971	183,878	201,558	
1972	239,111	365,421	51,897
1973	323,958	489,961	52,446
1974	315,734	780,557	113,484
1975	351,667	694,364	234,116
1976		1,047,234	290,909

SOURCE: *1977 Sourcebook of Criminal Justice Statistics*. U.S. Dept. of Justice (Washington, D.C.: G.P.O.). 1977, p. 516.

* This description of the marihuana distribution system is adapted from the descriptions in Goldman,[7] the *Wall Street Journal*,[8] and the *Ann Arbor Observer*.[15]

Table 8-2   Marihuana Distribution Network

Level	Price per Pound	Typical Parcel Size	Number of Customers
Colombian syndicate	$80–$100	Few thousand lbs.	
Smuggler	$300–$350	Few thousand lbs.	4–5
Distributor	$340–$400	500–1,000 lbs.	10
Wholesaler	$375–$425	50–100 lbs.	10
Dealer	$400–$500	1–10 lbs.	10–20
Street seller	$500–$700	1 oz.–1 lb.	30
User or $5-bag seller	—	—	—

creased much more rapidly than the number of arrests for use or sale of marihuana.

Having bought a few hundred-pound bales of marihuana from the importer, for $300 to $350 a pound, the distributor sells his marihuana in fifty- or hundred-pound lots to wholesalers for a $50 per pound profit. These wholesalers then break their shipments down into much smaller lots—ten to fifty pounds per lot—and sell them to ten customers, who are also wholesalers or "pound-dealers" at a $25 per pound profit. (Sometimes, especially in larger cities, there may be another level of wholesaler before the dealer level. These smaller wholesalers may throw sampling parties at a protected apartment or "smokeasy" for their dealer-customers.)[16] Pound-dealers cut their marihuana into one- to ten-pound parcels and sell these parcels at a profit of $20 to $35 a pound to the street dealers. The street dealers break the marihuana into smaller parcels yet—pounds, "lids" (one-ounce packages), or $5 bags—and sell them to marihuana smokers. A street seller will usually have about thirty regular customers. His profit margin rises as the size of the parcel he sells decreases and as the time since the arrival of the last large wholesale shipment increases. On the average, street sellers can expect to make $100 to $200 profit per pound of marihuana sold. Table 8-2 summarizes the model of the marihuana distribution system discussed in this section.

Size, Trends, and National Income

In this section, we consider estimates of the size and income of the marihuana distribution industry. In our chapters on heroin and cocaine, we used both demand and supply figures to estimate the size of the corresponding industry. However, supply estimates are not very useful in discussing the marihuana industry. While heroin and cocaine are derivatives of plants which grow in reasonably well-specified regions of the world, the marihuana plant is a weed which can grow abundantly throughout the world—even in small gardens and basements in metropolitan areas.[17] While all of the heroin and cocaine used in the United States must be imported, more and more of the marihuana used in the United States is grown domestically. When federal enforcement efforts slow down the flow of marihuana from abroad, farmers in the United States take up the slack and increase their own production, and individual users find it expedient to "grow their own." This diversity and unpredictability in production patterns of the marihuana plant make supply estimates difficult and unreliable.

Fortunately, the demand-side picture is much clearer. A number of groups have been conducting household surveys during the 1970s to estimate the number of marihuana users. These groups have used careful surveying techniques to collect and analyze their data. Table 8-3 summarizes the results of these household surveys for 1971, 1972, 1974, 1976, and 1977.

Researchers report that nearly all those who said they had used marihuana in the previous month are regular users; so, we will use the last two columns in Table 8-3 as a measure of the number of regular users. This number has doubled in the period 1971–1977—an average annual rate of increase of 12 percent. However, in the 1972–1977 period, the average annual rate of increase was a much smaller 5 percent. During this latter five-year period, regular use by young adults, ages 18 to 25, remained fairly steady. It is this age. group that accounts for more than one half of the regular marihuana users. Young users, ages 12 to 17, have been the fastest-growing population of regular users, increasing at an annual rate of 18 percent during the 1971–1977 period and even the 1972–1977 period. In 1971, 6 percent of American youth used marihuana regularly; by 1977, this percentage had grown to 16 percent.

The middle columns in Table 8-3 tabulate the numbers of Americans that have used marihuana at least once in their lives. Since these figures are cumulative, it is not surprising that they increase so steadily. Still, the percentages are startling, especially for young adults between the ages of 18 and 25. In 1971, 39.3 percent of young American adults had smoked at least one marihuana cigarette; by 1977, this percentage had risen to over 60 percent!

Table 8-3   Surveys of Marihuana Use

Year	Group (ages)	Population of Group (millions)[f]	Lifetime Use Percentage	Lifetime Use Number (millions)	Use in Last Year Percentage	Use in Last Year Number (millions)	Use in Last Month Percentage	Use in Last Month Number (millions)
1971[a]	Youth (12–17)	24.62	14.0	3.45			6.0	1.48
	All adults (≥ 18)	136.66	15.0	20.50			5.0	6.96
	Young adults (18–25)	27.96	39.3	10.99			17.3	4.84
	Total (≥ 12)	161.28		23.95				8.44
1972[b]	Youth (12–17)	24.87	14.0	3.48			7.0	1.74
	All adults (≥ 18)	139.24	16.0	22.28			8.0	11.14
	Young adults (18–25)	29.30	47.9	14.03			27.8	8.14
	Total (≥ 12)	164.11		25.76				12.88
1974[c]	Youth (12–17)	25.22	22.6	5.70	18.6	4.69	11.6	2.93
	All adults (≥ 18)	144.15	18.9	27.24	10.3	14.85	7.0	10.99
	Young adults (18–25)	30.12	53.2	16.02			25.5	7.68
	Total (≥ 12)	169.37		32.94		19.54		13.02
1976[d]	Youth (2–17)	24.97	22.5	5.62	17.9	4.47	12.4	3.10
	All adults (≥ 18)	149.47	21.3	31.84	11.5	17.19	7.9	11.81
	Young adults (18–25)	31.52	52.9	16.67	34.0	10.72	24.6	7.75
	Total (≥ 12)	174.96		37.46		21.66		14.90
1977[e]	Youth (12–17)	24.63	28.2	6.94	21.8	5.37	16.1	3.96
	All adults (≥ 18)	152.09	24.5	37.26	12.8	19.47	8.2	12.47
	Young adults (18–25)	32.03	60.1	19.25	38.6	12.37	27.7	8.87
	Total (≥ 12)	176.72		44.20		24.84		16.43

[a] National Commission on Marihuana and Drug Abuse, *Drug Use in America: Problem in Perspective* (Washington, D.C.: U.S. Government Printing Office, 1973). See also William A. Glenn and Louise G. Richards, *Recent Surveys of Nonmedical Drug Use: A Compendium of Abstracts* (Rockville, Md.: National Institute on Drug Abuse, 1974).

[b] *Ibid.*

[c] Herbert Abelson and Ronald B. Atkinson, *Public Experience with Psychoactive Substances* (Rockville, Md.: National Institute of Drug Abuse, 1975).

[d] Herbert Abelson and Patricia M. Fishburne, *Nonmedical Use of Psychoactive Substances: 1975/76 Nationwide Survey Among Youth and Adults* (Princeton, N.J.: Response Analysis Corp., 1976). See also U.S. Department of Justice, Law Enforcement Assistance Administration, *Sourcebook of Criminal Justice Statistics* (Washington, D.C.: U.S. Government Printing Office, 1977).

[e] Herbert Abelson, Patricia M. Fishburne, and Ira Cisin, *National Survey on Drug Abuse: 1977* (Rockville, Md.: National Institute on Drug Abuse, 1977).

[f] U.S. Department of Commerce, Bureau of the Census, *Estimates of the Population of the United States by Age, Sex, and Race: 1970 to 1977*, Series P-25, No. 721 (Washington, D.C.: U.S. Government Printing Office, 1977).

Table 8-4   Distribution of Regular Marihuana Users

Frequency of Use	Percentage of Regular Users	Annual Number of Uses in Each Category	Annual Number of Uses Per Regular User
3–4 times a day	10	1278	127.8
Once a day	15	365	54.8
3–4 times a week	20	182	36.4
Once a week	15	52	7.8
2–3 times a month	15	30	4.5
Once a month	25	12	3.0
Total	100		234.3

How much marihuana was consumed by the users tabulated in Table 8-3? To answer this question, we need to estimate the smoking habits of regular marihuana users. A number of surveys have asked questions regarding the frequency of use.[18–20] Putting together the results of these surveys, we have estimated a use pattern for regular users as described in Table 8-4. In compiling this table, we have assumed that the *average* "more-than-daily" user smokes marihuana three to four times a day. Table 8-4 estimates that there are roughly 234 uses per regular marihuana smoker each year—a figure we will round off to 240 in our calculations. Note that the "more-than-daily" users account for more than one half of the marihuana users.

To estimate how much marihuana is smoked each year, we need to bring the irregular users into our discussion and to estimate how much marihuana is consumed "per use." For 1974, 1976, and 1977, we can use the last four columns in Table 8-3 and subtract the number of people who used marihuana in the past month from the people who used marihuana in the last year to estimate the number of irregular users. We will interpolate the corresponding percentages to estimate the number of irregular users in 1971 and 1972. We will further assume that each of these irregular users used marihuana twice a year. Since the usage by irregular users accounts for such a small fraction of the total marihuana consumption, the estimate of two uses per year per irregular user could vary by a factor of five or ten without having much of an impact on the total annual consumption.

How much marihuana is consumed per "use?" Few of the above surveys addressed this question. The 1972 report of the National Commission on Marihuana and Drug Abuse estimated that the average marihuana cigarette weighs .5 grams, with "cigarettes used

Table 8-5 Annual Marihuana Consumption (all figures in millions)

	1971	1972	1974	1976	1977
(1) Number of regular users (from Table 8-3)	8.44	12.88	13.02	14.90	16.43
(2) Number of annual uses by regular users (row 1 × 240)	2,025.6	3,091.2	3,124.8	3,576	3,943.2
(3) Number of irregular users (from Table 8-3)	4.22	6.44	6.52	6.76	8.41
(4) Number of annual uses by irregular users (row 3 × 2)	8.44	12.88	13.04	13.52	16.82
(5) Total number of users (row 1 + row 3)	12.66	19.32	19.54	21.66	24.84
(6) Total number of uses per year (row 2 + row 4)	2,034	3,104	3,138	3,590	3,960
(7) Grams of marihuana consumed per year (1 gram per use)	2,034	3,104	3,138	3,590	3,960

in eastern states generally smaller than those rolled in the west. Most data indicates that for the large majority of users one half to one cigarette is sufficient to 'get high' in intermittent-moderate users, although often two or more cigarettes were smoked to achieve additional effect. . . . Current American daily users appear to consume one to two cigarettes per occasion."[21] (This passage refers to the work of Jones[22] and McGlothlin.[23, 24]) For the purpose of our estimates, we'll assume that the average marihuana user consumes one gram of marihuana per use, that is, two one-half gram cigarettes. Table 8-5 summarizes our estimates for the amount of marihuana consumed each year. Note that consumption increased at an average annual rate of 5 percent between 1972 and 1977.

Finally, we convert these consumption estimates into dollar amounts by estimating the total retail value of the marihuana consumed and the national income of the American marihuana distribution industry. To carry out these financial estimates, we will need two more figures: the average retail price of a gram of marihuana and the percentage of the gross receipts that are paid to foreign exporters or spent on distribution-related expenses.

The U.S. Drug Enforcement Administration publishes yearly estimates of the street price of illegal drugs.[25] We list these prices for a gram of marihuana in row 2 of Table 8-6. However, using a report of the National Narcotics Intelligence Consumers Committee, the Internal Revenue Service arrived at an estimate of $1.26 per gram in 1976 compared to the DEA estimate of $.64 per gram. (See IRS data.[26] These figures are comparable with our figures in Table 8-2.) Agreeing with Reuter that the IRS estimate appears unreasonably high,[27] we will use the DEA estimates as our lower estimates of the street price and a price of $1 per gram in 1976 as a basis for our upper estimates of the retail price of marihuana. Since the DEA did not publish estimates for the retail price in 1971 and 1972, we will use 60 cents a gram as an estimate of the street price in 1972 and forego estimates for 1971. (DEA estimates for 1973 and 1975 were 63 and 65 cents per gram, respectively.) The resulting total retail value of the marihuana consumed is listed in row 4 of Table 8-6.

To compute the national income, we need to deduct from the total retail value the outlays to foreign exporters and the expenditures and losses on distributional activities. All these expenses vary widely with the region of production and the method of smuggling. The expenditures for smuggling a planeload of marihuana from Colombia are much greater than the expenditure of smuggling a boatload of Mexican marihuana or of raising the drug domestically. Table 8-2 is based on the situation in which the American smuggler buys his marihuana from a large Colombian boat in the American coastal waters—a situation where dollar outlays to foreign exporters are large but distributional expenses rather small. Using figures in Table 8-2, one notes that the $90 per pound paid to the Colombian syndicate was 15 percent of the $600 per pound street value. Using DEA and National Narcotics Intelligence Consumers Committee estimates, the Internal Revenue Service estimated that total expenses including payments to foreign exporters, distribution and legal expenses, and losses due to domestic seizures totaled 14.4

Table 8-6   The Economics of the Marihuana Distribution Industry

Year	*1972*	*1974*	*1976*	*1977*
(1) Estimated quantity consumed (in metric tons)	3,104	3,138	3,590	3,960
(2) Lower average retail price per gram (DEA estimate)	$.60	$.56	$.64	$.69
(3) Higher average retail price	$.94	$.88	$1.00	$1.08
(4) Total retail value (in $ billion)	$1.86–$2.92	$1.76–$2.76	$2.30–$3.59	$2.73–$4.27
(5) Dollar outlays to foreign exporters and expenditures and losses on distributional activities (.15 × row 4, in $ billion)	$.28–$.44	$.26–$.41	$.35–$.54	$.41–$.64
(6) Annual national income of the marihuana distribution industry (row 4 − row 5, in $ billion)	$1.58–$2.48	$1.50–$2.35	$1.96–$3.05	$2.32–$3.63

percent of the total retail value.[26] Consequently, we will use these figures to estimate that the national income of the marihuana distribution industry is 85 percent of the total retail value of the marihuana consumed. As indicated in the last row of Table 8-6, these estimates yield a national income of about $2 billion for 1972 and 1974, $2.5 billion for 1976, and $3 billion for 1977.

Benefits and Costs to User and Seller

As mentioned in the introduction to this chapter, the principal benefits that a marihuana user may experience include an increased sense of well-being; an enhanced sensitivity to colors, sounds, patterns, textures, and tastes; a feeling that time and space have expanded; a relaxation of inhibitions; and a dreamy, carefree state of relaxation. The intensity with which these effects are felt depends on the psychological make-up of the user, the setting in which the marihuana is consumed, and the potency of the marihuana being used.

These psychological effects are often accompanied by some subtle physical effects, including a moderately increased heart beat, a dilation of the conjunctival blood vessels (including a reddening of the eyes), and a drying of the mouth.[28-30] Marihuana users rarely, if ever, develop any physical dependence on the drug, although a few may develop some psychological dependence—similar to that of tobacco users. Neither do marihuana smokers develop a tolerance for the drug. If anything, regular users may develop a reverse tolerance, in that they will need less marihuana to reach a "high" than a novice will. The active ingredient in marihuana, THC, may accumulate in the body so that a regular user may already have a basic dose and need only a small additional amount to experience the effects.[31, 32]

Larger doses can intensify some of these psychological reactions. They may also lead to rapidly changing emotions and sensory images, fragmentary thought with disturbed patterns of association, dulling of attention, an altered sense of self-identity, and even fantasies and hallucinations. Very large doses can, in rare cases, trigger more serious adverse reactions, from a simple depression to panic to a psychotic breakdown.[33-35] Even small doses may impair the user's psychomotor performance, adversely affecting ability to drive a car or operate any form of machinery. This impairment, although potentially dangerous, appears to be weaker than that resulting from moderate alcohol consumption.[36]

Since marihuana smoking is similar to cigarette smoking, many of the long-term lung problems associated with cigarette smoking also apply to marihuana cigarettes.[37-39] Although marihuana leaves are different from tobacco leaves, marihuana smoke also contains some proven cancer-causing chemicals. While it is true that a regular marihuana smoker will consume many fewer cigarettes than a regular tobacco user, marihuana produces more tar per milligram than tobacco does. Marihuana smokers also inhale more deeply and hold the smoke in their lungs much longer than cigarette smokers do.

In general, we have very little conclusive information about the effects of long-term marihuana use. Further careful and objective research is needed to assess marihuana's true impact on its regular users.

Of course, the black market status of marihuana sales, possession, and consumption adds some significant costs to the marihuana user. Because of the long vertical distribution chain in the marihuana distribution industry and the significant risks that members of this chain take in smuggling or distributing the drug, the marihuana user must pay a premium price for the drug. The black market status also prevents the user from obtaining reliable information about the quality and purity of the drug. This problem came to a head in the late 1970s in the Southwest when regular users discovered that much of the Mexican marihuana they were smoking had been sprayed in the fields with the herbicide Paraquat by Mexican authorities. The possibility that Paraquat could cause an irreversible fibrosis of the lungs touched off a serious panic among the millions of regular users in the Southwest.

The black market status of marihuana also provides the user with the usual costs due to the risk of arrest, prosecution, fine, and imprisonment. Unfortunately, as the President's Office of Drug Abuse Policy admitted, the penalties for drug use or even possession are "more damaging to an individual than the drug itself" and have resulted "in inducting large numbers of otherwise law-abiding young people into the criminal justice system."[40] As a result of the penalties in force on states' statutes in 1970, anyone possessing marihuana faced a *minimum* sentence of five years without parole in Alabama and two years without probation in Colorado.[41] In Georgia, Louisiana, and Utah, a first sale of marihuana to a minor could lead to life imprisonment, and a second sale could lead to the death penalty. In Massachusetts, simply being in the company of a person who had illegal marihuana was a felony punishable by up to five years in prison. Between 1969 and 1972, nearly every state amended its marihuana penalties so that by 1972 simple possession of an ounce or less of marihuana was a misdemeanor in all but eight states.

As usual, these risks of long sentences and steep fines are the major costs to members of the marihuana distribution industry. The principal benefits are the high profits which smugglers and salesmen can command in return for their acceptance of these risks.

Endnotes

1. Brecher, Edward M., and editors of *Consumer Reports*. 1972. *Licit and Illicit Drugs*. Boston: Little, Brown and Co., p. 403.
2. Andrews, George, and Simon Vinkenoog, eds. 1967. *The Book of Grass: An Anthropology of Indian Hemp*. New York: Grove Press, p. 34.
3. Fuqua, Paul Q. 1978. *Drug Abuse: Investigation and Control*. New York: McGraw-Hill, p. 124.
4. DeLong, James V. 1972. "The Drugs and Their Effects," in Wald and Hutt (eds.), *Dealing with Drug Abuse*. New York: Praeger Publishers, p. 100.
5. Fuqua, *Drug Abuse*, p. 135.
6. Grinspoon, Lester. 1971. *Marihuana Reconsidered*. Cambridge, Mass.: Harvard University Press, pp. 110–116.
7. Goldman, Albert. 1979. *Grass Roots: Marihuana in America Today*. New York: Harper and Row, pp. 52–54.
8. *Wall Street Journal*. 1980. "The Pot Trade." July 16, July 22, July 29, August 4, and August 8.
9. *Ibid.*
10. *New York Times*. 1980. "California Marihuana Farms Yield a Billion-Dollar High." July 13, 1980.
11. Goldman, *Grass Roots*, pp. 156–157.
12. *Ibid.*, p. 161.
13. *Ibid.*, p. 159.
14. *Wall Street Journal*, "The Pot Trade," August 4, 1980.
15. *Ann Arbor Observer*. 1978. "Merchant of Marihuana." February.
16. Goldman, *Grass Roots*, pp. 13–18.
17. *Ibid.*, pp. 30–32.
18. National Commission on Marihuana and Drug Abuse. 1973. *Drug Use in America: Problem in Perspective*. Washington, D.C.: U.S. Government Printing Office, p. 90.
19. Glenn, William A. and Louise G. Richards. 1974. *Recent Surveys of Nonmedical Drug Use: A Compendium of Abstracts*. Rockville, Md.: National Institute on Drug Abuse, p. 60.
20. National Commission on Marihuana and Drug Abuse. 1973. *Drug Use in America: Problem in Perspective. Appendix*. Washington, D.C.: U.S. Government Printing Office, p. 113.
21. National Commission on Marihuana and Drug Abuse. 1972. *Marihuana: A Signal of Misunderstanding. Appendix*. Washington, D.C.: U.S. Government Printing Office.
22. Jones, R. T. 1971. "Tetrahydro-cannabinol and the Marihuana Induced Social 'High' or The Effects of the Mind on Marihuana." *Annals of the New York Academy of Science* 191:155–165.
23. McGlothlin, W. H. 1971. "Marihuana: An Analysis of Use, Distribution, and Control." Prepared for the Department of Justice, Washington, D.C. (June).
24. McGlothlin, W. H. 1972. "Use and Effects of Cannabis." Prepared for National Commission on Marihuana and Drug Abuse.
25. U.S. Department of Justice, *1977 Sourcebook*.
26. U.S. Department of the Treasury. Internal Revenue Service. 1979. *Estimates*

of *Income Unreported on Individual Income Tax Returns.* Washington, D.C.: U.S. Government Printing Office, p. 141.

27. Reuter, Peter. 1980. "A Reading on the Irregular Economy," *Taxing and Spending* (Spring), pp. 65–71.
28. DeLong, "The Drugs and Their Effects," p. 99.
29. Fuqua, *Drug Abuse,* p. 138.
30. Drug Abuse Council. 1980. *The Facts About "Drug Abuse."* New York: The Free Press, pp. 165–166.
31. DeLong, "Drugs and Their Effects," p. 102.
32. National Commission, *Drug Use, Appendix,* p. 29.
33. DeLong, "Drugs and Their Effects," pp. 100–101.
34. Fuqua, *Drug Abuse,* pp. 135–136.
35. Goldman, *Grass Roots,* pp. 58–65.
36. Drug Abuse Council, *The Facts,* p. 172.
37. Goldman, *Grass Roots,* p. 242.
38. Drug Abuse Council, *The Facts,* pp. 170–171.
39. *Ann Arbor News.* 1980. "Marihuana smoking safe? It's not so, researchers say." October 11.
40. Office of Drug Abuse Policy. 1978. *1978 Annual Report.* Washington, D.C.: U.S. Government Printing Office, pp. 28, 30.
41. Brecher, *Licit and Illicit Drugs,* pp. 419–420.

Additional References

DUPONT ROBERT L., AVRAM GOLDSTEIN, and JOHN O'DONNELL, eds. 1979. *Handbook on Drug Abuse.* Washington, D.C.: U.S. Government Printing Office.

KAMSTRA, JERRY. 1974. *Weed: Adventures of a Dope Smuggler.* New York: Harper and Row.

NAHAS, GABRIEL G. 1973. *Marihuana—Deceptive Weed.* New York: Raven Press.

WALD, PATRICIA, and P. HUTT, eds. 1972. *Dealing with Drug Abuse.* New York: Praeger Publishers.

Part IV

PRODUCTION AND DISTRIBUTION OF ILLEGAL SERVICES

Chapter 9

FRAUD ARSON

Definition, Numbers, and Trends of Arson Fires

The American Heritage Dictionary of the English Language defines arson as "the crime of maliciously burning the building or the property of another, or of burning one's own for some improper purpose, as to collect insurance." A number of groups, including the Arson Leadership Seminar, have taken this to be the working definition of arson.[1] Arson is a unique crime in that an investigation must be conducted before one knows whether a crime was committed. Such investigations are not as common and as careful as they could be, and there are a number of reasons why arson may not be detected even after a careful investigation. Most police, fire, and insurance experts take it for granted that one-half of those fires whose causes are classified as unknown—and probably a number of those classified as accidental—are actually caused by arson. According to Boudreau *et al.*:[2]

> *Fire reports classify the causes of fire into five main categories: i)* accidental *(defective equipment, electrical wiring, careless smoking, children playing with matches, and other unintentional causes), ii)* natural *(lightning, etc.), iii)* incendiary *(intentionally set fires, including fraud fires), iv)* suspicious *(suspected of being incendiary), and v)* unknown cause *(no cause established). Legally, the cause of a fire must be assumed to be accidental or natural until proven otherwise.*

Table 9-1 summarizes the statistics for building fires in 1974. The statistics were compiled by the National Fire Protection Association. Note that 9 percent of the building fires and 17 percent of the building fire losses in 1974 were attributed to arson. If one assumes that 50 percent of the fires of unknown cause are arson-induced, one

Table 9-1 Building Fire Statistics for 1974

Cause of Fire	Number of Fires	Percentage of All Fires	Loss Value	Percentage of All Dollar Losses
All causes	1,270,000	100	$3,260,000,000	100
Accidental or natural	996,400	78	$1,460,000,000	45
Incendiary or suspicious	114,400	9	$563,000,000	17
Unknown causes	159,200	13	$1,237,000,000	38
Incendiary or suspicious plus one-half unknown cause	194,000	15	$1,181,500,000	36

SOURCE: Adapted from Annual Report in *Fire Journal*, Sept. 1975 (Boston: National Fire Protection Association).

Table 9-2 Arson Fires and Losses, 1974–1975

Basis	1974 Number	1974 Dollar Loss ($ million)	1975 Number	1975 Dollar Loss ($ million)
Incendiary or Suspicious				
Building fires	114,000	563	144,100	634
Motor vehicle fires	42,000	9	41,600	12
Wildfires	31,000	44	28,200	62
Total	187,000	616	213,909	708
Incendiary or Suspicious Plus One-Half Unknown Cause				
Building fires	194,000	1,182	212,800	1,259
Motor vehicle fires	277,000	58	270,700	81
Wildfires	31,000	44	28,200	62
Total	502,000	1,284	511,700	1,402

SOURCE: Adapted from Boudreau et al., *Arson and Arson Investigation: Survey and Assessment*. 1977. (Washington, D.C.: U.S. Government Printing Office), p. 14.

finds that arson accounted for 15 percent of the building fires and 36 percent of the building fire losses for 1974.

These figures do not include motor vehicle fires and wildfires (uncontrolled fires in forest and watershed areas). There were 640,000 motor vehicle fires in 1974, resulting in a total loss of $135 million. An estimated 6.6 percent, or 42,000, of these were estimated to be incendiary or suspicious in origin, with a loss value of $9 million. If one adds to these figures one-half of the 464,000 motor vehicle fires of unknown cause, one arrives at a total of 274,000 fires (42.9 percent of all vehicle fires), for a loss of $58 million. Table 9-2 summarizes the data for arson fires in buildings, motor vehicles, and forests for 1974 and 1975.

In summary, the National Fire Protection Association estimated that 31 percent of all fires in 1974 were intentionally set. The property loss for these fires was estimated at $1.3 billion or 36 percent of all fire dollar loss. This latter percentage lies conveniently between the 20 percent estimate of the National Fire Incident Reporting System and the 40 to 50 percent estimate of the Alliance of American Insurers.

In 1974, there were 11,600 deaths and 123,000 injuries due to fires from all causes. An estimated 1,000 people, including 45 firefighters, died in incendiary or suspicious fires in that year. This latter estimate does not include the many additional deaths that occurred in arson fires which were officially listed as "fires of unknown cause."

Table 9-3 illustrates the dramatic increase in the number and property costs of arson fires from 1964 to 1977. (No figures for arson fires were reported for 1976.) During this period, the number of incendiary or suspicious fires increased 571 percent at an average annual growth rate of 14 percent, while the property damage in these fires increased 1,704 percent at an average annual rate of 24 percent. Of course, these figures do not take into account inflation

Table 9-3   Estimated "Incendiary, Suspicious" Building Fires in the United States, 1964–1975

Year	Number (000s)	Percent Annual Increase	Property Damage ($ million)	Percent Annual Increase
1964	31	—	68	—
1965	34	9.6	74	8.8
1966	38	11.8	94	27.0
1967	45	18.4	141	50.0
1968	50	11.1	131	(7.1)
1969	57	14.0	179	36.7
1970	65	14.0	206	15.1
1971	72	10.8	233	13.1
1972	85	18.1	285	22.3
1973	94	10.6	322	13.0
1974	114	21.3	563	74.8
1975	144	26.3	634	12.6
1977	177	—	1,159	—

or the increasing sophistication of arson detection techniques. However, it is striking that during the 1964–1974 decade, the number of incendiary and suspicious building fires increased more rapidly than that of any other crime category.[3]

Fraud Arson

Fires are deliberately set for many different reasons. The most common motive is revenge or spite. Arson fires are also set by young vandals looking for excitement, criminals trying to destroy evidence of a crime, pyromaniacs enjoying the excitement connected with fires, and rioters caught up in a violent protest. Table 9-4 summarizes the results of three studies of motives of arsonists.

In our study of the underground economy, we are concerned solely with arsons from which some economic profit is made. As cited in Boudreau *et al.*:[4]

In a common type of insurance fraud, a person may buy a property, generally a vacant building in an economically depressed section of the city—and insure it for more than it's worth. A fire will then result in a substantial profit on the investment. . . . For example, in 1969 a man bought two properties in central St. Louis for $6,000 and placed the deeds in the names of two straw parties. Within two years, there had been a serious fire of suspicious origin in each property, with the insurance payments totalling $33,424. This same property owner had received over $415,000 in insurance payments for 54 fires occurring within a two-year period (he was indicted for arson for one of these fires in early 1972).

Table 9-4 Motives of Arsonists in Three Studies

Motive of Arsonists	Robbins-Robbins (1967)		Inciadri (1970)	Steinmetz (1966)
	% of Adult Subjects	% of Juvenile Subjects	% of Subjects	% of Subjects
Revenge	47	5	58	41
Excitement or pyromania	30	14	18	49
Vandalism	10	80	4	—
Crime concealment	9	2	7	7
Insurance fraud	4	0	7	3
Institution transfer	—	—	7	—

SOURCES: Boudreau *et al.*, *Arson and Arson Investigation*, pp. 22–23, and Steinmetz, "Current Arson Problems," *Fire Journal*, Sept. 1966.

Businesses may resort to arson when, for example, they build up a large inventory of unsaleable seasonable goods at the end of the season or their plant becomes outmoded or requires extensive renovation. The foreclosure of a mortgage, adverse market conditions, or obsolete merchandise may induce a businessman to try to profit from his situation through the use of arson.

Poor economic conditions over the last twenty years have generally been accompanied by an increase in incendiary and suspicious fires.[5, 6] As Table 9-3 indicates, significant jumps in both the number and cost of arson fires have occurred during the recessions of 1969–1970 and 1974–1975.

During the recession of 1975, a latex-rubber-products plant was destroyed by fire in Shelton, Connecticut. The plant's profitability margin had been severely reduced by environmental pollution problems and stiffening competition from polyurethane manufacturing. A year before the fire, the plant, along with four others in the vicinity, was sold by the B. F. Goodrich Company to Grant Sheet Metal Company for $13 million. Immediately after the sale, the new owners began laying off workers and reducing inventories. On the evening of March 1, 1975, three dynamite charges detonated, several widely scattered 55-gallon drums of gasoline erupted into flame, and almost immediately the entire three and one-half block plant was engulfed in flame. After Grand Sheet Metal filed insurance claims totaling about $62 million, federal authorities lodged charges of arson and conspiracy against the plant's owner and nine other men. While the owner was found innocent, a number of the others were found guilty of the charges filed against them. Incidentally, 900 Shelton residents were left unemployed because of the fire, and Shelton's unemployment rate jumped from 10 percent to 15 percent. (For more details, see NFPA[7] and Katchmer.[8])

The operation of a professional arson ring was described by Boudreau *et al.*:[9]

> *In some of this country's larger cities, professional arson rings have operated to defraud the insurance companies of millions of dollars. One such ring was uncovered in Detroit in 1974 when 57 persons were charged with 186 counts of arson. In a typical operation of the ring, a mortgage company employee alerted a crooked repair contractor, who was a member of the ring, of an impending foreclosure. The contractor persuaded the homeowner to contract with him for fire damage repairs. The contractor then arranged for a professional "torch" to set a fire when the insured was absent. After the fire, the contractor repaired the building with substandard materials (which*

*would readily burn next time) at a substantial profit, while the
homeowner netted a small amount after paying off the torch.*

Detroit police reported that top arsonists received an average of
$1,500 per fire and that the best of the professional torches are
involved in up to 100 fires a year.[10]

In his testimony to the U.S. Senate, Clifford Karchmer described
the business and criminal backgrounds and the elaborate schemes of
professional arsonists in the 1960s and 1970s.[11] He concluded that
the professional arson rings are "filled with organized crime figures
from every segment of the underworld." Using interviews with
investigators and prosecutors and an extensive research of case files,
Karchmer and his associates at the Battelle Law and Justice Study
Center have compiled an elaborate description of the economic
organization of arson rings.[12] The arson entrepreneurs or master
torches they describe enter the arson-for-profit enterprise after
some involvement in white-collar crime, such as bank, real estate,
or automobile insurance fraud. As the organizers of the arson ring,
they enlist the services of specialists in several fields and act as the
middlemen who bring together the willing buyer (businessman,
homeowner) with the willing sellers (torch, white-collar criminal) of
fire and fraud. These arson rings are loosely disciplined organizations whose hallmark is the early discovery, technological sophistication, and aggressive marketing of new crime schemes.

> *The entrepreneur attracts business by offering the client an insur-
> ance payment prospect that far exceeds what the client could obtain if
> he burned the property himself, or enlisted the services of a lone
> firesetter. He does this by drawing upon the skills of other criminals
> . . . to inflate the insurance coverage and increase the amount of dam-
> age, and thus the total amount of the fraudulent loss. Also, by orga-
> nizing all of his services into a "package deal" and by advertising the
> existence of this package, the entrepreneur can expect to be contacted
> by businessmen who hear of his lucrative service. For his part, the
> arson entrepreneur takes a percentage of the insurance settlement.
> Evidence in several recent prosecutions places the range of the entre-
> preneur's fee at between 10 and 25 percent of the insurance set-
> tlement.[13]*

There appear to be few reliable figures on what percentage of
arson fires are set to defraud insurance companies and what the
costs associated with such fires are. Boudreau *et al.* report:[14] "The
now defunct Fraud and Arson Bureau of the American Insurance
Association conducted 4,393 investigations of incendiary and suspicious fires throughout the United States in 1965. Of these, 836 (or

19 percent) were considered to have been set for recovery of insurance, amounting to $46 million. Of 1,703 fires established as arson in Ohio, North Carolina, and Pennsylvania during the years 1950 through 1955, 275 (or 16 percent) were found to have been insurance fraud fires."

The Metropolitan Chicago Loss Bureau, in a careful study of 80 percent of arson or arson-suspected fires in Chicago, found that one of every seven arson fires was set to defraud insurance companies. Since Chicago's fire problems are typical of the nation's problems, we will use the "1-of-7" figure in our arson-for-fraud computations. (See Figure 7 in Lucht.[15]) On the other hand, arson for fraud constitutes a much higher percentage of the property loss figures as compared with other arson fires. For example, even though the figures for Steinmetz's 1966 study of arson fires in Detroit (listed in Table 9-4) indicate that only 3 percent of the fires studied were set for fraudulent purposes, such fires accounted for almost 50 percent of the property loss of all arson fires.[16] Conversations with arson researchers have suggested that the property damage in arson-for-fraud fires is 30 to 40 percent of the property damage due to all arson fires.

Let's translate these rates into figures for our 1974 and 1975 data. Table 9-2 indicates that 194,000 arson building fires caused $1.182 billion in property damage in 1974. Using the above rates (1-of-7 and 35 percent, respectively), we are led to estimate 27,714 building fires set to defraud insurance companies, resulting in a property loss of $413.7 million in 1974. Similar calculations lead to an estimate of 30,400 arson-for-fraud fires in 1975, resulting in a property loss of $440.65 million.

There are two basic questions in the arson-for-fraud investigation for which no one appears to know the answer. First of all, how much profit is being made by those who are burning their own homes or businesses to defraud insurance companies? Each of these properties had some market value which the owner could receive by legitimately selling his home or business in the open market. The property loss figures quoted in Tables 9-1 and 9-2 are estimates by fire departments of the market value of the property destroyed. No figures are available as to the amounts that insurance companies paid in the arson fires. The compilation and publication of such data would be an invaluable aid in understanding the magnitude of the fraud arson problem.

In some of the arson incidents described above, arsonists filed insurance claims for five times the market value of their property. A person who intended to burn his home or business to make a profit would probably insure his property for an amount much above its market value to compensate himself for the risk involved in the crime of arson. On the other hand, a person who burns his business simply to replace outdated equipment or a homeowner who feels that he cannot meet his mortgage payments may be satisfied with insurance payments at or below the market value. In addition, in some of the cases labeled fraud arson, the insurance companies may be able to establish enough proof of fraud that they will pay substantially less than the value of the insurance policy, if anything at all. Sophisticated statistical analysis of one month's sample of arson fires has led D. J. Icove to the conclusion that the ratio of insured value to actual value of property destroyed by arson fire is 1.5 to 1.[17] We'll use this ratio in our calculations. Under this assumption, the insurance payments for arson-for-fraud fires would total $620.55 million in 1974 and $660.98 million in 1975. The net profits for the property owners would be $206.85 million in 1974 and $220.32 million in 1975.

A second important unanswered question in the investigation of fraud arson is: How much are the professional torches making each year? Since arson is a crime done in secret and easily disguised, we may never have a good estimate on this important figure. One can safely assume that the torch's fee rises with the size and value of the property to be destroyed. Karchmer's investigations[8, 12, 18] into several recent prosecutions place the range of the torch's fee at between 10 percent and 25 percent of the insurance settlement. The torch's fee was 10 percent of the insurance payment in an arson conspiracy described by Battle and Weston.[19] However, articles in *Psychology Today*[20] and *Newsweek*[10] describe estimates by some arson investigators that "top arsonists make an average of $1,500 a fire." We can compute a gross upper bound for the torches' fees if we assume a fee of $1,500 for each fraud arson incident. This computation leads to a figure of $41.55 million for 1974 and $45.6 million for 1975. If, on the other hand, we assume that torches received 10 percent of the insurance settlements and were involved in two thirds of the fraud arson fires or that they received 10 percent of the property value and were involved in all the fraud arson fires, we would arrive at profit figures of $41 million for 1974 and $44 million for 1975. Since these two sets of figures are similar, we will use them as our upper estimates on the torches' profits for these years.

Costs and Benefits in Fraud Arson

As discussed in the previous section, there are a number of ways that a businessman or property owner can benefit from an arson fire on his property. For example, he may be able to lessen or avoid the economic impact of a pending bankruptcy. The landlord of a vacant building or the owner of slum real estate may be able to collect more from his fire insurance than he would collect from renting or selling his property. The more able these property owners are to overinsure their buildings or businesses, the greater is their incentive to instigate a fraud arson. A further incentive to commit arson is the ease with which this crime is committed. The arsonist needs no more than some gasoline and a match, although a more sophisticated arsonist might use materials or liquids already present in the targeted building or some odorless accelerant.

Of course, the arsonist and the property owner that hires him face the risk of arrest and fine or imprisonment. However, studies of arrest data indicate that such risks are truly minimal. In 1974, only 9 percent of all incendiary or suspicious fires resulted in an arrest, two percent resulted in a conviction, and 7/10 of one percent resulted in a jail sentence. By way of comparison, a similar study of the seven FBI index crimes (murder, rape, robbery, aggravated assault, burglary, robbery, and motor vehicle theft) indicates an average arrest rate more than twice that of arson, an average conviction rate more than three times as high, and an average incarceration rate more than four times as high.[21]

The costs of arson to government and society are high indeed. It is estimated that there were 6,000 arson investigators, both public and private, in the United States in 1975.[22, 23] Most of the private investigators are employed by insurance companies. Since many of the investigators employed by public agencies, such as police and fire departments, have other duties in addition to arson investigation, Boudreau et al. estimate that there were 5,000 full-time equivalent arson investigators in 1975.[24] The salaries of these investigators amounted to nearly $100 million. In addition, governments must also undergo substantial judicial and penal costs in their anti-arson expenditures.

To date, no detailed studies have been made to determine the economic costs to society of arson, especially fraud arson. In 1972, the National Commission on Fire Prevention and Control computed the total annual costs of *all fires* as follows:[25]

Property loss	$2.7 billion
Fire department operations	$2.5 billion
Burn injury treatment	$1.0 billion
Operating cost of insurance industry	$1.9 billion
Productivity loss	$3.3 billion
Total	$11.4 billion

The Commission's report supplied no further basis for these calculations. Their estimate indicates that their computed total cost to society of fire is 4.2 times the direct property costs. This would bring the total cost of arson to society in 1974 to $5.4 billion and the total cost of fraud arson in building fires to $1.74 billion in 1974 and $1.85 billion in 1975.

These latter figures are gross underestimates of the total cost to society of fraud arson because they omit some of the most important costs of fraud arson. They do not include the losses from businesses that must close and from jobs that are interrupted or destroyed. As indicated by the description of the arson fire at the Shelton rubber plant, such losses can be considerable. They do not include the judicial and penal enforcement costs nor the erosion of the tax base as property values fall. Finally, they do not include cost figures for the 1,000 citizens, including 45 firefighters, who died in incendiary and suspicious fires in 1974.

Summary

Table 9-5 summarizes the estimates we have made in this chapter regarding arson-for-fraud building fires in 1974 and 1975.

Table 9-5   Arson-for-Fraud Figures for 1974 and 1975

	1974	1975
Number of Arson-for-Fraud Building Fires	27,700	30,400
Property Loss in the Fires (in $ million)	$413.7	$440.65
Total Cost to Society (in $ million) (Low Estimate)	$1,738	$1,859.73
Insurance Payments in the Fires (in $ million) (1.5 × Item 2)	$620.6	$660.98
Property Owners' Profits (in $ million) (Item 4 − Item 2)	$206.9	$220.33
Upper Estimate for Profits of Professional Torches (in $ millions) (10% of Item 2)	$41	$44

Endnotes

1. U.S. Department of Commerce. 1976. *Arson: America's Malignant Crime.*
2. Boudreau, John F., Quon Y. Kwan, William E. Faragher, and Genevieve C. Denault. 1977. *Arson and Arson Investigation: Survey and Assessment.* Report to U.S. Department of Justice, Law Enforcement Assistance Administration. Washington, D.C.: U.S. Government Printing Office.
3. *Ibid.*, pp. 16–17.
4. *Ibid.*, p. 20.
5. Teague, P. E. 1976. "Arson: The Growing Problem." *Fire Journal* (March), p. 3.
6. *Business Week.* 1975. "Bad Times Are Good Times for the Arsonists" (February 17).
7. National Fire Protection Association, Fire Analysis Department. 1976. "The Shelton Affair: The Hidden Costs of Arson," *Fire Journal* (March), pp. 22–24.
8. Karchmer, Clifford. 1977. "The Underworld Turns Fire into Profit," *Firehouse Magazine* (August), reprinted in *Congressional Record—Senate*, October 4.
9. Boudreau *et al.*, *Arson and Arson Investigation*, pp. 20–21.
10. *Newsweek.* 1974. "Detroit: The Torches' Game." November 25, pp. 42–43.
11. Karchmer, "Underworld Turns Fire into Profit."
12. Karchmer, C. *et al.*, Battelle Law and Justice Study Center. 1978. "Development of a Technical Assistance Manual on Strategies to Combat Arson-for-Profit." Battelle Law and Justice Study Center Preprint.
13. *Ibid.*, p. 31.
14. Boudreau *et al.*, *Arson and Arson Investigation*, p. 23.
15. Lucht, D. A. 1978. *Arson—A National Perspective.* Washington: U.S. Department of Commerce.
16. Steinmetz, R. C. 1966. "Current Arson Problems, Part I," *Fire Journal* (September), pp. 23–25, 31.
17. Icove, D. J. 1979. *Principles of Incendiary Crime Analysis.* Ph.D. dissertation. University of Tennessee, Knoxville.

18. Karchmer, C. 1978. "How to Fight the Arson Racketeer," *Journal of Insurance* (March-April), pp. 22–25.
19. Battle, B. P., and P. B. Weston. 1954. *Arson, a Handbook of Detection and Investigation*. New York: Arco Publishing Company, p. 244.
20. Horn, J. 1976. "Building-burners for Hire," *Psychology Today* 9 (February).
21. Boudreau *et al.*, *Arson and Arson Investigation*, pp. 29–30.
22. Kerr, J. W. 1975. "Incendiarism: An Overview and an Appraisal. Report on a Conference on Arson and Incendiarism." National Academy of Sciences, Washington, D.C., July 29–30, 1975, p. 4.
23. Boudreau *et al.*, *Arson and Arson Investigation*, p. 36.
24. Boudreau *et al.*, *Arson and Arson Investigation*.
25. National Commission on Fire Prevention and Control. 1973. *America Burning. The Report of the National Commission on Fire Prevention and Control.* Washington, D.C.: U.S. Government Printing Office.

Additional References

CARAWAY, C. W. 1976. "Incendiary Fires in Industrial Occupancies," *Fire Journal* (March), pp. 28–33.
CARTER, ROBERT E. 1963. "Arson in Virginia: Detection and Prosecution," *The Fire and Arson Investigator* 13 (Jan./March):27.
Citizens League Committee on Arson, Minneapolis, Minnesota. 1978. *We Make It Too Easy for the Arsonist*. Minneapolis: Citizens League.
COPPOCK, WILLIAM G. 1978. "Arson for Fun and Profit," *Best's Review* 79 (November):32, 34, 36, 38.
GOLD, L. H. 1962. "Psychiatric Profile of a Firesetter," *Journal of Forensic Science* 7:404–417.
GRIMES, MARTIN E. 1977. "The National Problem of Arson," *Fire Journal* (September):67–72, 103.
HEINEKE, J. M. 1975. "Modeling Arson—An Exercise in Qualitative Model Building," *IEEE Transactions Systems, Man and Cybernetics*, V (July):457–463.
INCIARDI, J. A. 1970. "The Adult Firesetter, A Typology," *Criminology* (August):145–155.
JACKSON, RALPH J. 1976. "The Insurer's Role in Arson Prevention," *Fire Journal* (March), pp. 45–47.
Journal of American Insurance. 1974. "Arson-Epidemic in America," *Journal of American Insurance* (Fall), pp. 1–5.
Journal of American Insurance. 1978. "Target-Arson," *Journal of American Insurance* 53 (Winter):12–15.
KERR, E. 1958. "Southerners Who Set the Woods on Fire," *Harpers* (July):28–33.
LEVY, W. 1975. "Arson—The Rising Flame," *Journal of Insurance* 36 (March-April):21–32.
LEWIS, N. D. C., and H. YARNELL. 1951. *Pathological Firesetting (Pyromania).* Nervous and Mental Disease Monographs. New York: Coolidge Foundation.
MACDONALD, JOHN M. 1977. *Bombers and Firesetters*. Springfield, Ill.: C. C. Thomas.

MAY, R. E. 1974. "Arson, the Most Neglected Crime on Earth," *Police Chief* (July), p. 32.

National Fire Protection Association. 1976. *Arson—Some Problems and Solutions.* Boston: National Fire Protection Association.

PEDLAR, J. F., and R. E. TIGHE. 1976. "The Forgotten Crime," *International Fire Chief* 42(4):3–4.

PRIAR, LAWRENCE L. 1956. "The Rising Trend in Fraud Fires," *Fire and Arson Investigator* (July-September).

ROBBINS, E. AND L. ROBBINS. 1967. "Arson with Special Reference to Pyromania," *New York State Journal of Medicine* (March 15), pp. 795–798.

ROTTENBERG, S. 1976. "Social Response to Incendiary Fire-Equipment Systems Improvement Program." Washington, D.C.: LEAA, U.S. Department of Justice.

SHAVER, PAUL A. 1962. "Report of the Arson Committee," *The Fire and Arson Investigator* 13 (July-September):63.

STRAETER, R. L. 1955. "Insurance Motive Fires," *Journal of Criminal Law, Criminology and Police Science* 46:277–280.

STUERWALD, JOHN E. 1970. "Arson," *Encyclopedia Americana* 2. New York: Americana Corporation.

TEAGUE, P. E. 1976. "Action Against Arson," *Fire Journal* (March), p. 3.

U.S. Department of Justice, Law Enforcement Assistance Administration. National Institute of Law Enforcement and Criminal Justice. 1979. *Arson: A Selected Bibliography.* Washington, D.C.: U.S. Government Printing Office.

U.S. News and World Report. 1975. "Behind Alarming Rises in Fires for Profit." May 12, pp. 61–62.

Chapter 10

ILLEGAL GAMBLING

In 1967, the President's Commission on Law Enforcement and Administration of Justice issued its Task Force's report on the economic impact of crimes.[1] This report estimated that the $7 billion GNP of the illegal gambling industry made up 87 percent of the total GNP for the production of all illegal goods and services—far outstripping the combined figures for narcotics, loan-sharking, prostitution, and illegal liquor activity. The report declared, "There is universal agreement among law enforcement officials that gambling is the greatest source of revenue for organized crime and the crime that involves by far the largest amount of money."[2] The report leaves a clear impression that an accurate estimate of the size of the GNP of the illegal gambling industry will go a long way to estimating the total impact of all illegal production.

The Commission asked the National Opinion Research Center to estimate the amount illegally bet on horse racing each year, believing that this amount would be the major component of the revenue for all illegal gambling. However, the Commission eventually rejected the NORC estimate of $3.3 billion for illegal horse race betting as being too low. It preferred instead to issue the general statement that "estimates by experts of the annual amount of illegal gambling vary from $7 to $50 billion. . . . Total annual profits are estimated at $6 to $7 billion."[3]

As we will see, more recent findings cast doubt on many of these conclusions of the 1967 Task Force. For example, it is generally agreed that bettors wager much more money on football and baseball with bookmakers than they do on horse racing. In addition, the takeout from the numbers game appears to be substantially larger than that of illegal horse betting (see Table 10-3 on page 207). Some careful analysts, such as Peter Reuter and Jonathan Rubinstein, are even questioning the assumed link between gambling and organized crime.[4]

In this chapter, we will look at five types of illegal gambling: sports betting with bookmakers, horse betting with bookmakers, sports parlay cards, numbers, and illegal casinos. We will describe and contrast four recent studies of the amount of illegal gambling and examine the structure of these illegal games.

Our estimates of the volume of illegal gambling in the United States in 1974 are mainly derived from the Report of the Commission on the Review of the National Policy toward Gambling.[5] These estimates are substantially lower than the 1967 estimates of the President's Task Force. We estimate that Americans wagered between $5 and $10 billion in 1974 and that, after the payoffs to the winners, the takeout to the illegal gambling industry was between $1 and $2 billion.

Estimates of American Gambling Intensity

To estimate the percentage of the population that gambles illegally each year and to get an idea of how much is actually wagered, we will study and compare four surveys of America's gambling habits—two local and two national.

The first of these surveys was carried out in 1971 by the Illinois Institute of Technology and the Chicago Crime Commission and entitled "A Study of Organized Crime in Illinois." Its purpose was "to determine the nature and extent of organized crime in the State of Illinois." An integral part of this study was a household survey conducted by the IIT Research Institute "to obtain some quantitative indicators of the extent of gambling and heroin usage in the population . . . and to measure public knowledge and public opinion of organized crime and its possible relationships with the police, the prosecutors, the courts, and the political system."[6]

To encourage truthful answers for sensitive questions on gambling and heroin, the interview procedures included the use of the Warner technique of probabilistic sampling in which the choice of a colored ball from an urn before the answer to each question allows the respondee a degree of anonymity in his response. For example, if the respondee chooses a red ball, he must tell the truth; if he chooses a blue ball, he need not answer truthfully. The interviewer

Table 10-1   Market for Crime Services in Illinois

Attribute	Percentage of Urban Illinois Population	Percentage of Chicago SMSA Population
Bet on sports events	27	28
Gamble with pinball machines, match-books, or jar games	19	19
Bet on policy, numbers, or bolita	11	9
Place off-track bets with bookies	7	7
Have used heroin	5	4
Have had first hand contact with organized crime	20	22

SOURCE: IIT Research Institute and the Chicago Crime Commission. 1971. *A Study of Organized Crime in Illinois.*

does not know what color ball the respondee has picked, although he does know how many balls of each color were in the bowl.

Table 10-1 indicates the results of the IIT household survey for the urban population of Illinois and for the Chicago metropolitan area. The urban population is three quarters of the total population of Illinois. The percentages are maximum-likelihood estimates. No attempt was made by the survey to estimate how much money was spent on gambling or drugs and how much sports betting involved only wagers between friends. The survey found that most Chicago and urban Illinois residents believed that organized crime was currently operating in their county and corrupting the police, prosecutors, judges, and city and county employees.

In early 1972, a little more than a year after the IIT study, Oliver Quayle and Company conducted two surveys of the betting habits and attitudes of adult residents of New York City for the Fund for the City of New York. The Fund was mainly concerned with the feasibility of legalizing the numbers game and sports betting, two of the largest illegal gambling enterprises in the city and in the state of New York. The report of the Fund's findings and conclusions was published in November 1972 in the booklet *Legal Gambling in New York: A Discussion of Numbers and Sports Betting.* We'll refer to this booklet as "Fund for N.Y.C." Its two appendices contain the results of the Quayle Company's household surveys.

To gather data for this study, trained members of Quayle's staff conducted over 600 personal interviews with adult residents of New York City. Interviewees were asked what games they bet on, how frequently they bet, how much money they wagered, with whom they bet, and what their attitude was toward legalized gambling. The interviewer promised complete anonymity in their sessions but did not use any specific technique to encourage completely honest responses. Among the major findings of the Quayle survey were the following:[7]

1. Eight in ten adult residents of New York City bet money at some time or other on games of chance or sporting events.
2. Some 36% in total say they bet on sports such as football, baseball, basketball, and horse racing. Thirty percent of adults have bet on horse racing; 25% bet on at least one of the other three sports.
3. A quarter of the city's population plays the numbers. Nearly all of these would be willing to play a legalized state game, if it were made convenient enough to play.
4. Forty percent of numbers players play the game daily; another 30% play two or three times a week. The typical bet is one dollar.
5. Heavy sports bettors ($500 or more a year) constitute 5% of the adult population and 19% of the sports betting population. Such bettors account for 85% of all dollars bet on football, with three quarters of their bets placed with bookmakers.
6. More adults placed bets on baseball (18% or 1 million people) than on football (15%) or basketball (13%). However, 41% of the money bet was bet on football games.
7. Seventy-two percent of sports bettors reported that most or all of their bets are made strictly with friends or acquaintances—legal bets. (This implies that 7% of the adult population—28% of 25%—make illegal sports bets, either with bookmakers or parlay cards.) However, over 60% of the total amount wagered in 1972, $428 million, was bet with bookmakers.
8. Sports bettors are in favor of legalized sports betting and would participate in such a legalized system if it were available.

Table 10-2 summarizes the participation rate, total amount wagered, payout percentage, the gross receipts after the payout, and

Table 10-2 Illegal Gambling in New York City

Activity	Percentage of N.Y.C. Residents that Participate	Take-Out Rate	Total Amount Wagered	Total Take-Out = Total Wager Minus Payoff	Net Industry Profit
Numbers	24%	47%	$576,204,700	$270,816,200	$58,000,000
Sports betting with bookmakers		4.5%	$428,360,000	$19,276,200	$4,000,000
Sports card betting	7%	60 to 80%	$35,410,000	$24,787,000	?
Horse race betting with bookmakers	< 24%*	17%	$83,643,000	$14,219,300	?
Total	?	29%	$1,123,617,700	$329,098,700	?

SOURCE: *Legal Gambling in New York: A Discussion of Numbers and Sports Betting.* 1972. New York: Oliver Quayle and Co.

* This figure represents the estimate that before off-track betting was legalized in New York City, 24 percent of all sports bettors made horse racing bets with bookmakers.

the net industry profit for each of the four types of illegal gambling that the Fund for the City of New York studied. Since New York City already has a legal off-track betting system, the Fund did not perform as complete an analysis of illegal horse race betting as it did for the other games.

We turn now to surveys and estimates of the illegal gambling habits of the entire population of the United States. In November of 1973, a year and a half after the Quayle survey, Alfred King estimated the extent of illegal gambling in the United States for the U.S. Department of Justice. Mr. King noted that the Quayle survey for the Fund for the City of New York estimated that, among those who used the services of bookies for sports betting, betting with bookies accounted for 37.8 percent of their total off-track horse betting. He assumed that this same percentage held for all persons who bet on horses, so that bookies accounted for 37.8 percent of all off-track horse betting. He next calculated the dollar value of bookmaker horse race bets in New York City in the first six months of 1973, based on the published dollar value of legal OTB bets. He computed a weekly average for illegal horse racing bets and compared this average with the weekly average of arrests for illegal horse race gambling by the Federal Government's strike forces in New York City. On the basis of this calculation, a factor of expansion was computed and was used to project not only illegal horse bets in New York but all illegal bets throughout the country on the basis of the bets uncovered by Federal Strike Forces nationwide. (For more details, see Melnick and Crocker.[8])

The Department of Justice announced that their estimate for the total volume of illegal gambling in 1973 lay somewhere between $29 and $39 billion. A partial breakdown of this figure can be found in the report by the Commission on the Review of the National Policy toward Gambling.[9] For example, the Department's estimate of illegal sports betting in New York City was $2.8 billion (compared with the estimate of $428 million by Quayle for such gambling).

The most extensive survey of the extent of gambling (both legal and illegal) in the United States was performed in the summer of 1975 by the University of Michigan Survey Research Center for the Commission on the Review of the National Policy toward Gambling. The Commission, which we will call "The National Gambling Commission" for brevity's sake, was charged with surveying "what is known about each form of gambling," "who should regulate it and how," and what are "the possible consequences of its legalization."[10] The Commission published its report in the fall of 1976 in four volumes—a final report[5] and three appendices.[9, 11, 12] The second appendix described the SRC's "Survey of American Gambling Attitudes and Behavior" and compared this study to the earlier Department of Justice report.

The primary purpose of the SRC survey was to produce information about: (1) the attitudes of the public toward gambling and its legalization, (2) the proportion of the population that participates in gambling activity, (3) the possible impact of legalization, and (4) a set of persons known as compulsive gamblers. The SRC completed a total of 1,736 interviews for its survey, with a response rate of 75.5 percent. Participants were selected at random from the U.S population. Interviews were conducted at the residences of the respondents and lasted an average of 90 minutes. The interviewers were "professionally trained to detect evasive efforts and to note any reservations about the sincerity of responses on the interview schedules. Evasive responses were reported for less than 1 percent of the sample."[13] Table 10-3 summarizes the findings of the survey with regard to the extent of gambling participation in the United States.

Table 10-3   Take-Out and Handle for U.S. Gambling, 1974

Activity	Take-Out Rate (%)	Total Take-Out ($ million)	Estimate of Total Amount Wagered ($ million)
Legal			
Horses at Track	16.0	$1,247	$7,930
OTB, New York	21.0	171	967
Legal Casinos	15.0	1,004	6,076
Bingo	33.0	551	1,735
Lotteries	55.0	374	639
Total Legal	19.3	$3,347	$17,347
Illegal			
Sports Books	4.5	105	2,341
Horse Books	16.6	227	1,368
Numbers	54.0	575	1,064
Sports Cards	60.0	115	191
Casino Games	15.0	19	110
Total Illegal	20.5	$1,039	$5,074
Total Legal and Illegal	19.6	$4,385	$22,421

SOURCE: Commission on the Review of the National Policy toward Gambling, *Gambling in America: Final Report* (Washington, D.C.: U.S. Government Printing Office, 1976), p. 64.

Table 10-4   Comparison of Published and SRC Estimated Data for Legal
              Wagering in the United States

Legal Gambling Activity	Sample Estimate of Total Handle ($ million)	Published Data of Total Handle ($ million)	Survey % Over/Under
Horses at track	$7,930	$7,512	+5.6
OTB, New York	967	786	+22.9
Legal casinos	6,076	6,693	−9.1
Bingo	1,735	1,672	+3.8
Lotteries	639	681	−6.2
Total legal handle	$17,347	$17,345	−0.0

The SRC presumed that their survey would underestimate the total "handle" (that is, amount of money wagered) because of faulty memory, reluctance to report, and underrepresentation of gamblers who wagered very large amounts. Consequently, it collected the official reports of the total handle for the *legal* games it studied and compared this total with the total legal handle estimated by the SRC survey. As Table 10-4 indicates, the difference between these two totals was less than one tenth of one percent. The SRC suggested that this statistical concurrence pointed to the validity of their estimates for the illegal handle.

How, then, does one explain the difference between the $29 billion estimate of the Department of Justice and the $5 billion estimate of the SRC survey for the total handle of illegal gambling? Other very rough studies which we haven't mentioned suggested estimates more in line with that of the Justice Department. The F.B.I. released figures stating that gambling officials made $750 million in payoffs to law enforcement people, suggesting that even the Justice Department's estimate was too low. The Bureau of Alcohol, Tobacco, and Firearms, an agency of the U.S. Treasury with responsibility for the administration of the federal wagering excise and occupational stamp taxes, extrapolated estimates from other agencies to suggest a total illegal handle of $67 billion. Even the 1967 President's Commission on Law Enforcement and Administration of Justice came up with an estimate of a yearly illegal handle of $20 billion.[14] None of these estimates was as carefully derived as those of the SRC and of the Department of Justice.

The Justice Department estimates are based on the following assumptions: (1) the rate of arrests for illegal operations in New York City is the same as the arrest rate for the rest of the country; (2) the rate of arrest for (illegal) horse race betting is the same as the rate of arrest for all other kinds of illegal betting; (3) the 37.8 percent rate computed by the Quayle survey for illegal horse race betting is an accurate figure.

There are obvious difficulties with each of the first two assumptions. The use of apprehension data is problematic, especially if the efforts of law enforcement agencies are unevenly distributed across the nation or among different forms of gambling. Reuter and Rubinstein suggest that the Department of Justice had a higher sampling fraction in New York than elsewhere since federal antigambling efforts there were "built around wiretapping, and the rate of surveillances per capita was higher in New York than in other major cities."[15] This could give "an upward bias" to the Department of Justice figures.

The Department's use of the Quayle survey also raises some questions since it assumed that all horse bettors use bookmakers to the same extent as horse bettors who are also sports bettors. Because sports betting is the main service of bookmakers, any sports bettor who wants to bet on horses with a bookie is likely to have already established contact with one.

On the other hand, the University of Michigan SRC survey used some sophisticated and reasonably careful sampling techniques in their study. Not only does their computation of the amount of legal gambling from their survey match very closely the amount reported in official records of legal gambling, but their estimates of participation rates in legal and illegal sports betting are similar to the corresponding estimates in other surveys. While the Quayle survey found that 25 percent of New York City residents gambled on sports and the IIT survey found that 27 percent of urban Illinois residents bet on sports, the SRC survey found that 28 percent of the American population bets on sports—32 percent in the Northeast and 30 percent in the North Central area. While the Quayle survey found that 7 percent of New York City residents bet on sports with bookies, the SRC survey found that 6 percent of the residents of the Northeast did so. However, there are discrepancies in participation rates in the numbers game. The IIT survey estimates that 11 percent of urban Illinois residents and 9 percent of Chicago residents bet on numbers; the Quayle survey found that 24 percent of New York City residents bet on numbers. However, the SRC survey estimated that only 8.1 percent of residents of the Northeast and 2.2 percent of residents of North Central states bet on numbers. Conversations with researchers who have studied the numbers game in New York City indicate the following patterns in numbers betting:

(1) the game is truly an urban game so that urban estimates should be much higher than general nationwide estimates, and (2) the actual participation rate of numbers betting in New York City is somewhere between the above figures of 8 and 24 percent.

There are other more important indications, however, that the SRC survey erred on the low side. The Quayle survey found that most of the volume of sports wagering was concentrated among a rather small number of sports bettors. For example, 27 percent of all football bettors—those betting $500 or more a year—accounted for 85 percent of the dollars bet. The sample design of the SRC survey "did not account for the possibility that most illegal gambling is concentrated among a relatively small group of people. If there were as many as 500,000 people in the nation who bet an average of $50,000 annually, the sample used by the SRC has a very small chance of producing good results of their gambling activity."[16] If such a group were missed in the sample and the SRC estimate were accurate for the rest of the population, "the true amount of illegal betting might exceed $30 billion a year."[17]

Conversations with researchers familiar with the New York City sports betting environment report that a substantial number of bettors wager over $1,000 a week with bookmakers there. Furthermore, there are games just about every week that involve 100 to 125 bettors and handles of $250,000.

The SRC survey estimated that the total handle of illegal gambling in the United States was $5,074 million in 1974. Since there is sufficient cause to suspect that this estimate is low, we will double the SRC estimate to obtain a figure that should be an upper bound on the total illegal handle.[18] Thus, we feel safe in estimating that between $5 billion and $10 billion was wagered in illegal bets in 1974. Assuming that the takeout rate of 20.5 percent calculated for the aggregate illegal gambling is correct—the takeout rate for legal gambling was a rather similar 19.3 percent—one arrives at a takeout somewhere between $1 billion and $2 billion for illegal gambling in 1974.

We'll look now at some of the games in detail.

Numbers and Policy

Both the National Gambling Commission and the Quayle survey found that the total takeout of numbers games represented more than one half of the total takeout for all illegal gambling. The numbers game is a simple lottery game. On any day of the week (except Sunday) the numbers player picks a three-digit number from 000 to 999. Before 2:00 p.m., he wagers from twenty-five cents to ten dollars with a numbers "runner" that his number will be the day's winning number. Most players bet $1 or $2 each day that they participate. The runner (sometimes called "writer" or "seller") records the number on a piece of paper, delivers the money to a "pick-up man" or controller, who in turn passes the wager on to the "bank," the central headquarters or processing office.

Later that evening, the player learns the identity of the winning three-digit number. If it matches his choice, that is, if he correctly predicted all three digits of the winning number in their proper order, the winning player meets his runner in some predetermined prominent place that evening or the next morning and collects an amount equal to 600 times the amount of his wager. He tips his runner 10 percent of this amount and usually places his bet for the next day's drawing.

The winning number is usually determined by betting totals or payoff odds on selected races at horse racing tracks. Two systems used in New York are the "Brooklyn" number—which is simply the last three digits of the selected race track's parimutuel handle for the day—and the more common "New York" number, which is more complicated, combining the payoff odds for win, place, and show horses in the first seven races.

There are a number of variations on the standard bet. In "bolita," the player wagers on the first two or last two digits of the final winning number. The winning payout in bolita is 60 times the amount bet. In "single action," there is a separate bet on each digit of the winning number. Payoff here is seven times the amount bet.

"Policy" is a two-digit variation of the numbers game. There are two variations, one using 100 numbers and the other 78 numbers. In both versions, the payoffs are 60 to 1. Policy is the dominant lottery in Chicago.[19]

A major advantage to the player of the various numbers games over the legal state lotteries is the opportunity for the player to choose his own number. Players often bet on numbers of some personal significance. Thus, players can employ "hunches, favorite numbers, sentimental numbers, or, most frequently, dreams. The usual way dreams and events are transformed into numbers is via dream books or dream cards. Dream books are published lists of objects, events, or feelings, each of which is magically assigned a number. In a black ghetto, half a dozen different titles of these books may be for sale in local stores."[20] To protect themselves from heavy losses, numbers operators "cut" some of the most popular numbers from the list of 1,000 eligible numbers, for example, 100, 200, . . . 900, 111, 222, . . . 999, or traditionally lucky numbers like 711.

In the study commissioned by the Fund for the City of New York, the Quayle Company found that 24 percent of the adult population bet on numbers in 1972, with the amount wagered approximately $600 million. The report of the National Gambling Commission found that nonwhites, Italians, divorcees, and city-dwellers had higher proportional rates of participation. "Play is proportionally much heavier among blacks and Puerto Ricans . . . . There is a strong feeling in black and Puerto Rican neighborhoods that numbers is 'their' game. Its lore is part of the community fabric. Runners and controllers are well-known figures."[21]

Figure 10-1 illustrates the organizational framework of the numbers business. At the bottom of this organization are the runners, who accept the wagers directly from the bettors. A runner may operate from a stationary place of business or he may be a mobile salesman over some specified territory. In the former case, he may be a neighborhood bartender, newsstand dealer, office messenger, elevator operator, union shop steward, or a small businessman. He will often be a regular bettor himself. Sometimes he'll accept bets on credit or make small loans.

The runners are the most exposed agents in the organization and thus take the highest risk with the police. Consequently, they are paid a commission of 25 percent of their receipts. In addition, they are usually tipped 10 percent of winning payoffs.

Runners drop off their money and slips at a specified secret "drop" to a controller, the middle man in the three-tiered numbers organization. The location of this transfer point is changed daily, sometimes hourly. The controller operates as an area manager. Not only does he tabulate the daily collection, but he also maintains the records of a large number of runners and makes payoffs with money from the central bank. He may employ some security lookouts and some bet-recorders to assist him.

Controllers receive between 5 and 10 percent of the total receipts. However, they often use some of this money to buy protection from local police officers.[22-24]

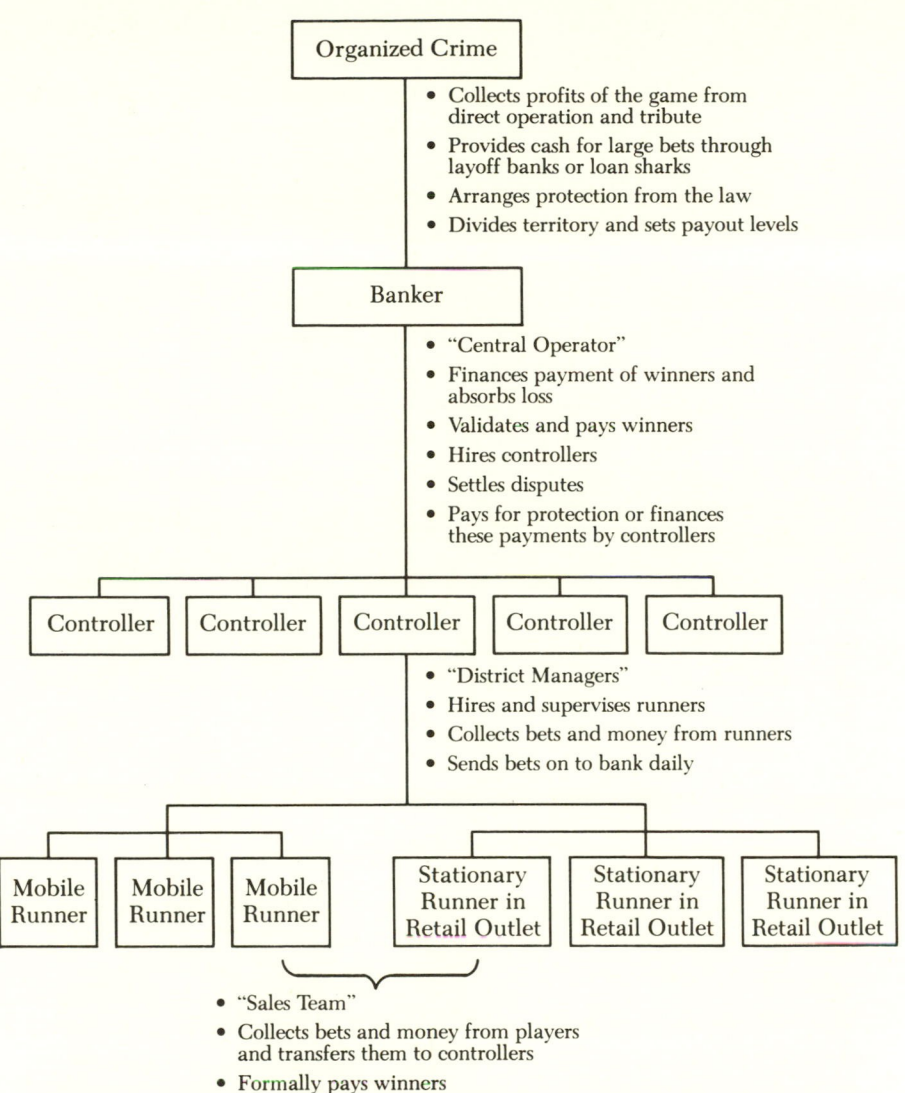

Figure 10-1 Illegal Numbers Game Structure. *(Source: Fund for the City of New York, Legal Gambling in New York: A Discussion of Numbers and Sports Betting, New York: Oliver Quayle and Co., 1972.)*

The controller forwards the day's receipts to the banker, the manager of the numbers game. "Just as the runner insulates the controller from the police, the controller acts as a buffer shielding the banker. Security measures are an essential element in the controller's operation . . . . The bank's pickup man, often with a car or taxi waiting, makes a quick stop to collect from the controller . . . . Because pickup men can provide the police department with a good lead to the banker, decoys or relay teams are frequently used to foil pursuers."[25] In a few cases, pickup men bring receipts directly from the runner to the central bank.

Besides collecting the final receipts and providing the winners' payout money, the central banker has a staff to keep a running audit of his games. He may also have to pay off policemen, bail bondsmen, and lawyers. The banker assumes all the financial risk in a game. "If a banker notices a particularly heavy play on a given number, threatening a loss for the day if the number wins, he may choose to cut his risk by turning some or all of these wagers to a layoff bank—a bank with sufficient capital to cover large hits. If the heavily-played number wins, the layoff bank provides funds to pay the winners. If the number does not win, the layoff bank keeps the money wagered."[26]

The Fund for the City of New York estimated the operating costs and profit for a typical bank which pays 600 to 1 as listed below.[27] The numbers represent percentage of total sales. The payback to winners is less than 60 percent because of the effect of cutting numbers.

Sales costs to runners	25%
Sales costs to controllers	5%
Net payback to winners	57.5%
Protection	5%
Office costs	2%
Total costs	94.5%
Profit	5.5%

Scarne[28] and Kaplan and Maher[29] arrive at similar estimates. For a game that pays back 500 to 1 instead of 600 to 1, the estimated payback to winners is 48.5 percent and the estimated profit is 14.5 percent. The Fund for New York City estimates that in a single year $600 million is wagered on numbers in New York City.[30] Of this amount, $282 million is kept by the numbers business, which eventually realizes a net profit of $58 million a year. Kaplan and Maher estimate the total number of New York City residents who work for the numbers business as somewhere between 10,000 and 100,000, the vast majority of which are runners.[31] Rados discusses both estimates and actual cases of salaries of employees at different levels in the numbers business.[32] He estimates that the average full-time runner earned between $5,000 and $7,500 in 1970. While this is a reasonable tax-free income, Rados reminds us that runners work for truculent masters, without job security, paid vacations, hospitalization, or pensions, while enduring the constant risk of shakedowns, arrests, and even jail.

The National Gambling Commission estimated that $1,064 million was wagered on numbers games nationally in 1974 and that the takeout rate was 54 percent, yielding a total takeout of $575 million. Following the procedures described at the end of the previous section, we will estimate the total handle of the numbers games as somewhere between $1 billion and $2 billion, with a total takeout of between $500 million and $1 billion.

Betting on Sports

The National Gambling Commission points out that "in terms of gross volume of betting, sports wagering is the number one form of illegal gambling in the United States."[33] It also estimated that 28 percent of the American adult population bet on sports in 1974. Similar estimates were made by the Quayle survey for the Fund for the City of New York and by a January 1971 Gallup Poll. Although most of these bets were simply with friends, a significant proportion of them did use the services of a bookmaker. In terms of dollars bet, the Quayle survey found that only 24 percent of the total amount bet on football games was composed of strictly private wagers between friends, while 67 percent of the dollar amount, or $188,590,000, was bet through bookmakers. The remaining 9 percent, or $24,960,000, was bet on betting cards or sheets.

As described in the Quayle survey, the bookie's role is[34]

> *that of a broker between those who want to bet on one team and those who want to bet on the other. For this service, he takes a commission on the total amount wagered. His goal is to equalize the amount bet on each side, so that the losses of one set of customers will cover the winnings (less his commission) of the other. To attract the same amount of money to each team, he employs either (in the case of baseball) betting odds or a point spread (football and basketball).*
>
> *The point spread is a handicap for the stronger team. If the Jets are listed as a seven-point favorite over the Vikings, Jet backers win only if their team wins by more than seven. If the Jets win by exactly seven points, it is a betting tie and all wagers are returned.*

Typically, a bookmaker requires the bettor to put up $11 for every possible $10 payoff, and the bulk of his income comes from that extra dollar. If his books are in balance—that is, with an equal number of bettors on both sides—the bookmaker will keep 4.5 percent of his total football and basketball handle as his commission.

Complications arise for the bookie when the bets are not balanced, that is, when one team attracts a significant majority of the bets. If bets on this team win, the bookie could lose a significant amount of money. When an imbalance occurs, the bookie can change the point spread to attract more bets for the other team in an attempt to equalize the betting. However, if the final margin of the game were to fall between these two point spreads, then the bookie could lose *all* bets.

Alternatively, a bookmaker receiving asymmetric bets at his point spread can reduce his risk either by trading bets with other bookies or by laying off his excess bets with a larger bookmaking operation. In the first case, a bookmaker receiving many more bets for team A than for team B can trade bets with a bookmaker that has an excess of bets on team B. In the second case, the bookmaker would turn over his excess bets on team A to a "bank" which would then keep the commission (or "vigorish") on the amounts bet. In extreme cases, a bookmaker may find that neither individual bookmakers nor the larger bookmaking operations will be willing to accept layoff money at mutually acceptable spreads.

According to Canes, "Most contacts between bookmakers and bettors take place by telephone, with some bookmakers using screening devices such as code words or answering services, others placing calls to their clients at appointed hours from public telephones, and still others operating from rented private homes or businesses."[35] The bookkeeper may also hire a "writer" to transcribe the bets, a "tabber" to keep track of the bets and to decide when to change the spread and when to lay off a bet, and possibly an accountant.

A bookmaker's operation is described in the Quayle survey as follows:[36]

> *A typical (bookmaker's) office might have 22 runners who take bets from clients directly or provide them with telephone access to the office by use of a code word . . . . The runner may be regarded as the bookmaker by his clients . . . . A runner keeps one-half of his customers' losses. If, in a given week, his customers are net winners, the runner is in the red to the office and must clear his debt before he begins to collect his share of the profits again.*
>
> *On the average, runners for such an office may collect $750 a day in horse racing bets and $3,500 a week in football wagers. If there is no other action, the office handles $99,000 on horse racing and $77,000*

on football a week. If all bets are in balance, the office retains about $16,500 from its horse racing action and $3,500 from football—a total of $20,000. Half of this goes to the runners, who average about $450 per week. (There are wide variations in income among runners. Some may have expenses, such as gratuities to good customers who are heavy losers.) The office has a weekly payroll of roughly $1,500, including the manager's salary.

If an office had a smaller horse racing business, as most policy estimates indicate, runners would average $300 or less a week and the net profits would be less than 2%. Canes estimates that "85,000 people in the United States today derive income from bookmaking activities."[37]

A person who wants to begin placing bets with a bookmaker will usually require an introduction from an established customer, followed by two to six months of informal contact, before the bookmaker will accept a bet. Meanwhile, the bettor can use a trusted bookmaker customer to place his bets with the bookmaker.

The National Gambling Commission describes the typical sports bettor as a single, white male between 25 and 44 years of age who lives in the Northeast or North Central United States. As family income increases, the proportion of people betting on sports increases, as does the mean proportion of family income wagered.[38]

The National Gambling Commission's SRC survey estimated that the total amount wagered on sports bets with bookies was $2.341 billion. At a takeout rate of 4.5 percent, this would yield a takeout of $105 million to the bookmaking industry. Following our discussion of the possible underestimating by SRC of the amount of gambling with bookmakers, it seems safe to estimate a total handle of between $2 and $4 billion and a total takeout of between $100 and $200 million due to illegal sports books in 1974.

Betting on Horses

Bookmakers came into prominence in the 1870s when they were licensed by horse racing tracks to accept wagers at a particular track facility. In return, they paid the track a daily fee. Horse race bookmakers eventually included wagers on sports events at a much later date—basically as a courtesy to some of their wealthy customers. The National Gambling Commission's survey reported that 35 percent of the U.S. adult population placed a bet at a racetrack in their lifetimes, while 14 percent placed such a bet in 1974. "About 7½% placed an illegal bet on the horses with a bookmaker sometime in their life, while about 2½%, or 3.6 million people, did so in 1974. The total volume of horse bets with bookies was about 1.4 billion dollars in 1974."[39]

What type of person bets on horses with bookmakers? The National Gambling Commission survey notes that five times as many men as women placed an illegal bet on horses in 1974. In contrast to the trend in illegal sports betting, a greater proportion of the nonwhite than white population bet illegally on horses, although people with Italian- and Spanish-speaking backgrounds had a higher participation rate than all other ethnic groups. As income increases and as age decreases, there is a steady increase in the percentage of people who report betting horses with a bookie. Also, those who are divorced or separated showed above-average participation.

The National Gambling Commission also reported that:[40]

> *The basic information needed by both bookmaker and player is derived from a 'scratch sheet,' which provides such facts as jockeys, post positions, time of races, probable odds, and handicappers' picks. Winning bets placed through a bookmaker are paid at the same payoff as at the track, with the bookmaker's profit deriving from that portion which, at the track, would go for expenses and taxes. As a rule, a horse bookmaker can gross 15% of his wagers and can net approximately 11%. As in sports betting, layoff facilities are utilized by a bookie who receives an excess of wagers on one horse. Depending on the odds, layoffs are made at the track itself, in the form of a large wager on the bookie's favored horse; this not only enables the bookmaker to use track winnings for making payoffs but reduces the amount of the track's potential payoff."*

Horse race betting is far more profitable to a bookmaker than is sports betting. In horse race betting, he can gross 15 to 17 percent of the amount wagered, while the best he can do in sports betting is 4.5 to 8.3 percent. His actual profit is about 11 percent of the amount wagered on horses but less than 3 percent of the amount wagered on sports. According to the Fund for the City of New York, "In terms of profit to the bookmaker, $1 bet on horse racing is worth $3.80 wagered on football or basketball."[41] In addition, because of the layoff system which the race track provides, the bookmaker takes a much smaller financial risk in horse race betting.

The SRC survey estimated a total handle of $1.368 billion in 1974 for illegal gambling on horse racing. At a takeout rate of 16.5 percent, this would yield a total takeout of $227 million.

Sports Parlay Card Betting

Bettors whose low volume of bets is uninteresting to a sports book-maker are often attracted to parlay cards or pool cards. Such cards exist for betting on baseball, basketball, and football. The Quayle survey found that five times more money was bet on football parlay cards than on baseball or basketball cards.

A typical football parlay card lists about ten professional games and twenty college contests, each with a point spread. A bettor picks at least three games and turns in a numbered stub that shows his selections and the amount of his wager. He loses his bet if any of the teams he has chosen loses *or ties*.

Pool card spreads differ from those set by bookmakers for single game action in that the cards are fixed at the most common margins of victory (for example, 3, 6, 7, 10, 14 points). In particular, they never use half-point spreads. The reason for such spreads is to bring about as many tie games as possible and thus add to the card-seller's advantage. The Fund for the City of New York reviewed point spreads printed during the season by the *New York Times* and found that they brought about ties in six games out of 182—an edge for the poolseller of 5.4 percent.

Cards are printed at the beginning of each week and distributed no later than Tuesday. As a result, the line in parlay card betting does not have the flexibility to reflect changes that occur during the week. The cards are distributed at such places as factories, offices, newsstands, and schools, with ready access to the public. In many ways, the operations of a parlay card business are much more like those of a numbers game than those of a bookmaking operation. As in numbers, runners are used as agents to pass out cards, collect stubs and wagers, and pay off winners.

A player must bet on at least three or four games. If he bets on ten or more games and misses only one game, he will receive a consolation prize. However, the odds against the bettor rise rapidly the more selections he makes. Assuming that each game is a 50-50 proposition, the odds against picking three winners in three games are 8 to 1, while the payoff is $4 for each dollar bet. Thus, the pool card operator would, on the average, retain 50 percent of the amount wagered on such bets. Table 10-5 describes the odds, payoffs, and operator's average gross profit depending on how many games the player bets on his card. These figures assume that the player will pick correctly in one-half of the games he selects. They do not take into consideration the considerable advantage which the

Table 10-5   Odds and Payoffs on Football Cards

Number of Games Played	Payoff on $1	Odds Against Winning	Probable % Retained by Operator
3 out of 3	$4	8–1	50
4 out of 4	$10	16–1	37.5
5 out of 5	$15	32–1	43
6 out of 6	$25	64–1	61
7 out of 7	$50	128–1	61
8 out of 8	$100	256–1	61
10 out of 10	$250	1024–1	80
9 out of 10	$150	1024–10	
12 out of 12	$500	4096–1	80
11 out of 12	$300	4096–12	
16 out of 16	$5,000	65,536–1	88
15 out of 16	$3,200	65,536–16	

SOURCE: Adapted from Fund for the City of New York, 1972, p. 47.

operator enjoys from the fact that he wins all tie bets.
As explained by the Fund for the City of New York:[42]

> *The game's very high profit margin greatly simplifies the poolseller's operations. Rarely if ever does he need to lay off bets. He is unconcerned with fixed games . . . . Poolselling has a lower status in the illegal gambling hierarchy than bookmaking. It is, in fact, disdained by police and bookies alike. Bettors are regarded as suckers in the same class as numbers players, and sellers as small-time operators. Booking records seized by the police reveal no evidence that bookies engage in poolselling and there is a feeling, among bookies at least, that selling pool cards would be beneath their dignity.*
>
> *In the aggregate, however, poolselling is a lucrative business. The Quayle study (for the Fund for the City of New York) found that football bettors make pool bets regularly. Only 28 percent bet a single three- or four-game card per week. Most bet cards with more picks, which offer odds on which the seller retains an average of 53 percent to 90 percent of the bets. It is reasonable to estimate that a poolseller's markup is between 60 percent and 80 percent of the $35 million spent on pool cards by New Yorkers each year. That amounts to $21 million to $28 million, before expenses.*

In their calculations, the National Gambling Commission estimated that poolsellers kept 60 percent of the total amount wagered on sports cards.[43] At this rate, the takeout on the $191 million which the SRC estimated was wagered on sports cards in 1974 was $115 million.

Illegal Casinos

"With the repeal of prohibition in 1933, former bootleggers developed renewed interest in gambling ventures. During the 1930s, illegal casinos were established in every major city."[44] The 1950 Kefauver committee investigations brought national attention to the existence of many illegal casinos. The resulting increase in law enforcement activities, together with the passage of a series of federal antigambling statutes in the early 1960s, forced most of the illegal casinos to close. A few small illegal casinos exist, generally offering only blackjack, dice games, and, recently, backgammon.

The National Gambling Commission estimated that $110 million was wagered nationally in illegal casinos in 1974.[45] It estimated that the owners of these casinos kept 15 percent of the total amount gambled, or $19 million. During the same year, it estimated that $6,076 million was wagered at legal casinos, with the same 15 percent takeout rate. Thus, the total handle at illegal casinos was less than 1.8 percent of all casino betting.

Costs and Benefits

Here we will consider the costs and benefits of illegal gambling to the individual gambler, to the organizers of illegal games, to government, and to society as a whole.

The principal benefits that gamblers experience when they gamble legally or illegally are the intrinsic value of the activity itself as entertainment and the possibility of winning money. Gambling can be a stimulating and exciting activity in which an individual exercises varying degrees of commitment, decision making, and fantasizing. The excitement of gambling can and often does compensate for a dull or tedious work activity.[46] The extra riskiness of *illegal* gambling can heighten this effect. In addition, the illegal gambler not only has a much broader spectrum of games to play, but also has a better opportunity to avoid reporting any winnings on his income tax returns.

Of course, in all professional gambling arrangements gamblers lose money in the long run since the games' organizers set the odds in their own favor in order to earn a profit. Furthermore, under the usual economic assumption of "diminishing marginal utility," the decrease in utility that accompanies the loss of $100 in income is greater than the increase in utility corresponding to a gain of $100 in income. As a result, if one ignores the recreational value of gambling, even a bet at fair odds involves an economic loss. (See, for example, Samuelson[47] or Hirshleifer.[48])

The casual, occasional gambler also risks the possibility that his enthusiasm for the game will lead to excessive or compulsive gambling, a state which is usually accompanied by a degeneration of work, family, and social life.[49, 50]

Persons who engage in illegal gambling face more risks than their legal counterparts. If apprehended, they can be arrested and fined or imprisoned. Even if they win their bet, they may not receive their winnings because of the dishonesty of the game's organizers or confiscation of all bets as a result of police action.

The organizers and managers of illegal gambling games benefit not only from the profits they make but also from the easy avoidance of income taxes, occupational tax stamps, and wagering excise taxes. On the other hand, they face the usual costs associated with illegal activities, that is, the possibility of arrest and fine or imprisonment. To reduce this possibility, they must take extra security precautions and pay bribes to police and government officials. Operators of illegal gambling games also face the risk that despite their "layoff" precautions they can be bankrupted if they receive too many wagers on the winning number or team.

Government at all levels incurs extensive enforcement costs as a result of the illegal gambling industry. For example, federal, state, and metropolitan governments have organized special task forces to crack down on illegal gambling operations. (Unfortunately, the U.S. Justice Department does not keep records of the amount of money and time spent on gambling investigations and prosecutions each year.)[51] Government also suffers a cost in lost tax revenue as a result of the nonreporting of individual players' winnings and of organizers' revenues, and failure to pay the gambling excise tax.

The question of whether or not to legalize some or all gambling ventures has sparked a vigorous debate over the costs and benefits of gambling to society. Many have claimed that gambling, especially illegal gambling, harms society by (1) encouraging an inequitable distribution of wealth; (2) separating money from its function as a reward for honest work and effort, thus leading to job dissatisfaction; and (3) introducing too large an element of chance in what should ideally be a well-ordered society. The "inequitable distribution of wealth" argument comes from the finding that lower income groups wager a slightly higher percentage of their income than do higher income groups, especially in games like numbers and legal lotteries.[52,53] However, Weinstein and Deitch argue that the relatively higher gambling expenditure for lower income groups is due more to frequency of play rather than amount bet. Thus, such gamblers may be deriving more entertainment value for their betting habits. Regarding arguments (1) and (2), Weinstein and Deitch found that gamblers appear to be as aware as nongamblers that gambling is not a profitable activity. Furthermore, as mentioned earlier, the excitement that gambling generates can compensate for the dullness of assembly-line jobs and thus help workers in such jobs tolerate their tedious but necessary occupations.

As mentioned earlier, illegal gambling organizations can benefit society by providing employment for tens of thousands of individuals who are officially listed as being unemployed. On the other hand, from a macroeconomic point of view, one can argue that organized gambling subtracts from the national income since it involves simply sterile transfers of money between individuals, creating no new money, yet absorbing time and resources.[54] This point of view neglects the important recreational component of gambling.

Illegal gambling induces many more costs to society than legal gambling does. It often provides money for the underworld activities of crime syndicates. Most law enforcement officials believe that illegal gambling provides the main financial support for crime syndicates.[1, 9, 55] Others—Reuter and Rubinstein,[15] for example—downgrade such links, pointing to the fragmentation and low profitability of illegal gambling operations in New York City.

Illegal gambling also hurts society because it inevitably leads to some police corruption. The New York Commission to Investigate Allegations of Police Corruption, otherwise known as the Knapp Commission, found direct evidence of such corruption in half the New York City police department's plain clothes divisions and allegations of corruption in the others.[56] Unlike any other illegal business, a successful gambling operation requires the unrestricted freedom to contact clients on a regular, routine basis. "Without the cooperation of the police, either by protecting gambling organizations or by ignoring their existence, organized illegal gambling cannot be carried on profitably."[57] The Knapp Commission concluded, "The most important effect of corruption in the so-called gambling control units is in the incredible damage their performance wreaks on public confidence in the law and police."[58]

Illegal gambling can lead directly to other types of crime in that an unsuccessful gambler may resort to theft, embezzlement, or loan-shark deals to pay off his gambling debts. In addition, sports betting, especially by athletes themselves, has occasionally led to scandals, such as The Black Sox Scandal, which have damaged the integrity of organized sports.

Endnotes

1. The President's Commission on Law Enforcement and Administration of Justice. 1967. *Task Force Report: Crime and Its Impact—An Assessment.* Washington, D.C.: U.S. Government Printing Office.
2. *Ibid.*, p. 52.
3. *Ibid.*
4. Reuter, Peter, and Jonathan Rubinstein. 1978. "Fact, Fancy, and Organized Crime," *The Public Interest* 53 (Fall):45–67.
5. Commission on the Review of the National Policy toward Gambling. 1976. *Gambling in America: Final Report.* Washington, D.C.: U.S. Government Printing Office.
6. IIT Research Institute and the Chicago Crime Commission. 1971. *A Study of Organized Crime in Illinois.*
7. Fund for the City of New York. 1972. *Legal Gambling in New York: A Discussion of Numbers and Sports Betting.* New York: Oliver Quayle and Co.
8. Melnick, D., and R. Crocker, 1976. "A Review of Two Studies on Gambling in the United States," in *Commission on the Review of the National Policy toward Gambling.*
9. Commission on the Review of the National Policy toward Gambling. 1976. *Gambling in America. Appendix 3. Summaries of Commission Hearings.* Washington, D.C.: U.S. Government Printing Office, pp. 15–16.
10. Commission, *Gambling in America. Final Report,* pp. ix, 1.
11. Commission on the Review of the National Policy toward Gambling. 1976. *Gambling in America. Appendix 1. Staff and Consultant Papers, Model Statutes, Bibliography, Correspondence.* Washington, D.C.: U.S. Government Printing Office.
12. Commission on the Review of the National Policy toward Gambling. 1976. *Gambling in America. Appendix 2. Survey of American Gambling Habits and Behavior.* Washington, D.C.: U.S. Government Printing Office.
13. Commission, *Gambling in America. Appendix 2,* pp. x–xi.
14. Commission, *Gambling in America. Final Report,* p. 64.
15. Reuter and Rubinstein, "Fact, Fancy, and Organized Crime," pp. 60–61. Reprinted with permission of the author from *The Public Interest,* No. 53 (Fall 1978). Copyright 1978 by National Affairs, Inc.
16. Melnick and Crocker, "A Review of Two Studies," p. 10.
17. *Ibid.*, p. 11.
18. Commission, *Gambling in America. Appendix 3,* p. 523.
19. Commission, *Gambling in America. Final Report,* pp. 172–173.

20. Herman, Robert D. 1976. *Gamblers and Gambling*. Lexington, Mass.: Lexington Books, p. 118.
21. Fund for N.Y.C., *Legal Gambling in New York*, p. 9.
22. *Ibid.*, p. 26.
23. Rados, David L. 1976. "The Numbers Game: An Economic and Competitive Analysis," *Quarterly Review of Economics and Business* 16:30.
24. Kaplan, Lawrence, and J. Maher 1970. "The Economics of the Numbers Game," *American Journal of Economics and Sociology* 29 (October):400.
25. Fund for N.Y.C., *Legal Gambling in New York*, p. 27.
26. *Ibid.*, p. 28.
27. *Ibid.*, p. 31.
28. Scarne, John. 1961. *Scarne's Complete Guide to Gambling*. New York: Simon and Schuster, p. 165.
29. Kaplan and Maher, "The Economics of the Numbers Game," p. 402.
30. Fund for N.Y.C., *Legal Gambling in New York*, p. 30.
31. Kaplan and Maher, "The Economics of the Numbers Game," p. 401.
32. Rados, "The Numbers Game."
33. Commission, *Gambling in America. Final Report*, p. 174.
34. Fund for N.Y.C., *Legal Gambling in New York*, p. 36.
35. Canes, Michael E. 1976. "The Market for Pro Football Betting," in William R. Eadington (ed.), *Gambling and Society*, p. 112. Courtesy of Charles C. Thomas, Publisher, Springfield, Ill.
36. Fund for N.Y.C., *Legal Gambling in New York*, p. 42.
37. Canes, "The Market for Pro Football Betting," p. 113.
38. Commission, *Gambling in America. Final Report*.
39. *Ibid.*, p. 177.
40. *Ibid.*, p. 174.
41. Fund for N.Y.C., *Legal Gambling in New York*, p. 41.
42. *Ibid.*, pp. 46, 48.
43. Commission, *Gambling in America. Final Report*, p. 64.
44. *Ibid.*, p. 176.
45. *Ibid.*, p. 64.
46. Newman, O. 1972. *Gambling: Hazard and Reward*. London:. Athlone Press.
47. Samuelson, Paul. 1976. *Economics* (Tenth edition). New York: McGraw-Hill, p. 425.
48. Hirshleifer, J. 1965. "Investment Decisions under Uncertainty—Choice Theoretic Approaches," *Quarterly Journal of Economics* 79(4):532.
49. Commission, *Gambling in America. Appendix 2*, p. 438.
50. Martinez, Tomas. 1976. "Compulsive Gambling and the Conscious Mood Perspective," in Eadington.
51. Commission, *Gambling in America. Appendix 3*, p. 785.
52. Weinstein, D., and L. Deitch. 1974. *The Impact of Legalized Gambling*. New York: Praeger.
53. Commission, *Gambling in America. Appendix 2*, p. v.
54. Samuelson, *Economics*, p. 425.
55. King, Rufus. 1969. *Gambling and Organized Crime*. Washington, D.C.: Public Affairs Press.
56. New York Commission to Investigate Allegations of Police Corruption and the

City's Anti-Corruption Procedure. 1972. *Commission Report.* (Also known as
Knapp Commission Report.)
57. Rubinstein, J. 1976. "Gambling Enforcement and Police Corruption," in Commission on the Review of the National Policy toward Gambling, p. 600.
58. New York Commission, *Commission Report,* p. 89.

Additional References

ALLEN, DAVID D. 1952. *The Nature of Gambling.* New York: Coward-McCann.
BOLEN, D. W. 1976. "Gambling: Historical Highlights and Trends and their Im-
plications for Contemporary Society," in William R. Eadington, ed., *Gambling
and Society.* Springfield, Ill.: C. C. Thomas.
BURKE, DUANE V. 1976. "The Legalization of Gambling in the United States: An
Analysis and Forecast," in Eadington.
CONKLIN, JOHN E. 1977. *Illegal, But Not Criminal.* Englewood Cliffs, N.J.: Prentice-
Hall.
CORNISH, D. B. 1977. *Gambling: A Review of the Literature and Its Implications for
Policy and Research.* London: Her Majesty's Stationery Office.
DOWNES, D. M., B. P. DAVIES, M. E. DAVID, and P. STONE. 1976. *Gambling,
Work and Leisure: A Study Across Three Areas.* London: Routledge and Kegan
Paul.
EADINGTON, WILLIAM R., editor. 1976. *Gambling and Society.* Springfield, Ill.:
C.C. Thomas.
FOWLER, FLOYD J., T. W. MARGIONE, and F. E. PRATTER. 1978. *Gambling Law
Enforcement in Major American Cities.* Washington, D.C.: U.S. Government
Printing Office.
HERMAN, ROBERT D., editor. 1967. *Gambling.* New York: Harper & Row.
HERMAN, ROBERT D. 1976. "Motivations to Gamble: The Model of Roger Caillois,"
in Eadington.
IGNATIN, GEORGE and ROBERT F. SMITH. 1976. "The Economics of Gambling" in
Eadington (1976).
JOHNSON, J. A. 1976. "An Economic Analysis of Lotteries," *Canadian Tax Journal*
24:639–651.
KUSYSZYN, I. 1972. "Gambling Addict vs. the Gambling Professional," *Interna-
tional Journal of Addictions* 7:387–393.
LONGSTREET, STEPHEN. 1977. *Win or Lose.* Indianapolis: Bobbs-Merrill.
MERCHANT, L. 1973. *The National Football Lottery.* New York: Holt, Reinhart,
and Winston.
MERCHANT, LARRY. 1973. "Bet, Book, and Handle," *Sports Illustrated* 39(10):67,
68.
PANKOFF, L. D. 1968. "Market Efficiency and Football Betting," *Journal of Busi-
ness* 41(2):203.
SCHUETZ, RICHARD J. 1976. "Sports, Technology, and Gambling," in Eadington.
SMITH, VERNON. 1971. "Economic Theory of Wager Markets," *Western Economic
Journal* 9.
TURNER, WALLACE. 1965. *Gamblers' Money: the New Force in American Life.*
Cambridge: The Riverside Press.

Chapter 11

LOAN SHARKING

Every Monday is payday for Boston City Hospital's nonprofessional employees. However, many of these employees will run out of cash before then and will need some money to finance their weekend plans. Fortunately for many of them, Jimmy makes his rounds of the hospital every Friday, offering to loan employees spending money for the weekend. He deals in straight cash with no questions asked and no papers to sign. He'll return again Monday afternoon after the paychecks arrive so that the employees can pay back their loans. Jimmy charges his borrowers a dollar for every five dollars he lends them. If a borrower can't pay the principal on payday, he need pay only the 20 percent interest charge every Monday until he is ready to pay off the principal.[1]

On a larger scale, an insurance company executive needed $10,000 in a hurry to replenish some company accounts that he had been using for personal expenses. Because of his need for speed and secrecy, he approached a loan shark organization for a $10,000 loan at a simple interest rate of 5 percent a week. Since this was his first loan, the organization made an arrangement so that it would automatically receive a large percentage of his commissions. However, when the executive developed repayment difficulties, the loan shark threatened to inform the insurance company of the entire situation. The borrower immediately raised the necessary money and paid off his loan to the organization.[2]

Loan shark organizations operate in all the major cities of the United States, where they are one of the main sources of revenue for large-scale criminal organizations. Lending agreements between borrowers and loan sharks have three principal characteristics: (1) a high rate of interest, generally 20 percent a week (1040 percent a year) for large loans; (2) a more or less explicit understanding that the borrower is pledging his physical well-being and that of his family as collateral for the loan; and (3) a belief by the borrower that the lender has connections with criminal organizations which would enable the lender to use force on the borrower in case of default.

In fact, the loan shark rarely has to resort to violence to collect his loan. The borrower's anxieties about violence, fostered by media stories about the operations of criminal organization, and the borrower's need for future loans encourage regular, amicable payments by the borrower. Most borrowers, including the hospital employees discussed earlier, consider their loan shark a good friend and valuable asset and would not even consider reporting his activities to the police. As a result, there is an impregnable wall of secrecy about the loan shark industry—a wall which few writers or law enforcement officials have been able to penetrate. The only close-to-thorough study of the loan shark industry was the 1968 Harvard Ph.D. dissertation of John Seidl—a report which was later circulated as a monograph by the Law Enforcement Assistance Administration of the Justice Department. Seidl's research forms the foundation for most of our discussion of the loan shark industry in this chapter.

Typical Transaction

As our examples indicate, there are actually two loan shark markets—one for small loans and one for large loans. The small loan market handles loans under $1,000, with $150 to $400 being typical amounts.[3] Interest charges on small loan shark loans are independent of the market interest rate. Neither do they depend on the law of supply and demand or on relationships between marginal revenue and marginal cost. Instead, they are traditional prices that were established in the 1920s and have not changed since. There are two basic methods of paying interest on small loan shark loans. In most such loans, the interest ("vigorish" or "juice") is 20 percent a week and is due every week. The principal of the loan can only be paid off in one lump sum, or occasionally in two lump sum payments. A less common arrangement is the "pay down" with an interest fee of 20 percent for a six- to ten-week period. In this case, the borrower repays the total (principal plus interest) in six to ten equal weekly installments. Curiously, one will find one or the other of these two methods of payment in any given metropolitan area—but never both.[4]

For large loans, there is usually no installment paying. The interest rate is usually 5 percent a week and the principal is repaid in one or more lump sum payments, depending on the agreement negotiated at the time of the initial loan. Generally, the loan shark is not anxious to have the principal repaid, preferring a long, steady stream of 5 percent interest payments.

Loan shark borrowers are typically people with an urgent need for money and the inability to borrow the desired funds through normal lending channels. This inability may stem from lack of necessary collateral, a questionable purpose for the loan, or impatience with the red tape in the traditional lending channels. For example, one loan shark who worked a waterfront neighborhood in South Philadelphia had 100 regular customers—most of whom were housewives who needed money for food or clothes, had little access to conventional loans, and enjoyed the convenience of negotiating a loan without leaving their homes.[5] Large loan borrowers fall into three main categories: owners of a small business in need of working capital, speculators or promoters in need of venture capital, or individuals—especially gamblers—in need of personal funds to pay for their spending habits or illegal activities.[6] Some industries, like the jewelry and garment industries, which are characterized by keen competition, seasonal sales, thin capital, and the need to pay their skilled laborers even in the off-season, are prime candidates for a loan shark's services.

Besides lending out funds himself, the loan shark sometimes acts as a middleman by arranging a conventional loan for a borrower from a cooperative lending officer in a bank. The loan shark would receive a lump sum payment from the borrower for this service.

It is not easy for a potential new borrower to find a loan shark. Usually he would arrange to contact one through a "steer," such as a doorman, cab driver, elevator operator, newsstand operator, or, most frequently, a bookie. If the borrower works in a place that has a large blue-collar or nonprofessional work force, he can often search for a loan shark among his fellow employees. Occasionally, loan sharks actually drum up customers by waiting at gambling places for someone with an unusually large loss, or at a traditional lending institution for someone who has just had a loan application refused. At some banks, loan officers who direct unsuccessful loan applicants to a nearby loan shark could expect a substantial kickback as a result of the contact.[7]

For a first loan, a borrower generally must have a guarantor who would guarantee repayment of the principal. Once he has successfully negotiated and repaid a loan, he will not need a guarantor for future loans.

The loan transaction is a quick and simple process. The loan shark hands the borrower the principal of the loan in cash; they discuss the payback arrangement; they shake hands and go their own ways. No paper work, no credit references, no collateral but the physical well-being of the borrower and his family. Although this collateral agreement is rarely stated so explicitly, there is never any misunderstanding about it in the borrower-lender agreement.[8]

Despite the implicit tensions in this collateral agreement, the vast majority of loan shark transactions run smoothly. When the loan shark comes around to collect a week later, the borrower either pays back his principal plus interest or pays for one week's interest and carries the principal for another week. If he misses an interest payment, he will receive a reminder from his loan shark and a penalty will be added to his principal and/or interest. If he continues to miss, he will receive some harassment from his lender, possibly all-night phone calls. Further delinquency will bring implicit and later explicit threats. As a last resort, especially if he is not even trying to meet his payments, he may encounter the loan shark's enforcer and suffer a possibly severe or debilitating injury.

Very few loan shark transactions reach this last violent stage, for the lender and the borrower both have strong incentives to avoid violence.[9-11] From the loan shark's point of view, such violence can bring police attention to an occupation that thrives on secrecy, can discourage future borrowing, and can make repayment from the delinquent borrower even less likely. From the borrower's point of view, there are often other desperate possibilities which he can use to escape a beating. For example, he can try to raise money by some illegal means like robbery or embezzlement; or if he owns a small business, he can give his loan shark part or full ownership in the business. (See Salerno[12] for examples.) On rare occasions, in cases of disputes or a true inability to pay, the organization which backs the loan shark can arrange a "sit down" and work out an agreement to let the borrower off the hook. In no case would the compromise payment be less than the original principal and interest.[13]

The Loan Shark Industry

The ultimate source of the funds that are lent in loan shark transactions are the cash profits of large-scale criminal organizations.[14-16]

The head of the organization is the one ultimately responsible for supplying the money and directing the operations. He distributes several million dollars a year to his chief lieutenants according to their past successes and the strength of the market they cover, charging them interest of 1 percent a week. These lieutenants, who make up the second echelon of the loan shark industry, loan this money to the loan sharks on the street at an interest of 1½–2½ percent a week.[17–19] These loan sharks then loan the money to the industry's customers at rates between 5 and 20 percent a week, as described in the previous section. In the case of large loans—in the $100,000 to $1 million range—the syndicate's lieutenants may deal directly with the borrower.

In addition to these money handlers, a loan shark organization will generally employ an attorney, some accountants, and two or three enforcers.[20] (Kaplan and Matteis describe a loan shark operation in which the loan shark employed 19 runners to make the actual contact with borrowers. These runners held other full-time jobs and worked for the loan shark just two to three hours per week. This loan shark also employed five full-time, supervising bookkeepers at a straight salary of $200 a week each. Each bookkeeper kept records for three or four runners.) At one time, five recognized criminal organizations in New York City had 121 members engaged in loan sharking.[21] Every major urban area appears to have at least one loan shark organization, although such organizations appear to be non-existent outside the major cities.[22]

The vertical nature of the loan shark organization removes the loan shark on the street from the day-to-day operations of the criminal organization and thus insulates the top echelons of the organization from police and public scrutiny. The arrest of a loan shark will generally shed no light on the loan shark organization.[23] Another reason that law enforcement agencies know so little about loan shark organizations is the fact that borrowers from these organizations rarely complain to the police. Generally borrowers find their loan shark dealings to be friendly and convenient. But even if they do not, they will keep quiet because of fear of retribution, sympathy for the syndicate, or their own involvement in illegal activities.[24, 25]

In his dissertation, Seidl describes the organizational framework of the loan shark industries in New York, Detroit, Philadelphia, Cleveland, Chicago, and Boston.[26] New York City's industry is controlled by the city's five oligopolist criminal organizations. Through collusion and "conscious parallelism," these oligopolists set prices and establish the rules of competition for all criminal organizations in the area. They have either taken over or driven out of business any new independent criminal entrepreneurs. Naturally these oligopolists establish and enforce the operational rules for the loan shark industry, including the rules of competition. Among these rules are the prohibition of the indiscriminate use of violence, the ban on a loan shark dealing with another loan shark's customers, and the establishment of a fairly uniform schedule of interest rates.

A criminal cartel dominates Detroit's underworld and loan shark industry.[27] A tightly organized and controlled central organization allocates markets and settles disputes among smaller criminal organizations throughout the city. The few criminal organizations in Detroit that are not part of the cartel organization must pay an extortionate tax to the cartel for the right to operate. The cartel dictates and enforces the operational rules of Detroit's loan shark industry—rules which are similar to those of other urban underworlds, including allocation of territories, prohibition of competition, and standardization of interest schedules. Unlike the New York loan shark industry, the cartel in Detroit closely supervises the individual loan shark organizations and demands that only cartel money be used in loan shark transactions.

In a similar manner, large-scale criminal organizations provide funds and control the operations of loan shark operations in urban areas throughout the United States. In some cities, like Philadelphia and Cleveland, their control is not as tight as it is in New York and Detroit. In all the cities studied, the usury laws and banking practices which make high-risk lending impossible in legitimate loan operations lead to the establishment of a black market for such loans and thus indirectly provide protection from legitimate competition for the organizations that are willing to supply high-risk loans illegally. With the usury laws providing protection from the upper-world competition, the large-scale criminal organizations collude among themselves to limit underworld competition and thus allow the loan shark industry to collect monopoly rents from their enterprise. Similar criminal monopolies were created when passage of the Eighteenth Amendment brought about the establishment of a black market in the sale and distribution of alcoholic beverages.

Benefits and Costs to Borrowers

In the next section, we will use demand-side figures to estimate the size of the loan shark industry. First, we need to examine the factors which create a demand for loan shark funds.

The basic cause for the existence and growth of the loan shark market is the nonavailability in the legitimate business world of the funds and services that loan sharks provide. The key factors in this nonavailability are the usury laws present in many states and the traditional practices of legitimate lending institutions.

Most states have usury laws which prescribe maximum interest rates for loans made within the state. These usury laws are one of our oldest legal traditions. Their proponents either claim that high interest rates are against divine and natural laws, quoting Aristotle and the Old and New Testaments to support these claims, or they contend that such laws are necessary because of the unequal bargaining power between borrower and lender in loan transactions. One effect of usury laws is the limitation of the risk-taking ability of lending institutions, especially during periods of tight money. Individuals or firms that require high-risk loans are forced to look for such loans in the black market which develops in response to the usury laws.

The second key factor underlying existence of the loan shark industry is the operational procedure of legitimate lending institutions in their loan transactions. First of all, such lending procedures are rather formal, time-consuming, and involved, in comparison to loan shark lending services. They simply do not provide the secrecy, informality, speed, convenience, and availability that attract many borrowers to the loan shark market.[28] Secondly, traditional lending institutions rarely make available high-risk credit to individuals and firms in need of such funds. This practice is due in part to the conservative lending policies of these institutions, since the high risk entails a higher probability of default, or at least a more expensive collection process. This practice is further supported by the existence of usury laws and by the inability of commercial lenders to accept a borrower's body as collateral in loan agreements.

As a result, there are three circumstances under which a rational borrower may turn to the loan shark market to secure necessary funds:

1. The borrower may not have the collateral to support his application for a loan;

2. The loan requested may be a high-risk loan so that restrictions on interest rates and other banking customs may lead legitimate lending institutions to deny such a loan application, even if proper collateral is present;
3. The borrower may require a degree of speed, secrecy, or convenience unavailable among the legitimate options he is considering.

In the latter case, he may need the loan for purposes unacceptable to conventional institutions; for example, to pay off gambling debts, or to cover up embezzlements of company funds, or to continue dealing drugs despite a recent "bust."[29]

The above discussion describes the possible benefits to the customer in the loan shark industry. As indicated earlier, most loan shark loans are amicable transactions. Loan sharking is one crime that does not produce a distinct class of irate victims. A loan shark customer who had once borrowed $200 from his loan shark, Jimmy, in a transaction for which Jimmy drove across town during a midnight snowstorm, exclaimed to Seidl, "You just don't understand what a good friend Jimmy was."[30]

Of course, not every loan shark transaction runs so smoothly. Many borrowers must be affected by some fear and anxiety when they realize the risk of victimization should they be unable to continue their interest payments. This anxiety can affect their social well-being and their economic productivity. It can undermine family morale, welfare, and solidarity. The higher the possibility of default, the greater the emotional stress on the borrower and his family. This stress can lead to restrictions on the individual's freedom of movement as he tries to avoid his loan shark. It can lead to an impaired mental and physical capability and even to suicide. In efforts to avoid deliquency and to dampen his anxiety, a borrower in risk of default may turn to crime to raise the needed interest payments. Such crimes may include armed robbery (see Salerno, p. 61, for examples), embezzlement, cargo pilferage, stock fraud, prostitution, or assistance to gambling or burglary rings.[31] When the owner of a small business defaults on his loan, he may decide to give up all or part of the ownership of his business or its capital as payment on his loan. Criminal organizations have used such opportunities to acquire interests in legitimate businesses and thus to extend their influence and to obtain a means for "laundering" money obtained through illegal activities.

In his transactions in the black market in loans, the borrower is forced to pay a much higher price for his loan because of the monopoly status given to the loan shark industry by usury laws. Furthermore, he surrenders the possibility of using bankruptcy proceedings to help him keep his head above water when his debt load becomes greater than the combined value of his assets.

Extent and Trends

The secrecy that shrouds the loan sharking industry makes accurate estimates or even reasonable guesses of the size of this industry impossible to determine. A few writers have made some "off the cuff" estimates. The *Columbia Journal of Law and Social Problems* suggested that loan sharking may be the largest source of revenue for organized crime, and cited estimates from $350 million to $1 billion for its GNP in 1968.[32] Kaplan and Matteis suggested that "a conservative estimate would put the loan shark business in the United States in the $1 to $2 billion class."[33] The difficulty in estimating the size of the loan shark industry can be illustrated by the fact that in the 1979 Internal Revenue Service report on unreported income a guess was not hazarded as to the size of the industry.[34]

Seidl tried to fathom the size of the industry "by relating the availability of upperworld credit to actual and potential upperworld borrowers."[35] At least during the 1960s, the industry appears to have expanded rapidly. If one assumes that the loan shark industry is a component of the total financial institutional structure of our economy, and that its growth is analogous to other financial institutions in the economy, then the rapid growth of the loan shark industry can be estimated from the large growth in consumer credit issued by all types of financial institutions, the large growth of family debt service, the increasing share of family income that is used to service this debt, and the tremendous growth in bankruptcy filings in the United States.

Seidl used consumer finance company loan data to gauge the size of the small-loan market. Under the assumptions that the consumer finance industry is the small-loan lender of last resort, that the distribution of the requested amounts for rejected borrowers was similar to the distribution for accepted borrowers, and that there was only one loan per customer, Seidl estimated that consumer finance companies turned down 12 million borrowers requesting $4.1 to $4.5 billion dollars in loans in the late 1950s. To estimate the small-loan loan shark market in the late fifties, one need only make an assumption about what percentage of these rejected borrowers turned to loan sharks. If 50 percent did, then a reasonable estimate of the small-loan loan shark market is $2 to $2.2 billion in the late fifties. If 10 percent did, then the estimate becomes $400 to $450 million.

Secondly, Seidl estimated the demand in the late 1950s for large loans in the loan shark industry by small businesses—businesses with assets under $5 million. Using Federal Reserve data, he estimated that there were at most 5,440,600 small businesses at the time, and that 1,721,140 of these requested a loan from legitimate lenders, with the average loan being $10,000 per year. The question is: How many of these other 3.72 million small businesses turned to loan sharks to fulfill their borrowing needs? Surely, a large percentage of them did not need any kind of loan. Assuming an average loan of $10,000 and one loan per small business borrower per year, one can estimate that 743,892 small businesses borrowed $7.4 billion from the loan shark industry if 20 percent of this potential market turned to loan sharks. If only 1 percent turned to loan sharks, then 37,815 small businesses borrowed $372 million from loan sharks in the late 1950s.

To put these figures together to estimate the value-added of the loan shark industry—and Seidl did not push his estimates beyond this point—we will make the following reasonable, but unsubstantiated, assumptions: (1) that 10 to 50 percent of those who were turned down by consumer credit companies turned to loan sharks for loans; (2) that these borrowers paid the usual 20 percent a week interest and retained the principal from one to two weeks; (3) that 1 to 20 percent of those small businesses that did not borrow from legitimate lending institutions went to loan sharks; (4) that their average loan was $10,000; (5) that they paid 5 percent a week interest on their loans; and (6) that they paid off their loan in two to four weeks. The corresponding calculations are summarized in Tables 11-1 and 11-2.

Combining the smallest figures in Tables 11-1 and 11-2, we obtain a lower bound of $130 million. Combining the largest figures, we obtain $2.32 billion. Putting these together and taking into consideration the omission of large loans from loan sharks to individuals for *personal expenses*, we estimate that the national

Table 11-1 Estimates of Small-Loan Loan Shark Market

Percentage of individuals turned away by consumer credit companies that used loan sharks	10%	50%
Total loan shark loan	$.425 billion	$2.1 billion
One week's interest at 20% a week	$.09 billion	$.42 billion
Two weeks' interest at 20% a week	$.17 billion	$.84 billion

Table 11-2 Estimates of Small Business Loan Shark Market

Percentage of small businesses not obtaining a legitimate loan that obtained a loan shark loan	1%	20%
Total loan shark loan	$.372 billion	$7.4 billion
Interest for 2 weeks at 5% a week	$.037 billion	$.74 billion
Interest for 4 weeks at 5% a week	$.074 billion	$1.48 billion

income of the loan shark industry was between $200 million and $3 billion dollars in 1960—a range which is consistent with the estimates quoted at the beginning of this section.

We would like to make the corresponding estimates for the mid-1970s. The ideal way to update these estimates would be to rederive them, using more recent data. Unfortunately, updated data does not exist uniformly across all the indicators that we need to measure. We do know that total consumer credit continued to rise sharply between 1960 and the mid-1970s—with the average annual increase hovering around 9 percent. By comparison, the consumer price index increased an average of 3 percent a year during this period. In other words, from 1960 to 1973 the total consumer credit outstanding more than tripled, while the consumer price index rose 50 percent. On the other hand, toward the end of this period (especially during the 1970s) there was a significant loosening of credit restrictions—including the ready availability of credit cards and the establishment of revolving credit plans and checking account over-draft plans at legitimate lending institutions. The federal government also stepped in to make small business loans easier to obtain. These new legitimate credit options weakened some of the advantages of loan shark loans over bank loans. Taking these changes into consideration, we will update our lower estimate of the national income of the loan shark industry by using the 50 percent increase in the consumer price index between 1960 and 1973, and we will update our higher estimate by using the 216 percent increase in the amount of outstanding consumer credit between 1960 and 1969. These calculations lead to an estimated national income of between $300 million and $6.5 billion for the loan shark industry in the mid-1970s. The wide range in this estimate is due, of course, to the effective shroud of secrecy which covers the loan shark industry.

Benefits and Costs to Loan Sharks

We have already examined the benefits and costs which accrued to borrowers in the loan shark market. In this section, we will discuss the benefits and costs to the lenders.

The fact that the interest rates in the loan shark market have not changed from the traditional rates charged fifty years ago is an indication that the profit margins are comfortably high in the industry. As indicated earlier, these high profit margins result from the monopoly status given the loan shark industry by the black market status of high-risk loans. These profit margins are further increased because they escape state and federal taxation. This wealth, combined with the ability to help people out of pressing financial situations, allows the loan shark a measure of high social prestige and status in his community.

As a businessman in the lending industry, the loan shark is subject to some costs that are part of his job. These include the economic rent for the borrowed capital which he reloans to his customers, the wages he must pay his underworld and "upperworld" employees, and the risk that he may have repayment difficulties, either on the money he has borrowed from the criminal organization or on the money he has lent to his customers.

The loan shark also has some additional costs because of the illegal nature of his activity. In his daily operations, he may violate three different laws: the state usury laws which limit the interest rate that can be charged, the state banking laws which require the licensing of regular lending activities, and, finally, state and federal antiextortion laws which explicitly prohibit the use of force or even threats of force. Because of these laws, the loan shark faces a risk of arrest, prosecution, fine, and imprisonment. However, these risks are fairly low for loan sharking in comparison with other crimes. For one thing, violation of usury laws is a simple misdemeanor in most states. Secondly, the effective secrecy around the loan shark industry and the unwillingness of loan shark customers to talk about their borrowings make the risk of arrest very low indeed, and the risk of a successful prosecution even lower. To further reduce these risks, however, a loan shark may find it necessary to bribe police officers in his community—a cost which occurs frequently to loan sharks who work in the open among the employees of large firms or in large office buildings.

Benefits and Costs to Society

The existence of the loan shark industry produces both benefits and costs to society as a whole. In measuring the appropriateness of any governmental policy toward the loan shark industry, society needs to weigh and compare the benefits and costs involved.

One obvious benefit to society comes from the aggregation of the satisfaction which individual loan shark borrowers experience in their transactions with the industry, especially in their ability to obtain high-risk loans with a remarkable degree of secrecy, speed, and convenience. The loan shark industry is reasonably successful as a high-risk lending system that is responsive to borrowers with legitimate needs for high-risk loans. Seidl concluded from his interviews with borrowers and lenders that most of the funds borrowed from the loan shark industry are used for perfectly legitimate transactions.[36]

The loan shark industry also provides employment opportunities for a large number of people—many of whom may be listed as "unemployed" on official employment records. Furthermore, employment as a loan shark can be an avenue for upward social mobility and can result in an income redistribution that benefits a number of disadvantaged low-income urban dwellers.[37] The loan shark industry may also be a stabilizing force in the underworld, a fact which may reduce the need for violence there.[38]

On the cost side, the loan shark industry's monopoly profits provide one of the basic economic incentives for the maintenance of large-scale criminal organizations. Seidl comments:[39]

We do not like nor should we tolerate these types of organizations. They pose a threat to local pluralism; they evade large tax bills; they create incentives which result in increased levels of predatory crime; and they undermine social morale and public morality through their continual violation of the law. These are not evils of high-risk lending per se, but only of high-risk lending which can be controlled by large-scale criminal organizations.

In addition to receiving direct financial aid from loan sharking, criminal organizations have used loan sharking to infiltrate legitimate businesses and then use these businesses to launder their illegal profits into aboveboard funds.

Another major social cost of loan sharking comes from aggregating the individual borrowers' costs, especially the anxiety of the collateral agreement and its consequences. Society should not tolerate a lending system which relies on the threat of violence. This continuing extortion can lead to impaired family morale, welfare, and solidarity, the possibility of increased welfare expenditures, an increase in the crime rate as borrowers turn to crime to repay their debts, and the takeover of legitimate businesses by underworld interests.

The corruption which loan sharking breeds is another social cost of the industry. Many loan shark operations flourish in the open—a fact which could not occur without the knowledge and indifferent acquiescence of some local officials.[40] (See Endnote 11, p. 101, for examples of loan-shark-related police corruptions, and Endnote 7 for examples of corruption of bank officials as a result of loan sharking.) Furthermore, the very existence of loan sharking in some communities or factories can undermine the public's confidence in the effectiveness of their police departments. Loan shark borrowers contribute to this undermining of support for the law by their willing participation in an illegal activity.

Finally, because of the loan shark industry and the laws which create this industry, the government undergoes the costs which all illegal activities entail. These include the usual crime fighting costs by police, judicial, and correctional sectors in the law enforcement establishment. Loan sharking appears to take up a smaller percentage of these costs than most other illegal activities. Furthermore, because loan sharking is against the law, its profits will usually not be reported on state and federal income tax forms. As our earlier estimates indicate, the government may be losing over a billion dollars a year in tax revenues. In addition, its ability to avoid taxation gives the loan shark industry an unfair advantage over legitimate lenders in areas where there may be some competition between the two.

Endnotes

1. Seidl, John M. 1969. *Upon the Hip: A Study of the Criminal Loan Shark Industry*. Washington, D.C.: Law Enforcement Assistance Administration. U.S. Department of Justice, pp. 101–102.
2. *Ibid.*, p. 112.
3. *Ibid.*, p. 70.
4. *Ibid.*, p. 41.
5. *Ibid.*, p. 101.
6. Seidl, John M. 1970. "Let's Compete with Loan Sharks," *Harvard Business Review* 48:71.
7. Miller, Richard B. 1966. "The Impingement of Loan-Sharking on the Banking Industry," *Banker's Magazine* (Winter), p. 86.
8. Seidl, *Upon the Hip*, p. 50.
9. Seidl, *Upon the Hip*, p. 53.
10. Kaplan, Lawrence J., and Salvatore Matteis. 1968. "The Economics of Loansharking," *American Journal of Law and Sociology* 27:244.
11. "Loan Sharking: The Untouched Domain of Organized Crime," *Columbia Journal of Law and Social Problems* 5:96, 1969.
12. Salerno, Ralph F. 1971. "Banking and Organized Crime," *Banker's Magazine* 154 (Spring):59–63.
13. *Columbia Journal*, "Loan Sharking," p. 96.
14. Seidl, *Upon the Hip*, p. 32.
15. *Columbia Journal*, p. 94.
16. Kaplan and Matteis, p. 246.
17. Seidl, *Upon the Hip*, p. 39.
18. *Columbia Journal*, p. 94.
19. Kaplan and Matteis, p. 245.
20. Seidl, *Upon the Hip*, p. 101.
21. Kaplan and Matteis, "Economics of Loansharking," pp. 243–245.
22. Seidl, *Upon the Hip*, pp. 98–100.
23. *Columbia Journal*, "Loan-Sharking," p. 101.
24. Seidl, *Upon the Hip*, 102.
25. *Columbia Journal*, "Loan-Sharking," p. 101.
26. Seidl, *Upon the Hip*, pp. 62–86.
27. *Ibid.*, p. 68.
28. *Ibid.*, p. 127.
29. Goldman, Albert, 1979. *Grass Roots: Marihuana in America Today*. New York: Harper and Row, p. 20.
30. Seidl, "Let's Compete with Loan Sharks," p. 69.
31. *Columbia Journal*, "Loan-Sharking," p. 79.
32. *Ibid.*, p. 92.
33. Kaplan and Matteis, "Economics of Loansharking," p. 246.
34. U.S. Department of the Treasury, Internal Revenue Service. 1979. *Estimates of Income Unreported on Individual Income Tax Returns*. Washington: U.S. Government Printing Office, p. 134.
35. Seidl, *Upon the Hip*, pp. 138–157.

36. *Ibid.*, p. 95.
37. *Ibid.*, p. 167.
38. *Ibid.*, p. 171.
39. *Ibid.*, pp. 179–180.
40. *Columbia Journal*, "Loan-Sharking," p. 108.

Additional References

BEQUAI, AUGUST. 1978. *White Collar Crime: A Twentieth Century Crisis.* Lexington, Mass.: Lexington Books.

New York State. Temporary State Commission of Investigation. 1965. *An Investigation of the Loan-Shark Racket: A Report.*

President's Commission on Law Enforcement and Administration of Justice. 1969. *Task Force Report: Crime and Its Impact—An Assessment.* Washington: U.S. Government Printing Office.

SEIDL, JOHN M. 1978. "Loan Sharking," in Leonard Savitz and Norman Johnson, eds. *Crime in Society.* New York: Wiley (1978).

SEIDL, JOHN M. 1969. *Upon the Hip: A Study of the Criminal Loan Shark Industry.* Washington, D.C.: Law Enforcement Assistance Administration, U.S. Department of Justice. See pp. 204–239 for an extensive bibliography.

U.S. CONGRESS. Senate. Committee on Small Business. Impact of Crime on Small Business—1968. *Hearings 90th Congress. May 14–16, 1968.* Washington: U.S. Government Printing Office.

Chapter 12

PROSTITUTION

The existence of persons who do not have access to sexual gratification either through marriage or through mutual consent, combined with the existence of persons willing to trade sexual access for economic gain, leads to the situation where sexual access becomes explicitly an economic good. Yet, the "oldest profession" is one business enterprise that has rarely been studied from an economic viewpoint.[1]

As a working definition, we define a prostitute as any person who grants nonmarital sexual access to a number of clients by mutual agreement, and without emotional ties, for remuneration which provides part or all of that person's livelihood. This definition is a composite of the many operational definitions proposed in the literature on prostitution, varying from Lemert's characterization of it by barter, promiscuity, and emotional indifference[2] to Jennifer James's formulation of it as "any sexual exchange where reward is neither sexual nor affectional."[3] Although male and even transvestite prostitution are thriving phenomena throughout the country, we will restrict our attention in this chapter to female prostitution since it still is the most prominent form of prostitution.

Female prostitution is by no means a homogeneous occupation. One convenient way to classify prostitutes is by their occupational milieu—from streetwalkers who overtly solicit customers on the streets to call girls who work out of their apartments, soliciting business by telephone or by advertisements in sex-oriented publications. Most prostitutes ply their trade neither on the street nor in residential establishments. (This is based on a conversation with Priscilla Alexander of C.O.Y.O.T.E. See page 253.) These include house or brothel prostitutes who spend their working hours in houses specifically set up for prostitution, bar prostitutes, hotel prostitutes, and massage parlor prostitutes. Of course, there is some overlap in these categories. For example, streetwalkers or even call girls may enter a bar or hotel to drum up business. Another large category of prostitutes are the barterers who exchange sexual service for professional or other services or for material goods. (See especially Goldstein[4] and Boyer and James.[5]) Two important examples of barterers are drug addicts, who trade sexual services for expensive drugs such as heroin, and young runaways, who permit sexual access in exchange for food or a place to live.

Goldstein, in his study of the relationships between prostitution and drug use, divided the above categories into two large groups which he labeled "low class" and "high class."[6] In his sample of 43 prostitutes, he placed streetwalkers and barterers in the low class and call girls and massage parlor prostitutes in the high class. He found that most of the low class prostitutes were black, did not finish high school, and had previously worked at a blue-collar or clerical job for about $108 a week. On the other hand, he found that the high class prostitutes in his study were all white and that most had attended college and previously held white-collar, waitress, or entertainment jobs at an average weekly salary of $143. The low class prostitutes had a mean age of 26 and a mean age of first prostitution of 19. The high class prostitutes had a mean age of 28 and a mean first age of prostitution of 22.[7] (The mean age of 27 for the whole sample coincides with the mean age of the 83 prostitutes in Taylor's study of prostitution in Detroit in the thirties.[8])

Structure of the Industry

Unlike the highly structured heroin distribution industry, the prostitution industry is composed almost entirely of small, autonomous units with very little economic interaction between them. A typical unit is made up of either (1) a boss or manager (for example, pimp, brothel madam, massage parlor manager) and one or more prostitutes, working under the manager's direction, or (2) a single prostitute with only weak economic ties to others in the industry (for referrals or companionship, for example). There are, of course, exceptions to this general description. Verlarde describes a massage parlor where the employees formed a "sisterhood" to operate the parlor. The masseuses not only shared the management of the parlor but also treated each other as equals and supported each other in the stresses of their occupation.[9] It is reasonable to assume that such collectives also exist among other types of prostitutes.

The most unusual role in this whole framework is that of the pimp. In some cases, young girls considering prostitution seek out male partners or protectors and consider them an essential part of the life. In other cases, the pimp himself may convince the girl that prostitution would be a profitable occupation under his direction. The pimp provides the prostitute with psychological sustenance, stature, and, sometimes, love, and protects her from her clients and her competitors. He also serves as the major provider and decision maker, the price setter, and the controller of funds. In return, the prostitute promises to obey the "racket's 'four rules' governing her behavior toward her 'old man': no talking back, no lying, no holding back (money), and no 'chipping' (dating anyone else)."[10]

The pimp-prostitute relationship can range from romantic to impersonal; business-like to shockingly brutal.[5, 10–43] The major reference on pimps is Milner and Milner.[14] The prostitute will either give her pimp a flat percentage of her gross or she will give it all to him in return for his providing her with a comfortable life style from the proceeds. Despite the often exploitative nature of this relationship, a streetwalker will find it difficult to have protection and emotional stability without her relationship with her pimp:[15]

> *Prostitutes rely on pimps even more for psychological sustenance than they do for economic needs. The pimp fills an emotional void. In almost all cases, the relationship between a woman and her pimp is a purely voluntary one.*

The massage parlor manager is usually an entirely different kind of manager in the prostitution industry. Operating in a more formal, businesslike setting, his tasks are to hire his masseuses, if necessary to encourage his novice employees to perform sexual acts in addition to their straight massages, to collect the clients' fees, to keep the books, and to give the masseuse her 40 percent commission— almost a typical employer-employee relationship. Before 1970 there were relatively few massage parlors—most of them legitimate. Between 1970 and 1975 there was a quick surge in the number of massage parlors which specialized in sexual stimulation and prostitution. In one western metropolitan area with a population of one million, the number of massage parlors jumped from 3 to 150 between 1972 and 1976—at least 147 of which are houses of prostitution.[16] In another western city of 100,000, the number of massage parlors jumped from 1 to 22 between 1971 and 1975—at least 20 of these are houses of prostitution.[9, 17] Inspector Richard Dillon, the head of New York City's vice squad, asserts that 99 percent of today's massage parlors are houses of prostitution.[18]

If there is any link between prostitution and organized crime, it would be through the absentee ownership of chains of massage parlors by underworld figures.

Between the intensity of the pimp-prostitute relationship and the formalness of the massage parlor manager-masseuse relationship lies the moderately personal relationship between a brothel house madam and her employees. Like the massage parlor manager, the madam runs a complex business organization: hiring and firing employees, keeping records, and paying salaries. Unlike the massage parlor manager, she does not have a legitimate front to work with, so she must play a more personal role in attracting customers and prostitutes, being a hostess to their meetings, and effecting satisfactory working conditions with the police. Often, a madam will have to spend much of her work time training novice prostitutes and carefully supervising their first encounters. Heyl describes the teaching methods of a Midwestern madam who even used tapes to teach her novices such topics as: physical skills and strategies, verbal skills or "hustling," and prostitution world values.[10]

A typical brothel in the 1970s employed two to four prostitutes at any given time.[10, 19, 20] The madam kept 50 percent of the client's payments. The remaining 50 percent went to the prostitute, who would use part (4 percent) of her share to pay for her physician's exam and another part (16 percent) to pay for her room and board at the brothel if she lived there. The rest she would have to divide with her pimp, if she had one. (Before 1970, at least 90 percent of brothel prostitutes had pimps. Even the madam would often share her percentage with a pimp who would help supply her with prostitutes and aid her communication with her employees' pimps.)[10]

Other managers in the prostitution world are the managers of bars and hotels which offer the services of prostitutes. These managers pay the women who work for them a 40 to 50 percent commission. Besides these employers, the prostitutes, and their clients, there are a number of others who play an economic role in the prostitution business—the taxicab drivers and bellboys who refer prostitutes to potential customers for a commission, and the attendants who take care of services such as the linens or drinks in brothels or massage parlors.

Prices for the services of a prostitute are usually based on brothel prices. Streetwalkers charge roughly the same rate as house prostitutes and massage parlor prostitutes but earn a higher profit (before the pimp takes his cut) because they don't have to surrender 50 percent of the gross as the others do. However, streetwalkers must work a lot harder to drum up business. Their counterparts in brothels need only wait for their customers to come to them, and as a result may service twice as many customers a day.

It is reasonable to assume that the average price for the services of a streetwalker, or house prostitute, was $20 to $25 in 1974–1975. This figure is an average derived from several sources. Gray claims that in 1972 the price per trick ranged from $15 to $50, with many of the younger girls reporting an average of $25 per trick, with four to eight tricks a night.[21] Vorenberg and Vorenberg state that the standard rate in the legal brothels in Nevada is "about a dollar a minute; fifteen minutes minimum," adding that most customers pay "a lot more than fifteen dollars."[22] Heyl claimed that in 1974 "the minimum rate is $25."[23] Winick and Kinsie estimated an average fee per contact of $10 in 1970[24]—an amount that would be about $14 in 1975 dollars. It is also reasonable to assume that a streetwalker can turn three to four tricks on a typical night while a house prostitute can turn six to eight a night. Winick and Kinsie estimate that "the average full-time prostitute . . . has three clients daily."[25] As noted above, Gray reported that the younger streetwalkers she interviewed turned four to eight tricks a night.[26] Heyl states that on a good night a brothel prostitute "may turn eight to twelve tricks a night."[27] However, her earlier estimate that there were a total of 15 customers on any average night at a brothel implies that five to eight would be a more typical average day's work for a typical house prostitute.[28] Taylor reported that streetwalkers in Detroit averaged four customers a day in the thirties.[29]

Assuming that a prostitute works six days a week 50 weeks a year, and that a house prostitute splits her earnings 50-50 with her madam, we estimate that the average professional streetwalker and brothel prostitute earned from $18,000 to $30,000 a year in 1975. This figure compares well with the claim by C.O.Y.O.T.E.* (Call Off Your Old Tired Ethics) that the average streetwalker and house prostitute grosses from $20,000 to $25,000 a year. The figure is a bit below Sheehy's estimate of $50,000 for the average house prostitute

---

* C.O.Y.O.T.E. was formed on Mother's Day, 1973, by Margo St. James. Its principal goals are legal assistance for prostitutes and public education directed toward the eventual removal of all prostitution laws. Most researchers on prostitution consider C.O.Y.O.T.E. a valuable and reliable source of information on the industry.

and $70,000 for the average streetwalker in New York City.[30] It is close to the average of $36,000 established by a careful survey of sixty streetwalkers in San Francisco in 1977.[31] Using the $18,000 to $30,000 a year figures, a madam whose brothel services 15 customers a night would gross $45,000 to $56,250.

Massage parlor prostitutes have a slightly different scale. They are paid an hourly wage of $2 to $3 and charge $5 to $15 for a straight massage. Extras—from manual stimulation to intercourse—add $10 to $30 to each session. Thus a masseuse who sees five to six clients a day in an eight-hour day and earns a 40 percent commission will receive $14,000 to $40,000 a year. Only half of this amount will arise from straight massages. Her work will bring a yearly revenue of $22,500 to $81,000 to her parlor, with $15,000 to $54,000 of this coming from sexual services.*

Call girls, operating out of their apartments or meeting their clients at a place selected by mutual consent, make up the highest echelon in the world of prostitution. They spend more time with their customers—sometimes entire evenings—and try to develop a pleasant and more lasting relationship with a group of regular clients. Although call girls usually work alone, they require a network of call girl friends from whom they receive introductions to new clients and with whom they may share their own customers, either when the call girl is too busy or when her customer wants variety or the services of more than one girl for an evening's activity. Call girls may have pimps, but undoubtedly a smaller percentage of call girls than of streetwalkers have pimps.

A call girl charges a client $50 to $100 for a standard visit. This fee could be doubled when special services or a longer encounter are required.[32–35] Generally a call girl deals with one to three customers a night. Under the assumption that a call girl sees two customers a night, receives $75 per customer, and works six nights a week, 50 weeks a year, we are led to an average income of $45,000 for a call girl. This figure is supported by Greenwald's claim that the average call girl grossed $30,000 a year in the late sixties,[32] by Winick and Kinsie's statement that a call girl could gross as much as $40,000 in

---

* The sources for these estimates are the discussions about rates in Endnotes 16, 9, and 17. Although these authors use slightly different accounting methods, their estimates of the average massage parlor prostitute's salary are very close to ours: $12,000 to $36,000 per year (Rasmussen and Kuhn, p. 804) or up to $128 a day (Verlarde, p. 255).

Table 12-1 Summary of Revenue and Earnings Estimates, by Type of Prostitute

Type of Prostitute	Average Fee/Client	Average Clients/Day	Revenue Earned for Prostitution Industry	Yearly Income
Streetwalker	$20–$25	3–4	$18,000–$30,000	$18,000–$30,000
House prostitutes	$20–$25	6–8	$36,000–$60,000	$18,000–$30,000
Massage parlor prostitutes		5–6		
Legitimate services	$5–$15		$7,500–$27,000	$7,000–$20,000
Illegal services	$10–$30		$15,000–$54,000	$7,000–$20,000
Call girls	$50–$100	1–3	$45,000	$45,000
Bar prostitutes	$20–$25	4–6	$27,000–$45,000	$15,000–$27,000
Hotel prostitutes	$20–$25	4–6	$27,000–$45,000	$15,000–$27,000

1970,[35] and by Rosenblum's finding that the most established call girls in the group she studied earned about $48,000 a year.[36] (The novice in Rosenblum's group only earned $16,000 in her first year.) Sheehy estimated an annual income of $30,000 to $50,000 for an average New York City call girl.[37]

Bar and hotel prostitutes have not been discussed in the literature to the same degree that the other types of prostitutes have. It is reasonable to assume that their annual revenues lie somewhere between those of a streetwalker and those of a house prostitute. Table 12-1 summarizes the revenue and earning estimates that we have made in this section.

Just as there are many different kinds of prostitutes, there are surprising variations within each type, including different income patterns. In general, the four factors that determine the earnings potential within each type are beauty, intelligence, hustle, and the cost of living in the woman's working area.

Size and National Income of the Prostitution Industry

Having estimated the average yearly earnings of each type of prostitute, we need only to know the number of prostitutes in each type and the amounts of their occupation-related expenses to estimate the national income of the prostitution industry. Unfortunately there are no reliable estimates of either of these components.

A number of writers have made size estimates without indicating how they arrived at their figures or breaking down the estimates into types. Sheehy states, "Using the most current figures available, there are an estimated 200,000 to 250,000 prostitutes in the United States today. Taking the lower estimate, at only six contacts a day, and at the bottom price of $20 per 'trick,' the millions of clients of prostitution contribute to the support of the underworld the incredible sum of between seven and nine billion dollars annually. All of it untaxed."[38]

Vorenberg and Vorenberg claimed, "Probably more than half a million women work as prostitutes in America—some regularly, some from time to time . . . . There are about 100,000 arrests a year for prostitution and related crimes."[39] Bode refers to both of these estimates in his essay on prostitution.[40]

The difficulties in estimating the number of prostitutes nationally are also present in attempts at estimating the size in individual cities. For example, Winick and Kinsie estimated that there were 25,000 full-time prostitutes in New York City in 1968 with 8,045 prostitution-related arrests.[41] A few years later, the New York Women in Criminal Justice presented two more estimates of the New York City prostitution population: on one hand, an estimate of 40,000 by Samuel James, a psychiatrist who works with prostitutes in New York City; on the other hand, an estimate of 2,500 "hard-core" street prostitutes and West Side massage parlor prostitutes by a New York City police lieutenant.[42] NYWCJ adds that there were 2,838 arrests for prostitution in New York City in 1976 plus 2,620 arrests for loitering for the purpose of prostitution and 8,114 prostitution-related disorderly conduct arrests in the Manhattan South area. Given that there is such diversity in the size estimates for one city, it's not surprising that hard figures for the national population are so difficult to obtain.

While agreeing that "between 250,000 and 550,000" women may be working at prostitution on a more or less full-time basis, Winick and Kinsie used arrest records to estimate a lower bound for the size of the prostitute population in 1968. Using the FBI Uniform Crime Report's figures of 42,388 arrests for prostitution and commercial vice, 99,147 arrests for vagrancy, and 98,230 arrests for curfew and loitering violations, they interpolated that "there were some 95,550 arrests for violation of prostitution or related laws"—a figure that they interpret as a "very conservative approximation of the number of full-time prostitutes." Assuming an average of three clients per day, six workdays a week, and a $10 fee per client, they estimated that "all full-time prostitutes earn about $894 million a year," with a yearly gross of $9,300 and a yearly net between $5,000 and $6,000 for the "average full-time prostitute."[43]

However, as Winick and Kinsie point out, arrest records are unreliable estimates of the numbers of prostitutes.[44] For one thing, an arrest certainly does not imply that the arrested person is guilty of prostitution. Secondly, many prostitutes will be arrested more than once a year while many others won't be arrested at all. (Heyl's madam was arrested eleven times from 1961 to 1963 and not at all from 1969 to 1974.[45] Goldstein reports that 24 of the 25 "low class" prostitutes in his study had been arrested at least once with the median being six arrests in seven years of prostitution.[46]) Thirdly, the relative intensity of police enforcement activity will vary from city to city and even from year to year. New York City has changed its laws and procedures against prostitution a number of times in the last fifteen years. In 1967 the state penal code reduced prostitution from a misdemeanor to a violation with a fifteen day maximum sentence. In 1969, the maximum penalty was increased to ninety days.[41] In 1976, the state legislature passed the "Ohrenstein Law" which prohibits loitering for the purposes of prostitution. This law was passed to aid the city's new crackdown on prostitution as it prepared to host the 1976 Democratic Convention.[40, 41, 47, 48]

However, arrest records are the only national data we can build on. At least they provide a rough picture of the year-to-year trends and, as far as prostitution is concerned, a number which is a definite lower bound for the number of prostitutes. Table 12-2 summarizes the arrest statistics for "prostitution and commercialized vice" for the years 1971 through 1976.

Another fact which compounds the problem is the growing number of teenage prostitutes. There may be as many as 500,000 teenage runaways working as prostitutes.* The Office of Human Development Services calculated that there were about one million *reported* runaways in 1977. If one assumes that half of these

---

* Telephone conversations in September, 1980 with Priscilla Alexander of C.O.Y.O.T.E. and Judy Seckler of the Office of Social Responsibility. See also Endnote 5, pp. 7, 42.

Table 12-2   Number of Arrests for "Prostitution and Commercialized Vice"

Year	Total	Female	Male
1976	70,200	49,631	20,569
1975	68,200	50,673	17,527
1974	68,400	51,710	16,690
1973	55,800	42,129	13,671
1972	51,600	38,236	13,364
1971	55,100	42,813	12,287

SOURCE: U.S. Department of Justice. 1977. *The Sourcebook of Criminal Justice Statistics.* Washington, D.C.: U.S. Government Printing Office.

Note: The entries in the second column are the estimated total number of arrests each year for "prostitution and commercialized vice," including reported arrests and estimates for the number of unreported arrests. The entries in the third column were obtained by multiplying the number in the second by the percentage of women among the reported arrests; similarly for the fourth column.

runaways are female and that only half of the actual runaway population is reported, then one is led to believe that there were one million runaway girls in 1977, all searching for a quick way to earn money in a new metropolitan area. It is certainly possible that half of these may turn to prostitution to support themselves. Many of these may be satisfied with bartering sexual access for a place to live and some meals.

We will have to use a wide range of numbers in our estimate of the prostitution population in the United States in the mid-seventies. We will take as our lower bound the number 80,000—a little less than twice the number of arrests for female prostitution each year during this period. This is a conservative figure because the arrest totals in Table 12-2 do not include the large number of prostitutes who either were not arrested or who were arrested for other prostitution-related charges (such as loitering or vagrancy). On the other hand, we have mentioned estimates that there are over 500,000 full-time and part-time prostitutes. We will take as our upper bound the estimate that there were 500,000 full-time equivalents in the mid-seventies, that is, 500,000 prostitutes earning incomes as described in Table 12-1. For example, this estimate includes the possibility that there were 300,000 prostitutes with incomes of the order of those described in Table 12-1 and 400,000 prostitutes (for example, barterers) with incomes one half this size.

Our next objective is to estimate the gross and net incomes of the prostitution industry. In the previous section, we estimated that the average full-time prostitute brought in gross yearly receipts from her clients as indicated in Table 12-1. Unfortunately, there is no systematic study of the distribution of the six types of prostitutes in Table 12-1 among the total prostitute population. (Goldstein comments on this need also.[49]) Clearly, the types that are most visible and therefore appear to be most abundant are the streetwalkers and massage parlor prostitutes. However, a source at C.O.Y.O.T.E. (Priscilla Alexander in a telephone conversation, September 2, 1980) insists that only a small percentage of all prostitutes are streetwalkers or "independents" (that is, call girls), while the vast majority work in some establishment of prostitution, such as brothel, bar, or massage parlor. Accordingly, we will work with the distribution of prostitutes described in Table 12-3, assuming that prostitutes who work in establishments make up about two thirds of the total, with massage parlor prostitutes being the most common of these. If we weight the gross revenues in Table 12-1 with the distribution in Table 12-3, we find that the average full-time prostitute earns a total of $40,000 a year for the prostitution industry, while earning a personal income of $27,000.

To arrive at a national income for the industry, we need to subtract the prostitute's costs of doing business. These costs can be considerable. Each prostitute must purchase seductive clothing and expensive beauty aids. Most want regular physicians' exams. Madams and massage parlor managers have to pay rent for their establishments—rents that can be especially high if their landlord realizes the illegal nature of their business. A call girl needs a luxurious, well-furnished apartment or meeting place to entertain her clients. For example, a novice call girl in Rosenblum's group "was earning about $15,000 a year, yet paying $600 a month in rent and spending a considerable sum on clothing and beauty aids."[50] Heyl's madam estimated that she had a gross weekly income of $4,000 and

Table 12-3 Hypothetical Distribution of the Types of Prostitutes

Type of Prostitute		Percentage of Total
Streetwalkers		20
Call girls		15
Total working in establishments		65
Massage parlor	25	
Brothel	15	
Bar	15	
Hotel	10	

business expenses of $1,350 in 1973–1974.[51] Some of her expenses were probably payoffs to local policemen to deter the harassment of her house. Winick and Kinsie estimate that the average full-time prostitute's earnings were 54 to 65 percent of her gross earnings.[43] They do not indicate whether the remaining 35 to 46 percent were business costs, manager's share, or both. Adler and Hilton discuss the high costs that prostitutes must pay.[52, 53]

We will assume that the average prostitute's business costs were 20 to 40 percent of her gross revenues. This assumption leads to a contribution of $24,000 to $32,000 (60–80 percent of $40,000) to the national income of the prostitution industry from the average full time prostitute. If we combine these figures with our estimate that there were the equivalent of 80,000 to 500,000 full-time prostitutes, we are led to a national income of the prostitution industry of between $1.9 billion and $16.0 billion. If we use Tables 12-1 and 12-3 to net out that part of the massage parlor's revenues that are related to legal activities, we find that the prostitution industry contributes between $1.7 billion and $14.4 billion to the national income of the underground economy. Our figures also estimate that the gross earnings of the prostitution industry were between $3.2 billion and $20 billion. These estimates can be compared with (1) the estimate of the President's 1967 Task Force on Crime that the gross income of the prostitution industry was $225 million in the mid-sixties[54]; (2) the estimate by Benjamin and Masters based on demand-side data that the prostitution industry grossed $2.25 billion a year in the fifties;[55] (3) the estimate by Sheehy that the prostitution industry grossed $7 billion–$9 billion in 1970;[56] (4) the estimate by the Internal Revenue Service that the "total unreported income" of the prostitution industry was $1.1 to $1.6 billion in 1976;[57] and (5) the statement by Bode that "prostitution is a $10 billion industry."[58]

The discussion in this section points to the need for more accurate figures on the size of the prostitution industry so that we can intelligently discuss policy questions regarding prostitution. We really do have very little knowledge about how many prostitutes there are and how they are distributed by type. Of course, the clandestine and illegal nature of the profession makes such estimates extremely difficult. There are three methods that could be used to achieve reasonable estimates.

First of all, one could choose a sample of urban centers, including the reputed centers of prostitution like New York and San Francisco, and carefully survey knowledgeable sources in these cities as to the size and distribution of the prostitute population in their area. Valuable sources would include police detectives or vice squad leaders, psychologists, social workers, medical clinics, and possibly nearby university personnel. The researcher would have to compile the estimates of these sources and then carefully extrapolate to estimate the size and distribution in the whole country. In our chapter on heroin, we described how Hunt[59] and others used such methods to estimate the size of the heroin-user population.

Secondly, there is one large area of the prostitution industry where one should be able to achieve accurate estimates—the massage parlor segment. Since these massage parlors operate with legitimate fronts, it should be a simple matter to tabulate how many massage parlors there are and how many masseuses they employ. One can then continue the sampling method of Rasmussen and Kuhn[60] or Verlarde[61] to develop an accurate picture of exactly what happens and at what price in a typical massage parlor.

Finally, one can estimate the size of the prostitution industry by working from the demand side instead of the supply side. One could undertake a careful survey of the sexual habits of American men like the 1948 "Kinsey Report,"[62] which found that the men in a representative community of 100,000 interviewed in the late 1930s and early 1940s had some 3,190 contacts with prostitutes in a week. (See summaries in Winick and Kinsie,[63] and in Benjamin and Masters.) Benjamin and Masters used the data of the Kinsey Report and an estimate of an average fee of $7 per encounter with a prostitute to estimate a gross income of $2.25 billion for the prostitution industry in 1964.[64] It's time for an updated demand-side estimate.

Trends

Prostitution may be the world's oldest profession, but it appears to be a continually evolving and changing profession too. For example, in the 1920s and 1930s the prostitution industry was much more highly structured than it is now. With the diminished influence of organized crime and the decline of the brothel, it is now much more a business of individual entrepreneurship.[65] The only exception to this trend has been the striking increase of massage parlor prostitution between 1970 and 1975, as discussed at the beginning of this chapter. In this same vein, the role of the pimp appears to be diminishing too. The madam in Heyl's study recalled that every prostitute she knew in the early 1960s had a pimp, and that even in the late sixties over 90 percent of the novice prostitutes she hired were committed to pimps.[66] However, in the mid 1970s most of the girls seeking work at her brothel were "outlaws"—women independent of the influence of a pimp. (See Heyl, pp. 132–133, Adler,[67] and Farrell[68] for discussions of the decline of the influence of pimps.) On the other hand, most of the streetwalkers interviewed in a 1977 San Francisco study supported a pimp.[69]

Of course, since we have few good figures as to the numbers of prostitutes, it is difficult to measure the trends in the size of the prostitute population. According to Winick and Kinsie,[70]

> *the only comparative figures on the incidence of prostitution over a period of years can be found in the community studies conducted by the American Social Health Association* . . . . The Association has developed a weighted scale for evaluating the relative amount of prostitution in a community. The scale considers the size of a community, its socioeconomic level, the amount and type of prostitution, as well as the extent to which it is flagrant or clandestine. When these dimensions are weighted and combined into a single numerical index, a maximum score of 100 is possible. A score of 76 to 100 describes a community with a great deal of flagrant prostitution.*

In Table 12-4, we list the mean score of the communities surveyed during the different eras of our country's history. The trend appears to be downward, but stabilizing.

Prostitutes have a different clientele now than they did twenty years ago. For instance, in past years it was often the prostitute who initiated young males into sexual experiences. With liberalized attitudes toward sex, this customer base, once the prostitute's strongest, has been eroded. One study found that in a twenty-year span the number of male students who had their first sexual experi-

Table 12-4   American Social Health Association's Prostitution Index

Era	Score
1920–1929	95
1930–1938	92
1939–1945 (W.W.II)	49
1946–1950	74
1951–1960	35
1961–1970	37

* Formerly the American Social Hygiene Association.

ence with a prostitute dropped from 25 to 7 percent.[71] The typical client of today's prostitute is a white workingman or businessman in his middle thirties or forties. Eighty to ninety percent of today's customers request fellatio (oral stimulation of the genitals) during their encounter.[72, 73]

Prostitutes themselves have changed too. As mentioned earlier, today's prostitute is a little more likely to be independent of the influence of a pimp. There are also many more teenagers (especially runaways) taking up prostitution to support themselves after a move to "the big city." *Newsweek* reported that arrests for prostitution of girls under 25 has increased from 24 percent in 1961 to 74 percent in 1971 in New York City.[74] Women twenty-two and younger accounted for half of the arrests for prostitution nationwide in 1976. Many of the social organizations concerned about prostitution have made teenage streetwalkers their top priority.

Finally, in the last ten years, many prostitutes, especially streetwalkers in large cities, have found it more profitable to rob their customers at their secluded trysting place than to grant them sexual access. Often, a group of prostitutes will work together with one or two going through the customer's pockets while another seductively keeps the customer's attention. In Gray's study of seventeen teenage streetwalkers, only four reported never having robbed a trick.[75] In New York and San Francisco, bands of prostitutes have often been responsible for unprovoked violent attacks on innocent passers-by. In one such incident, a prostitute threw acid at cartoonist Charles Addams when he did not respond to her beckoning.[76] House prostitutes and call girls who rely on a core of regular customers have not participated in this wave of prostitute-initiated crime.

Drugs and Prostitution

Prostitution and drug use have often been linked in the public mind—and with good reason. Goldstein, who carefully studied the relationship between prostitution and drug use, concluded, "It was just about impossible to find any prostitutes who had not used drugs. . . . Seventy percent [of the subjects of his study] reported being addicted to some drug during their lives."[77] Major questions concerning the prostitute's drug use have been (1) who uses which drugs, (2) why, and (3) is there a causal relationship between drugs and prostitution?

Goldstein found some strong relationships between type of prostitution and type of drug use.[78] "Low class" prostitutes (for example, streetwalkers) tended to use heroin and cocaine more than "high class" prostitutes. They were also likely to have begun their drug use at a young age. Many took up prostitution to support their drug habit, often bartering sexual services in return for a regular supply of drugs. A number of these women quit prostitution a short time after they kicked their heroin habit.

Goldstein found, on the other hand, that high class prostitutes were much more likely to use barbiturates and amphetamines than heroin. Most of these women began their drug use after they became prostitutes and used drugs to cope with the stresses and challenges of their jobs and to relax their inhibitions. There does appear to be rather easy access to all drugs in environments in which prostitution flourishes.

Costs and Benefits to the Prostitute

Before considering the costs and benefits associated with prostitution, we will summarize some of the major hypotheses concerning a prostitute's entry into the profession. Researchers have found that most prostitutes come from homes broken by separation or divorce and troubled by very poor relationships between parents and children. (See Endnote 8, p. 91; Endnote 19, p. 36; and Endnote 10, p. 12.) Many girls had been victims of incest, sexual abuse, or rape prior to their involvement in prostitution. (See Endnotes 31 and 79. For a different perspective, see Endnote 11, pp. 791–792.) In most cases, weak parental guidance enabled the girl to experience early, casual sexual intercourse to the exclusion of more usual noncoital sexual relationships. (See Endnote 79, p. 134; Endnote 11, p. 790; and Endnote 80, p. 195.) Drawn by the excitement of big city life, such young women often leave home, but soon find themselves unattached, unemployed, or poorly paid in their new urban environment. If they meet prostitutes in this new environment, or at least become aware of the high earning power of prostitution, they will be tempted to try it out. If they do enter the profession, they will soon find that prostitutes are forming an increasingly large part of their circle of friends—a fact which supports and encourages their establishment in their profession.

There is general agreement among prostitutes and researchers that a major (if not *the* major) stimulus to entry into prostitution is the high income it promises. Compare, for example, the average gross salaries of $20,000 to $50,000 described earlier with median annual earnings of $5,903 for full-time, female civilian workers in the United States in 1972.[81] As one prostitute interviewed by Millett stated:[82]

> *I don't think you can ever eliminate the economic factor motivating women to prostitution. Even a call girl could never make as much in a straight job as she could at prostitution. All prostitutes are in it for the money. With most uptown girls, the choice is not between starvation and life, but it is a choice between $5,000 and $25,000 or between $10,000 and $50,000. That's a pretty big difference. You can say that they're in this because of the difference of $40,000 a year. A businessman would say so. Businessmen do things because of a difference of $40,000 a year.*
>
> *It's very hard for women to earn an adequate living and so we do not have much economic choice—even the call girl. And the minority woman on the street—the poor woman—she has no choice at all.*

In short, prostitution represents a better way of life for many women that has been or might otherwise be available. Most prostitutes are relatively well adjusted to their professions.[83] Of course, their financial reward is enhanced by the fact that no income tax will be deducted from their earnings.

As Margo St. James, the founder of C.O.Y.O.T.E., explains, money may be the main reason for entry, but there are others: "Most whores do it for money—99 percent. Others for adventure—breaking the law, excitement, whore-cop relationship, getting back at men by giving them a lousy screw."[84] Other incentives are the feeling of independence which the profession affords or the need to find money to support a drug habit. (Rosenblum, p. 177, emphasizes the role which the feeling of independence plays as a precipitating factor.) As the prostitute quoted in Millet argues:[85]

> *For white women . . . the choice itself is a choice between working for somebody else and going into business for yourself. Going into business for yourself and hoping to make a lot of money. . . . Lots of whores are on junk; it's expensive. A junkie has very little choice.*

There are, of course, costs to this high earning power. One reason for the prostitute's high income may be the low status of her profession in society.[86] Another is the steep downward mobility in the occupation. As a prostitute gets older, her beauty often fades and her earning power decreases. She will need to compensate herself in her twenties for this future decreased earning power. These shadows lie heavily on the aging prostitute; a large percentage of prostitutes attempt suicide at some time during their lives.[87, 88]

Prostitutes also face extreme physical and health dangers. Independent streetwalkers must deal with a constant concern that they may be beaten or roughed up by their clients or by competing prostitutes. Prostitutes who rely on pimps for protection may suffer emotional and even physical harm because of the turbulent prostitute-pimp relationship. There is also the ever-present threat of venereal disease. Since VD can ruin their careers as well as their health, most prostitutes have regular physician's exams and inspect their clients' genitals for signs of disease before entertaining.

Finally, like all members of the underground economy, prostitutes face the risks of arrest and fine or imprisonment. We really do not know the extent of the risk for the average prostitute, especially since it changes as the intensity of police activity changes. Clearly, different types of prostitutes face different degrees of risk. For example, streetwalkers who must openly solicit customers in semipublic places face a much higher risk of arrest than do call girls, who make most of their arrangements by phone and use an elaborate security process to make sure that new customers are not undercover police officers.

Social Costs

In a famous early study of prostitution, Abraham Flexner[89] argued that the four principal social costs to society resulting from prostitution are personal demoralization, economic waste, spread of venereal disease, and the association of prostitution with social disorder and crime.[90] The hostility of many people toward prostitution stems simply from the feeling that sex as a business threatens our social and moral structure and that sexual relations are only appropriate when performed by a married couple (or at least in the presence of strong emotional ties). As a result, the United States is one of a small minority of nations that attempts the legal suppression of prostitution.

The illegal nature of prostitution requires that city, state, and federal governments spend large amounts of money to suppress its activity. Estimates of the cost involved in prosecuting a single prostitute—from the street to jail—range from $600 to $1200. A few years ago, Seattle spent $1 million a year for this purpose, a figure that is probably a good estimate for other cities of comparable size.[91] In 1977, San Francisco spent over $2 million to process 2,938 people arrested for prostitution.[92] These arrests have led to large populations of prostitutes in our jails and prisons, where they can learn new tricks and teach their tricks to other inmates. Over 30 percent of the women in our nation's jails are convicted prostitutes. This percentage is over 50 percent in New York. (Vorenberg and Vorenberg[84] and NYWCJ[3] attribute these figures to Professor Jennifer James of the University of Washington.) We must ask ourselves whether the costs of these programs match the benefits they achieve.

Like gambling operations, prostitution activities are open to the public view to the extent that they could not exist without the cooperation or at least the intentional disregard of law enforcement officials. Investigations have frequently discovered that police officers have accepted bribes in return for a promise to ignore prostitution in their district.[93, 94] Occasionally, these bribes have involved free sexual favors. The resulting loss of faith in our law enforcement system is another social cost involved in the legal suppression of prostitution.

The propagation of venereal disease is another important cost to society. Ninety percent of all professional prostitutes contract venereal disease in their lifetimes. Each infected prostitute can infect an average of twenty men before her VD symptoms appear and are discovered. (See Winick and Kinsie[95] for a description of how one infected prostitute had 310 contacts with truck drivers from all over the United States.) However, it is important to keep in mind that only 5 percent of all VD that occurs annually is related to prostitution. Teenage males represent the highest rate of infection now—a population which rarely interacts with prostitutes.[96, 97] As mentioned above, modern prostitutes take careful precautions to guard against VD, including regular exams and an automatic inspection of their client.

Another serious cost to society from prostitution is the high incidence of crime and drug use which exists in areas of prostitution. After Terre Haute's 54 brothels were closed in 1942, the number of robberies a year dropped from 48 to 13 and the number of aggravated assaults from 36 to 14. "In terms of every important index of antisocial behavior or community problems, Terre Haute was a healthier and safer city after the brothels closed, and there is reason to believe that the red light district had a good deal to do with the change."[98] Hawaii experienced a similar decrease in juvenile delinquency and antisocial behavior after its brothels were closed in 1944. Even venereal disease and rape declined sharply.[95]

There are clear, direct connections between prostitutes and crime. As described earlier, many prostitutes have found that robbing their customers is more lucrative than providing sexual service. We also discussed the heavy drug use among prostitutes—drug use that requires a milieu where drugs are readily available. Our chapter on heroin points out the strong effect of heroin use on property crime. So it is only natural that when prostitution declines, so does the crime rate.

A final most important social cost of prostitution is the existence of a large class of people who are held in low esteem and whose earning power declines abruptly with age.

Summary

Table 12-5 summarizes our economic estimates of the female prostitution industry for the mid-1970s.

Table 12-5   Summary of Economic Estimates of the Female Prostitution Industry

Number of prostitutes	80,000–500,000 full-time equivalents
Average income	$27,000 per year
Average gross contribution to the prostitution industry	$40,000 per year
Gross revenues of the industry	$3.2 to $20.0 billion
National income	$1.9 to $16.0 billion
Unreported national income	$1.7 to $14.4 billion

Endnotes

1. Davis, Kingsley. 1971. "Sexual Behavior" in R. K. Merton and R. A. Nisbet, eds., 1966, *Contemporary Social Problems*. 3rd ed. New York: Harcourt, Brace and World, pp. 316–317.
2. Lemert, Edwin. 1951. *Social Pathology*. New York: McGraw Hill. Chapter 8: "Prostitution and the Prostitute," p. 238.
3. New York Women in Criminal Justice. 1977. *Prostitution in New York City: Answers to Some Questions*. New York: NYWCJ Publication, p. 1.

4. Goldstein, Paul J. 1979. *Prostitution and Drugs*. Lexington, Mass.: Lexington Books, pp. 37–38.
5. Boyer, Debra, and Jennifer James. 1980. "Easy Money: Adolescent Involvement in Prostitution," University of Washington Preprint, to appear in Kelly Weisberg, ed. *Woman and the Law: The Interdisciplinary Perspective*.
6. Goldstein, *Prostitution and Drugs*.
7. *Ibid.*, p. 55.
8. Taylor, Glen S. 1933. *Prostitution in Detroit*. Ann Arbor, Mich.: University of Michigan, Department of Sociology Publication, p. 83.
9. Verlarde, Albert. 1975. "Becoming Prostituted," *British Journal of Criminology*, 15:251–263.
10. Heyl, Barbara. 1979. *The Madam as Entrepreneur*. New Brunswick, N.J.: Transaction Books.
11. Gray, Diana. 1973. "Turning Out: A Study of Teenage Prostitution," *Urban Life and Culture*, 1:401–425, reprinted in Savitz and Johnson (1978):795.
12. Sheehy, Gail. 1971. *Hustling*. New York: Delacorte Press, pp. 6–7.
13. Millett, Kate. 1971. *The Prostitution Papers*. Reprinted 1975. Herts, England: Paladin Books, p. 79.
14. Milner, Richard and C. Milner. 1972. *Black Players: The Secret World of Black Pimps*. London: Michael Joseph.
15. New York Women in Criminal Justice, *Prostitution in New York City*, p. 8.
16. Rasmussen, Paul, and L.L. Kuhn. 1976. "The New Masseuse: Play for Play," *Urban Life* 5:271–292, reprinted in Savitz and Johnson (1978), p. 801.
17. Verlarde, Albert and M. Warlick. 1973. "Massage Parlors: The Sensuality Business," *Society* 2:56–61.
18. Vorenberg, Elizabeth, and James Vorenberg. 1977. "The Biggest Pimp of All: Prostitution and Some Facts of Life," *Atlantic Monthly* 239 (January):27–38.
19. Winick, Charles, and Paul Kinsie. 1971. *The Lively Commerce: Prostitution in the United States*, p. 158.
20. Sheehy, *Hustling*, pp. 197–218.
21. Gray, "Turning Out," p. 794.
22. Vorenberg and Vorenberg, "The Biggest Pimp of All," p. 29.
23. Heyl, *The Madam as Entrepreneur*, p. 133.
24. Winick and Kinsie, *The Lively Commerce*, p. 4.
25. *Ibid.*
26. Gray, "Turning Out," p. 794.
27. Heyl, *The Madam as Entrepreneur*, p. 134.
28. *Ibid.*, p. 99.
29. Taylor, *Prostitution in Detroit*.
30. Sheehy, *Hustling*, p. 216.
31. Lynch, T., and M. Neckes. 1978. *Cost Effectiveness of Enforcing Prostitution Laws*. San Francisco: Unitarian Universalist Service Committee.
32. Greenwald, Harold, 1970. *The Elegant Prostitute: A Social and Psychoanalytic Study*. New York: Walker and Co., p. 10.
33. Rosenblum, Karen. 1975. "Female Deviance and the Female Sex Role: A Preliminary Investigation," *British Journal of Sociology* 26:171.
34. Heyl, *The Madam as Entrepreneur*, p. 67.
35. Winick and Kinsie, *The Lively Commerce*, p. 177.

36. Rosenblum, "Female Deviance," p. 171.
37. Sheehy, *Hustling*, p. 226.
38. *Ibid.*, p. 4.
39. Vorenberg and Vorenberg, "The Biggest Pimp of All," pp. 31–32.
40. Bode, Ken. 1978. "New Life for the Oldest Profession," *New Republic* 1979 (July 8):22.
41. Winick and Kinsie, *The Lively Commerce*, p. 226.
42. New York Women in Criminal Justice, *Prostitution in New York City*, p. 21.
43. Winick and Kinsie, *The Lively Commerce*, pp. 4–5.
44. *Ibid.*, p. 4.
45. Heyl, *The Madam as Entrepreneur*, pp. 75, 93.
46. Goldstein, *Prostitution and Drugs*, p. 55.
47. Vorenberg and Vorenberg, "The Biggest Pimp of All," p. 33.
48. New York Women in Criminal Justice, *Prostitution in New York City*, pp. 12–15.
49. Goldstein, *Prostitution and Drugs*, p. 13.
50. Rosenblum, "Female Deviance," p. 172.
51. Heyl, *The Madam as Entrepreneur*, p. 99.
52. Adler, Polly. 1953. *A House is Not a Home*. New York: Rinehart, p. 309.
53. Hilton, George W. "The Prohibition: An Economic Analysis." U.C.L.A. Department of Economics Preprint.
54. President's Commission on Law Enforcement and Administration of Justice. 1967. *Task Force Report: Crime and Its Impact—An Assessment*. Washington, D.C.: U.S. Government Printing Office.
55. Benjamin, Harry and R. E. L. Masters. 1964. *Prostitution and Morality*. New York: Julian Press, p. 19.
56. Sheehy, *Hustling*, p. 4.
57. U.S. Department of the Treasury, Internal Revenue Service. 1979. *Estimates of Income Unreported on Individual Income Tax Returns*. Washington, D.C.: U.S. Government Printing Office, p. 134.
58. Bode, "New Life for Oldest Profession," p. 23.
59. Hunt, Leon. 1977. *Assessment of Local Drug Abuse*. Lexington, Mass.: D.C. Heath.
60. Rasmussen and Kuhn, "The New Masseuse."
61. Verlarde, "Becoming Prostituted."
62. Kinsey, A. C., W. R. Pomeroy, and C. E. Martin. 1948. *Sexual Behavior in Human Male*. Philadelphia: W.B. Saunders.
63. Winick and Kinsie, *The Lively Commerce*, p. 5.
64. Benjamin and Masters, *Prostitution and Morality*, p. 19.
65. Winick and Kinsie, *The Lively Commerce*, p. 5.
66. Heyl, *The Madam as Entrepreneur*, p. 132.
67. Adler, Freda. 1976. *Sisters in Crime: The Rise of the New Female Criminal*. New York: McGraw Hill, p. 65.
68. Farrell, Barry. 1977. "Part-time Pimping," *Chic* 1:27–28, 38, 93.
69. Lynch and Neckes, "Cost Effectiveness."
70. Winick and Kinsie, *The Lively Commerce*, pp. 5–6.
71. Geis, Gilbert. 1972. *Not the Law's Business? An Examination of Homosexuality, Abortion, Prostitution, Narcotics, and Gambling in the United States*. Rockville, Md.: National Institute of Mental Health, p. 182.

72. Winick and Kinsie, *The Lively Commerce*, p. 267.
73. Heyl, *The Madam as Entrepreneur*, p. 115.
74. *Newsweek*. 1971. "Prostitutes: The New Breed" (July 12), p. 78.
75. Gray, *Turning Out*.
76. Sheehy, *Hustling*, pp. 14–23.
77. Goldstein, *Prostitution and Drugs*, pp. 13, 15.
78. *Ibid.*
79. James, Jennifer, and J. Meyerding. 1977. "Early Sexual Experience and Prostitution," *American Journal of Psychiatry* 134:1381–1385.
80. Greenwald, H. 1969. "The Call Girl," in W. A. Rushing, ed., *Deviant Behavior and Social Process*. Chicago: Rand McNally.
81. United States Bureau of the Census. 1974. *Statistical Abstract of the United States: 1974*. Washington, D.C.: U.S. Government Printing Office.
82. Millett, *The Prostitution Papers*, pp. 34–35.
83. Winick and Kinsie, *The Lively Commerce*, pp. 24–25.
84. Vorenberg and Vorenberg, "The Biggest Pimp of All," p. 32.
85. Millett, *The Prostitution Papers*, p. 35.
86. Davis, Kingsley, 1966. "Sexual Behavior" in Robert K. Merton and R. A. Nisbet, eds., 1966. *Contemporary Social Problems*. New York: Harcourt, Brace & World, p. 347.
87. Winick and Kinsie, *The Lively Commerce*, p. 76.
88. Sheehy, *Hustling*, pp. 231–233.
89. Flexner, Abraham. 1914. *Prostitution in Europe*. New York: The Century Co., p. 11.
90. Goldstein, *Prostitution and Drugs*, p. 27.
91. Bode, "New Life for Oldest Profession," p. 23.
92. Lynch and Neckes, *Cost Effectiveness*.
93. New York Commission to Investigate Allegations of Police Corruption and the City's Anti-Corruption Procedures. 1972. *Commission Report*, New York: Commission. Also called the Knapp Commission.
94. Pennsylvania Crime Commission. 1974. *1973–74 Report*. St. Davids, Pennsylvania: Penn. Crime Commission, p. 101.
95. Winick and Kinsie, *The Lively Commerce*, p. 64.
96. *Ibid.*
97. James, Jennifer, *et al.* 1975. *The Politics of Prostitution*. Seattle: Social Research Associates.
98. Winick and Kinsie, *The Lively Commerce*, pp. 224–225.

Additional References

ESSELSTYN, T. C. 1968. "Prostitution in the United States," *American Academy of Political and Social Science, Annals* 377 (March):123–135.
GREENWALD, HAROLD. 1967. "Hypoanalysis of a Prostitute," *Journal of the Long Island Consultation Center* 5:33–39.
KAPLAN, LAWRENCE J., and DENNIS KESSLER. 1976. "The Economics of Prostitution," in Kaplan and Kessler, eds., *An Economic Analysis of Crime*. Springfield, Ill.: C.C. Thomas.

LEMERT, EDWIN. 1968. "Prostitution" in Edward Sagarin and D. MacNamara, eds., *Problems of Sex Behavior*. New York: Crowell, pp. 68–110.

McCULLOUGH, J. HUSTON. 1976. "The Ban on Prostitution: A Case of Economic Exploitation of Woman by Man." Ohio State University Economics Department Preprint.

SAVITZ, L., and N. JOHNSON, eds. 1978. *Crime in Society*. New York: Wiley.

STEIN, MARTHA L. 1974. *Lovers, Friends, Slaves*. New York: Berkeley Publishing Co.

U.S. Department of Justice, L.E.A.A. 1973, 1974, 1975, 1976, 1977, 1978. *Sourcebook of Criminal Justice Standards*. Washington, D.C.: U.S. Government Printing Office.

Note: For excellent bibliographies on prostitution, see Goldstein (1979) and Heyl (1979).

Chapter 13

POLICY ALTERNATIVES FOR THE ILLEGAL SECTOR OF THE UNDERGROUND ECONOMY

Our discussion of the structure and size of the illegal underground economy has included informal analyses of the costs and benefits that each sector of this economy brings to the producers and consumers within each sector and to society as a whole. This cost-benefit discussion leads naturally to a consideration of the policy alternatives available with regard to each sector. In effect, there are two basic policy questions that must be faced: (1) To what degree should the activities of each sector be legalized or regulated? and (2) What is the most effective way to enforce effectively the existing laws which have made the activities of these sectors illegal?

For some sectors, like fraud arson, there is universal agreement that stronger, more effective laws are needed to discourage the activity. For others, like prostitution and marihuana, an increasingly large percentage of the population has been urging a relaxation of current regulations.

We know too little about many of the illegal sectors to carry out an informed discussion of policy alternatives. Consequently, for many of the sectors we also list the important questions which must be answered before policy changes can be considered.

The Drug Sectors

The legalization question with respect to drugs has sparked a lively debate in the last few decades. While many have argued that laws against drug use and sale should be made stricter, others have argued that all such laws should be abolished. Groups seeking a compromise between these two extremes have suggested that the use of some drugs be decriminalized but not legalized; in such a setting drug use would be treated somewhat like illegal parking—a fine could be levied but there would be no entry on a person's criminal record.

Those who favor stricter drug laws or who at least oppose legalization base their arguments on the costs to users and to society that we have cited in our discussion in Chapters 6, 7, and 8. Each of the drugs can have strong debilitating effects. Heroin appears to have the worst effects, especially with prolonged use. Over a thousand deaths a year are attributed to heroin consumption. With continued use, its pleasurable effects diminish and more of the drug is needed to achieve the same high. If use is stopped abruptly, painful withdrawal symptoms can occur. Although cocaine and marihuana do not appear to have the addictiveness and tolerance effects that heroin has, their use may also entail some unhealthy side effects. For example, cocaine sniffers can develop an erosion of the nasal mucosa, while marihuana smokers are susceptible to all the smoke-related diseases that cigarette smokers face. In addition, cocaine or marihuana users may experience severe temporary psychoses.

In addition to these individual health costs, drug abuse can lead to major social costs. Unhealthy users cannot lead normal, productive lives. Furthermore, addicted heroin users may resort to theft to raise the money to support their expensive habit. Recall that Moore found that 44 percent of the income of the average heroin user in his model came from thievery.[1] While opponents of legalization may agree that the social costs of heroin are much worse than those of cocaine or marihuana, they argue that the latter drugs should be banned too, not only because they can have harmful effects on individuals and society but also because their use can lead to experimental use of heroin and other more powerful drugs.

Supporters of legalization feel that the costs to society of drug use do not outweigh the costs that antidrug laws bring to society. They argue that less harmful drugs, like marihuana and cocaine, may be less dangerous than alcohol and should not be treated differently. They compare the current illegal status of drugs to the prohibition of alcohol from 1920 to 1933. Clearly, Prohibition greatly reduced alcohol consumption and with it the amount of alcoholism and alcohol-related diseases like cirrhosis of the liver. Similarly, the current policy of prohibition of drug use has reduced the supply of these drugs, raised their prices, and reduced the aggregate harmful (and beneficial) consequences of their use. However, similar to the situation with alcohol in the 1920s, the prohibition of drugs has brought them black market status. Long vertical underground distribution systems have developed in response to this prohibition, leading to exorbitantly high prices and poor or uncertain quality. Furthermore, criminal organizations have been able to reap large profits by taking advantage of the black market status of these drugs. However, as Grinspoon and Bakalar argue, societies do not usually base their prohibition and legalization decisions on careful cost-benefit analyses:[2] "It is easy to say that it would be rational to examine whether the benefits of legalized cocaine would be so much less in proportion to the potential harm than the benefits of legalized alcohol, refined sugar, or handguns. But serious public debate about this question is unlikely because what society regards as rational is inseparable from its traditions and self-image."

On the other hand, the Drug Abuse Council argues:[3]

The enforcement of marihuana laws may have had an even more negative impact than alcohol prohibition on the relationship between the American people and their criminal justice system and legislative officials. Prohibition of use seemed to be applied selectively. This perception of unequal enforcement of the law alienated a substantial segment of the American people. These feelings of alienation led in some cases—perhaps in many—to active rejection of other laws and social conventions.

The fact that by 1977 one out of every four American adults had broken the law by smoking a marihuana cigarette is a sign of a tentative weakening in the American population's respect for the laws on which effective government is based. As a result, city, state, and federal governments began reassessing marihuana laws. In 1972, the National Commission on Marihuana and Drug Abuse had issued a comprehensive report recommending that possession of marihuana for personal use no longer be a criminal offense. Within eighteen months of the issuance of this report, Oregon became the first state to adopt legislation decriminalizing marihuana. It officially discouraged marihuana use by imposing a civil fine for possession of less than an ounce. Subsequently, ten other states—Ohio, Alaska, Colorado, Maine, California, Minnesota, Mississippi, North Carolina, New York, and Nevada—replaced jail sentences for simple possession by civil fines. These states make up one third of the population of the United States. In 1977, President Carter declared:[4]

Marihuana continues to be an emotional and controversial issue. Af-

ter four decades, efforts to discourage its use with stringent laws have still not been successful. More than 45 million Americans have tried marihuana and an estimated 11 million are regular users.

Penalties against possession of a drug should not be more damaging to an individual than the use of the drug itself; and where they are, they should be changed. Nowhere is this more clear than in the laws against possession of marihuana in private for personal use. We can, and should, continue to discourage the use of marihuana, but this can be done without defining the smoker as a criminal. States which have already removed criminal penalties for marihuana use, like Oregon and California, have not noted any significant increase in marihuana smoking. The National Commission on Marihuana and Drug Abuse concluded five years ago that marihuana use should be decriminalized, and I believe it is time to implement those basic recommendations. Therefore, I support legislation amending federal law to eliminate all federal criminal penalties for the possession of up to one ounce of marihuana.

Advocates of legalization of marihuana and cocaine also take issue with the frequent claim that these drugs lead to the eventual use of more dangerous drugs. Although surveys which measure the extent of drug use do provide some statistical association between the use of marihuana and that of other illicit drugs, these surveys usually show that the use of any specific drug can be statistically associated with that of any other drug.[5] (A recent survey by O'Donnell and others[6] found that 70 percent of American heroin users had their first drug experience with alcohol, and only 2 percent with marihuana.) Certainly a person who enjoys a marihuana-induced "high" is naturally well-disposed to the use of drugs in general. He or she may even develop a craving for something more exciting or challenging. However, Goldman argues:[7]

What has to be stressed is that the profound disposition in our society toward seeking pleasure through drugs is not something that can be checked by outlawing the mildest and most harmless of the popular euphoriants. Given the basic thrust, the process will continue whatever the legal status of marihuana.

When President Nixon closed down the Mexican border during Operation Intercept in 1969 and made marihuana scarce and expensive throughout the United States, many occasional marihuana smokers began experimenting with more dangerous drugs to fill the void. (See Chapter 8, Endnote 1, pp. 434–444, and Endnote 7, p. 100.) As indicated in the incidence graph in Chapter 6 (Figure 6-2), 1969 is the year that more people than ever before (or since) tried heroin for the first time. During the same year, a crackdown on marihuana use by American soldiers in Vietnam led to a major epidemic of heroin use among these soldiers. (See Chapter 8, Endnote 1, pp. 188–189.)

There are some people who would apply the arguments for legalization of marihuana and cocaine to the use of heroin as well. They cite recent studies by Hunt and Chambers[8] and by Hunt and Zinberg,[9] which provide strong evidence that there is a large (around three million) population of Americans who use heroin irregularly, are not addicts, live stable lives, hold steady jobs, and may not require any kind of treatment. This population may be four or five times larger than the population of addicts. The existence of this population would contradict the stereotype of heroin as an inevitably addicting drug that leads to a dysfunctional life—a stereotype upon which heroin treatment and control programs have been based. Further studies of this population of nonaddicted users are clearly necessary.

Given the current illegal status of heroin, cocaine, and marihuana, the government's goals are to discourage use of these drugs and to break up the organizations which have been profiting from their black market status. For example, the Office of Drug Abuse Policy[10] suggested to President Carter a federal policy that would attempt to reduce the frequency of cocaine abuse without unduly punishing the careful users:

> *The purpose of Federal policy and key to our national strategy is to maintain cocaine's high price and illegal status, in order to restrict consumption and limit negative health and social consequences. Domestically, it is important for the Federal Government to conduct research to increase our knowledge of the effects of compulsive, high-dose cocaine use, to monitor changes in incidence and prevalence, and to monitor patterns of cocaine use. Domestic penalties for simple possession of cocaine should not be reduced at this time. Unlike marihuana, cocaine possession laws have not resulted in inducting large numbers of otherwise law-abiding young people into the criminal justice system. There is also some reason to believe that the law may help to discourage use.*
>
> *Domestic law enforcement agencies should not single cocaine out for special attention since that approach seems of little practical benefit. . . . In order to reduce the availability of cocaine and increase the price, it is more effective to attack the distribution networks near the source before it dissipates and disappears in our domestic illegal market. . . .*

The federal government has found it particularly difficult to break up the organizations which have been profiting from the sale of illegal drugs. As we have seen, these organizations have developed structures which make them resilient to police attacks. Arrests of lower-level workers have had little effect on the organization, and people at the highest level of the system have built a very effective shield around themselves.

Moore suggests that the most effective place to attack this system and confiscate supplies is at the middle level—that of the "weight-dealers."[11] This level is low enough in the system that frequent transactions are made without the elaborate security strategies of higher levels. It is high enough that such dealers work with large quantities of heroin and would be difficult to replace. To attack this level effectively, police will have to rely on extensive undercover operations, including search warrant and wiretap investigations.

The policies described above require well-trained leadership to reach creative solutions to some of the problems posed. Congress can make sure that there are funds to train and coordinate such leadership and to carry out the above programs, including the necessary undercover operations. Congress should also ensure that federal funds are not being wasted on unplanned, counterproductive drug-law enforcement practices that may have only a temporary cosmetic effect.

In discussing effective policies against the spread of heroin use, one must keep in mind two socially and geographically distinct populations—the potential users who have not yet been introduced to heroin, and the current regular or irregular users. As mentioned above, there is strong agreement that 80 to 90 percent of heroin users were first introduced to the drug by a close friend in an informal setting. Such transactions among friends are relatively impregnable to narcotic enforcement efforts. Nor are they affected by the existence of treatment centers, since the introducer usually has only recently begun using heroin and feels neither the pangs of addiction nor the need for treatment at this early stage. Epidemiologists Leon Hunt and Carl Chambers argue that the only way that a program aimed at preventing new use of heroin can be successful is that it anticipate the locales of new use, focus on the individual new users, identify these new users early, and discover some way to induce the new unaddicted user to give up heroin.[12] Their studies of the national diffusion of heroin use indicate that this diffusion has followed population density and city size, moving from densely populated large cities to sparsely populated smaller cities, with a movement that is unaffected by police activity, by the curtailment of supply, or by any other intrinsic condition. However,

Moore uses simulation studies to argue that strangers do play a role in the propagation of heroin use—especially as a vector between different groups of friends.[13] He believes that even if narcotics enforcement strategies are limited to deterring stranger-to-stranger transactions, narcotics enforcement can have a significant effect on the rate at which heroin use spreads.

However, as Moore points out, the enforcement of narcotics laws against regular heroin users can have strong adverse effects on these users—direct effects such as police harassment, jail, poor self-image and stigmatization by society—plus such indirect effects as high prices, variable toxicity, and the general difficulties of holding a regular job and affording the necessities of life. Enforcement programs aimed at discouraging experimentation and encouraging new users to abandon the drug should not inflict too great a cost on current users, because of the indirect effect generated (for example, increased property crime). One way of making the effective price of heroin different for new and old users is to ensure that connections are very difficult to make. For example, there should be no area to which an inexperienced user can come and expect to find heroin. In addition, a wide variety of treatment programs should be available, along with creative diversion systems which keep arrested users out of jail. Jail terms do little to improve the behavior and condition of users; at the same time they make finding reasonable employment at a later stage much more difficult.

Fraud Arson

The rapid growth of the fraud arson segment of the underground economy has begun to catch the attention of the general public. Unfortunately, we know very little about the arson-for-fraud industry, and we have at present meager resources to discourage its rapid growth.

There are a number of straightforward questions about the size and impact of the arson industry which need to be answered. We need to take the guesswork out of the questions of just how many fires each year are caused by arson and what percentage of these are set for financial gain. In particular, insurance companies should be encouraged to estimate carefully the number of suspicious claims they receive each year, the total of the payments made for these claims, and the market value of the property involved. (See Simon et al.[14] for an example of a carefully done study of property values and fire losses.) In addition, as discussed in the previous section, detailed studies should be made to estimate much more carefully the economic costs to society of arson, especially fraud arson. These studies should take into account the vast loss of life, shutdown of firms, and decreased productivity that is attributed to arson fires. Even though the national income of the fraud arson industry is small compared to that of gambling and drug use, the actual costs to society from fraud arson are probably greater than those of illegal gambling and heroin. Once we have the answers to these questions, we can better decide how to allocate enforcement resources and how to set realistic goals in the battle against fraud arson. For example, even though the property loss resulting from arson fires was more than one half the property loss from all seven of the FBI index crimes in 1974, there were only 5,000 full-time equivalent arson investigators in 1974 compared to 100,000 full-time equivalent investigators for the index crimes.[15]

As part of this study, efforts should be made to establish the role of professional torches in the fraud arson picture. How many are there, how do they operate, what fees do they charge, do they operate across state lines, and are they connected to national crime syndicates? Armed with this information, Congress can encourage and, if necessary, initiate cooperative efforts of law enforcement agencies against fraud arson rings.

Of course, to make any impact on the stunning growth of the fraud arson "industry," one must find ways to increase the costs and decrease the benefits for would-be arsonists. One obvious way to increase these costs is to improve the dismally low arrest and conviction rate of arsonists. First of all, we need more efficient and effective means of determining whether or not a fire was started deliberately. This requires a substantial increase in the number of trained arson investigators and in the effectiveness of their detection devices. Unfortunately, many well-populated areas of the country have only one arson investigator to check out all suspicious fires. As a result, about 40 percent of building fire losses are due to fires "of unknown origin."

There are a number of reasons for the low rate of arson investigations. For one thing, an arson investigator must search carefully through filthy, smelly, and wet fire scenes. He must work quickly at the fire site before important evidence is burned or otherwise destroyed. Meanwhile, he faces exposure to foul weather and weakened building structures. After all this effort, he must put together a complex chain of circumstantial evidence to establish arson and implicate a suspect.

Another impediment to effective arson investigation has been the lack of cooperation between police and fire departments. Police have often felt that arson detection and investigation were concerns for fire departments, while the fire fighters have not been interested or trained in the pursuit of criminal investigations. To promote more effective joint action, the International Association of Chiefs of Police and the International Association of Fire Chiefs have recommended that fire departments take full responsibility for arson detection and that police agencies be responsible for the criminal investigation after the arson has been detected. This division of responsibility is not the current pattern in the United States. [16]

Arson investigators are further hampered by the lack of sophisticated equipment to help them in their work. Among the signs that they look for to establish arson as the fire's cause are the existence of multiple points of origin and the use of gasoline as a fire accelerant. The existing vapor-detection equipment used by investigators to locate traces of fire accelerants was actually developed for other purposes and is of limited value in arson investigations. A research and development program for equipment suitable for arson investigation is badly needed. [17]

Another way to increase the cost for would-be arsonists is to improve the conviction rate of 1.87 convictions per 100 arson fires. However, evidence in arson cases is not only difficult to find but usually circumstantial in nature. A complex circumstantial case must usually be developed, involving a heavy reliance on expert scientific testimony. Prosecutors need to be trained in the complexities which arise in arson cases.

Federal, state, and local governments can effectively raise the costs that arsonists face in committing their crime. They can ensure that an adequate number of arson investigators are properly trained to study effectively all suspicious fires. They can ensure that police and fire department task forces are established to divide the tasks properly and efficiently in arson investigations. [18] They can encourage and support scientific research on physical evidence in arson fires and on the development of more sophisticated arson-detection devices. They can support and make available many more mobile crime laboratories to aid arson investigators in their difficult task. They can train special prosecutors to handle the complexities that arise in arson cases. They can increase publicity so that the general public may be more aware of the extent and rate of increase of the arson problem.

Such a program can have an impact. The statistical analysis of Boudreau et al. implies that the average arson rate is lower for cities which have higher arrest or conviction rates.[19] In 1975, the city of Seattle, Washington, put into effect a number of the above policy suggestions, including the establishment of a special police and fire department arson unit, a substantial increase in the number and sophistication of arson investigators, and an intense publicity campaign. As a result, Seattle's arrest rate for arson now runs close to 50 percent. The number of arson cases dropped, from a total of 662 with a loss of $3.2 million in 1974 to a total of 518 with a loss of $1.8 million in 1977.[20]

Besides increasing the costs, there are also ways of decreasing the benefits to would-be arsonists by making it less likely that they will collect their insurance claims. Insurance companies have often been too eager to settle questionable claims quickly, both to uphold their reputations and to avoid legal suits. As a result, they have sometimes paid arsonists' claims without investigating carefully on their own or cooperating fully in police investigations. Historically, insurance companies have had to tread the fine line between the responsibility of sharing information with law enforcement authorities and the legal constraint of preserving the privacy of information concerning their clients.

There are a number of actions that insurance companies can take to eliminate the profit motive from arson. They can be more selective in their underwriting and in their claim adjusting by making sure that buildings and businesses are not substantially overinsured. They can try to be more aware of the financial condition of potential and current customers, looking out for bankruptcies that might lead to arson attempts.[21] As mentioned earlier in this section, they can expand their efforts to improve the reporting and investigating of possible arson fires and the prosecuting of possible arsonists. To this effect, sophisticated computer programs are becoming available to monitor and evaluate arson case information and to search for trends in recent arson incidents.[22, 23] To be most effective, these computer analyses should be coordinated nationally and a uniform method of incident reporting should be adopted. Finally, laws can be passed that would give insurance companies some more protection and flexibility when they handle cases in which arson is suspected.

Illegal Gambling

The discussion on gambling and its impact on American society poses a number of questions, the answers to which would clarify the impact of illegal gambling in American society. All three studies discussed in Chapter 10 took for granted that organized crime derives substantial revenue from illegal bookmaking and numbers games, although the National Gambling Commission's final report cast some doubt on the connection between illegal gambling and national crime syndicates like the Mafia. More recently, Reuter and Rubinstein have argued convincingly after a long and careful analysis of police files that the fragmentation and low profitability of illegal gambling in New York City suggests minimal syndicate control of such gambling there.[24] Additional studies of police files, similar to the Reuter-Rubinstein study, should be conducted to clarify the relationships between gambling and organized crime in all parts of the country. If the connections are weak, much of the work on legalized gambling will have to be redone.

We feel comfortable with the estimate that the total handle of illegal gambling in 1974 lay between $5 billion and $10 billion dollars. If there are enough gamblers who bet an average of $1,000 a week throughout the year, then the total handle would be much closer to the upper limit. It would be interesting to discover how much of such gambling exists and what percentage of the total illegal handle it comprises.

There is no way at present to estimate the trends in the intensity of illegal gambling. The only convincing national figures we have are the 1976 SRC data. If three or four different areas of the country, including New York City, were to make careful periodic estimates of the intensity of gambling, we could keep track of the national income of this rather large industry and possibly investigate the effect of different policies on the economic success of this industry.

As discussed in another chapter of this book, researchers have conducted a careful quantitative analysis of the costs to society of heroin consumption. In the chapter on illegal gambling, we listed some of the costs to society due to illegal gambling. It would certainly be beneficial to quantify these costs. One could then compare the figures for heroin with those for illegal gambling to help set priorities for police activities.

There appear to be three alternatives to the present method of dealing with illegal gambling: (1) increase police activity against illegal gambling, (2) legalize or at least decriminalize most gambling activities, and (3) encourage and support legal (possibly state-run) alternatives to illegal gambling. However, it is not clear that any one of these options has major advantages over the other options or over present policy. No reasonable amount of police activity will eliminate all illegal gambling. As the National Gambling Commission concluded in its final report, "gambling is inevitable." For example, the numbers game is played heavily in many black and Puerto Rican neighborhoods of New York and its lore is part of the community fabric. Before one increases police activity against illegal gambling at the expense of potential police activity against other illegal activities, one should measure the social costs and benefits of illegal gambling and compare these figures with those of other illegal activities. In fact, the National Gambling Commission reported that the New York City police actually relaxed their activities against small-time bookmakers in 1971 in an effort to cut down on police corruption.

The National Gambling Commission reported that there is broad support for the legalization of some gambling activities. It concluded that, since the mores of the people of a particular area play an important role, gambling should be dealt with at the state and local levels. It cautioned that a significant number of Americans believe that any form of gambling is wrong and that legalized gambling may undermine the work ethic for many citizens. Indeed, legalized gambling appears to create new gamblers.

Finally, there is the option of allowing state-run games to compete with illegal games. In 1976, states earned some $1.2 billion from legalized gambling, with parimutuel wagering accounting for $719.3 million and state lotteries for $462 million. States have expressed three motives for their legalization of certain gambling activities: revenue; competition for illegal gambling; and, in the case of present and proposed casinos in New England, a stimulus for the urban renewal and economic growth of certain areas. The National Gambling Commission emphasized that the first two of these goals are incompatible, since games that are truly competitive with illegal games must be highly flexible, inexpensive to run, retain a fairly small take-out, and be virtually untaxed. The Commission also found that if state-run gambling is viewed as a voluntary form of taxation, it is a regressive tax and one that is much more expensive to collect than income and sales taxes in terms of its administrative overhead. The Commission also noted that despite the introduction of the state-run off-track-betting system in New York, illegal book-making in New York City continued to increase.

Loan Sharking

In his detailed analysis of the loan-shark industry, Seidl summarizes the government's four policy options in dealing with this industry: continue current policy, publicize more, enforce more effectively, or change the current law and practices.[25]

One option is to continue present policies of enforcement. A careful cost-benefit analysis may indicate to some people that the benefits of the present high-risk lending system outweigh the costs listed in the chapter on loan sharking. Others may feel that a more careful study of the total loan shark picture is necessary before any policy changes can occur. A closely related policy option is to increase consumer awareness of the services offered by the loan shark industry in an attempt to increase competition in the industry and bring interest rates down. Proponents of this policy option would include those who believe that the threat of violence or some physical penalty is essential to high-risk lending. They may also believe that the present loan shark industry may be the most effective institution for high-risk lending, with an equitable mixture of service for those in need of quick, secret, or high-risk loans and punishment for those unable to manage their financial affairs within the reasonable constraints of traditional lending practices. On the other hand, such a policy would probably lead to increased business for loan sharks, increased violence—or at least the threat of violence—in loan shark transactions, and increased funding and vitality for the criminal organizations that depend on loan sharking as their main source of revenue.

A third policy option is to attack the loan shark industry with more efficient and effective law enforcement techniques, keeping in mind the dependency of criminal organizations on loan shark funds. An important component of such a campaign would be the establishment of permanent, adequately staffed police units at federal, state, and local levels, which would concentrate on the activities of large-scale criminal organizations. This was a major recommendation of the 1967 President's Commission on Law Enforcement. (See also *Columbia Journal of Law and Social Problems.*[26]) These units would need federal funding and coordination because of the scope and interstate character of many large-scale criminal organizations and the need for coordinated intelligence gathering. At present, only a few urban areas have such units staffed by more than ten people. This enforcement approach would also require that legislators pass laws to aid this campaign; for example, laws that would protect witnesses against loan shark activities and thus make the gathering of evidence easier, laws that would grant immunity to witnesses so that the activities of higher echelons in criminal organizations can be brought to light, laws that would make the possession of loan shark records a crime and thus lessen the need for the testimony of victims, and laws that would make loan shark extortion a felony and thus increase the possible costs of loan shark activities.

Of course, before embarking on this third policy, a careful cost-benefit analysis should be completed. Will these expensive and time-consuming efforts have much of an impact on underworld activities in general and on loan sharking in particular? What are the social costs of the increased powers which law enforcement authorities will receive? Recall that in many instances loan sharking is a "victimless crime"—one that rarely receives the attention or concern of the public or the media.

Another difficulty with the enforcement approach is that it does not attack the fundamental causes of the black market in high-risk loans on which loan sharks thrive. A fourth policy in regard to the loan shark industry is to attack these causes by promoting alternative lending systems" with the hope that we can stimulate what we like about loan sharking while discouraging aspects we don't like."[27] Key elements of this strategy would be the elimination of usury laws and a loosening of traditional lending practices. In effect, this policy would remove the black market for high-risk loans by allowing legitimate lending institutions to make high-risk loans at appropriately high interest rates. Such a policy should bring competition back into the high-risk loan market and remove excessively high monopolistic profits which loan shark organizations have been enjoying. At the same time, a more flexible lending service would have to be designed to compete with the speed, convenience, and secrecy of loan shark transactions.

Such a policy could decrease the flow of funds into the treasuries of criminal organizations. It would remove the secrecy from much of the loan shark industry's operation and could lessen corruption and enforcement costs. On the other hand, this policy would bring in a host of new problems to deal with—for example, how to protect the borrower from unnecessarily high rates by unscrupulous lenders, how to protect high-risk lenders from the increased probability of default which high-risk loans entail without allowing them to use physical threats to encourage repayment, and how to protect the integrity of the banking system in this less regulated situation.

All of these policies require that some sort of quantitative cost-benefit analysis be performed on the present loan shark industry and on the policy alternatives considered. Unfortunately, many of the critical costs—corruption and anxiety, for example—are difficult to quantify. Yet some attempt must be made in order to weigh these policy alternatives successfully. In addition, we need to have a better idea of the actual size of the present loan shark industry. To obtain such an estimate would require some effective police undercover work to study the supply side and some careful and discrete population surveys to study the demand side. Finally, it would be beneficial to know how the recent easing of credit restrictions has affected the growth of the loan shark industry. As discussed earlier, during the mid- and late 1970s lending institutions issued credit cards and circulated them widely, opened up revolving loan accounts, and introduced overdraft accounts to allow customers to write checks for amounts above the balance of their checking accounts. In addition, the federal government has made available loans to small businesses to overcome the relative disadvantages which small businesses had in borrowing funds for expansion or survival. All of these practices should have decreased the market for black market loans. Careful research is needed to determine whether or not they have and, if so, what further borrowing practices might turn even more borrowers away from the loan shark market.

Prostitution

The main questions that any government considering laws against prostitution must face are (1) whether or not prostitution in itself is a moral offense against the common good, and (2) if it is, are the costs of legal suppression of prostitution worth the benefits that attempts at suppression can yield?

Many of those who advocate stricter enforcement of laws against prostitution base their objections on their belief that prostitution is sinful and immoral. They also point to the high incidence of crime and drug use that occurs in areas where prostitution flourishes. Others who share their opposition to prostitution are concerned about the possible spread of venereal disease or the very low social esteem that prostitutes receive.

Many of those who favor looser enforcement or even abolition of laws against prostitution argue that governments should not be legislating morality. They argue that society may well be better off with legalized prostitution, which can be more carefully controlled, than with the current chaotic illegal industry. Legislation might allow funds currently spent on suppression to be spent combatting the negative side effects of prostitution.

A number of the proposed solutions to the problem of prostitution have been built on models in European countries where prostitution is more readily tolerated than it is in the United States. In Amsterdam and Hamburg, special old sections of the town are set aside for the operations of prostitutes. Outside these designated areas, prostitutes are arrested and fined. Within these areas, police officers are available to settle disputes, direct traffic, and prevent nonprostitution crime. In Hamburg, where some apartment buildings are set aside for prostitution, prostitutes must register with police and undergo weekly medical exams. In Copenhagen and Stockholm, authorities do not even treat prostitution as a crime. In counties of Nevada with populations of less than 200,000, licensed brothels may exist and pay taxes. Nevada law requires weekly VD exams and prohibits pimps. Brothel prostitutes must register as prostitutes, be fingerprinted, be checked by health authorities, and show clean police records. They must agree to stay at the brothel for specified periods of time and to stay away from certain parts of town—bars, casinos, and residential neighborhoods.[28, 29]

If one decides either that laws against prostitution are ill-founded attempts to legislate morality or that the costs of suppression outweigh the benefits they achieve, then governments should probably turn to eliminating the more damaging side effects of prostitution: the attendant crime and drug use, the possibility of VD infection, and the loss in value and self-esteem experienced by the aging prostitute. Indeed, given the close relationship between prostitution and drug use, even suppressive governments would achieve results in their campaign against prostitution by decreasing the flow of illegal drugs into their community, perhaps using suggestions we have made in regard to heroin. A decrease in drug use in an area should lead to a decrease in prostitution, especially streetwalking.

Another policy that a government could follow—whether or not it is interested in suppressing prostitution—would be to maximize opportunities and to provide as much support as possible for prostitutes ready to leave the profession. (In Goldstein's study[30] the mean age of first prostitution was 20, and the mean duration of prostitution was 6 years.) Such a policy should include intense probation supervision and vocational training for arrested prostitutes and the introduction of the prostitute into a milieu where few of her acquaintances are in the prostitution business. Support services could include shelters, child care, counseling, and a 24-hour hotline.[31] Ideally, one might employ former prostitutes to function as social workers in these endeavors. These policies would be most effective when used with prostitutes who are 26 or older and who therefore find the economic rewards of prostitution to be diminishing.

Turning to broader policies, stringent enforcement of the laws against sexual discrimination in the labor market may serve to diminish, for many attractive young women, the currently large gap between potential earnings in prostitution and the rewards of alternative jobs. Educational campaigns stressing the temporary nature of prostitution as a profession may also allow young women to assess more realistically the returns of prostitution. Finally, the general relaxation of sexual mores and the aging of the "baby boom" population may strike at prostitution from both the supply and the demand side.

Endnotes

1. Moore, Mark. 1977. *Buy and Bust*. Lexington, Mass.: Lexington Books.
2. Grinspoon, Lester, and James B. Bakalar. 1976. *Cocaine: A Drug and Its Social Evolution*. New York: Basic Books, pp. 234–237.
3. Drug Abuse Council. 1980. *The Facts About "Drug Abuse."* New York: The Free Press, p. 160. Copyright © 1980 by The Free Press, a Division of Macmillan Publishing Co., Inc.
4. Office of Drug Abuse Policy. 1978. *1978 Annual Report*. Washington, D.C.: U.S. Government Printing Office.
5. Drug Abuse Council, *The Facts*, pp. 174–195.
6. O'Donnell, John A., Howard L. Voss, Richard R. Clayton, Gerald T. Slatin, and Robin G. W. Room. 1976. *Young Men and Drugs—A Nationwide Survey*. Rockville, Md.: National Institute of Drug Abuse.
7. Goldman, Albert. 1979. *Grass Roots: Marihuana in America Today*. New York: Harper and Row, p. 245.
8. Hunt, L., and C. Chambers. 1976. *The Heroin Epidemics*. New York: Spectrum Publications.

9. Hunt, L., and N. E. Zinberg. 1976. *Heroin Use: A New Look*. Washington, D.C.: Drug Abuse Council, Inc.
10. Office of Drug Abuse Policy. *1978 Annual Report*. Washington, D.C.: U.S. Government Printing Office, pp. 30–32.
11. Moore, *Buy and Bust*.
12. Hunt and Chambers, *The Heroin Epidemics*.
13. Moore, *Buy and Bust*.
14. Simon, Herbert, R. W. Shephard, and F. W. Sharp. 1943. *Fire Losses and Fire Risks*. Berkeley, Calif.: University of California, Bureau of Public Administration.
15. Boudreau, John F., Quon Y. Kwan, William E. Faragher, and Genevieve C. Denault. 1977. *Arson and Arson Investigation: Survey and Assessment*. Report to U.S. Department of Justice, Law Enforcement Assistance Administration. Washington, D.C.: U.S. Government Printing Office, pp. 36–37.
16. *Ibid.*, pp. 33–34.
17. *Ibid.*, pp. 73, 93.
18. Krajick, K. 1979. "Arson Epidemic—Who Should Investigate?" *Police Magazine* 2 (July):4–16.
19. Boudreau *et al.*, pp. 39–54.
20. *Chicago Tribune*. 1978. "Seattle Puts Heat on Arson and Rate Falls" (November 26).
21. Herschbarger, Robert A., and R. K. Miller. 1978. "The Impact of Economic Conditions on the Incidence of Arson," *The Journal of Risk and Insurance* 45:275–290.
22. Icove, D. J. 1979. *Principles of Incendiary Crime*. University of Tennessee Ph.D. thesis.
23. Bryan, J. L., and D. J. Icove. 1977. "Recent Advances in Computer-Assisted Arson Investigation," *Fire Journal* 71:20–24.
24. Reuter, Peter, and Jonathan Rubinstein, 1978. "Fact, Fancy, and Organized Crime," *The Public Interest* 53 (Fall):45–67.
25. Seidl, John M. 1969. *"Upon the Hip": A Study of the Criminal Loan Shark Industry*. Washington, D.C.: Law Enforcement Assistance Administration, U.S. Department of Justice, pp. 181–190.
26. *Columbia Journal of Law and Social Problems*. 1969. "Loan-sharking: The Untouched Domain of Organized Crime," *Columbia Journal of Law and Social Problems* 5:123.
27. Seidl, *"Upon the Hip,"* 184.
28. Bode, Ken. 1978. "New Life for the Oldest Profession," *New Republic* 1979 (July 8):21–25.
29. Hilton, George W. "The Prohibition of Prostitution: An Economic Analysis." U.C.L.A. Department of Economics Preprint, p. 16.
30. Goldstein, Paul J. 1979. *Prostitution and Drugs*. Lexington, Mass.: Lexington Books, p. 15.
31. Lynch, T., and M. Neckes. 1978. *Cost Effectiveness for Enforcing Prostitution Laws*. San Francisco: Unitarian-Universalist Service Committee.

Chapter 14

SUMMARY AND CONCLUSIONS

In the previous chapters we examined in depth the principal sectors of the underground economy in the United States. In this chapter, we want to step back and look at the total picture. We will first compile our estimates of the sizes of the sectors in order to estimate the size of the total underground economy and to compare its size with standard measures of recorded economic activity. We will also compare our microeconomic approach with the macroeconomic techniques that others have used to estimate the size of the underground economy. Finally, we will consider the overall structure of the underground economy, discuss some of the reasons for the current concern about its existence and growth, and summarize some of the broad policy recommendations that our study suggests.

Before we put together our estimates of the sizes of the various sectors, we need estimates for some of the sectors we have not discussed, such as corporate tax evasion, forgery, and consumer fraud. After an extensive search of the literature and discussions with a number of experts, we were able to find estimates of the size of some of these sectors. We used 1974 figures from a study of the United States Chamber of Commerce to estimate the amount of bribery, embezzlement, computer crime, and various types of fraud (bankruptcy, check, consumer, credit card, insurance, and securities).[1] We used the 1980 testimony of Jack Key to the Senate Subcommittee on Investigations[2] to derive estimates for commercial bribery,[3] computer crime,[4] mail fraud,[5] illegal liquor sales,[6] and government fraud.[7] We used a report of the National Narcotics Intelligence Consumer Committee[8] to obtain estimates for drugs other than heroin, cocaine, and marihuana, under the assumption that the ratio of the retail value of these drugs to the retail value of the ones we studied was the same in 1974 as it was in 1977. We derived our figures for pornography from a 1980 report of the Philadelphia Crime Commission,[9] assuming that costs amounted to 40 percent of revenues. We estimated the amount of unreported corporate income using a report of the Bureau of Economic Analysis.[10] We obtained estimates for the amount of counterfeiting from Joseph Carlin, Special Agent in Charge, Counterfeit Division, United States Secret Service; to derive national income estimates, we assumed that the counterfeiters' costs of operations were 30 to 40 percent of the value of bills passed to the public and that one half of the counterfeiters' profits were factor incomes. Finally, we obtained estimates for the value of goods (other than drugs) smuggled into this country from Brian Lee of the U.S. Customs Service. To derive national income figures, we assumed that Customs agents intercepted half of all smuggled goods other than drugs, that costs were 30 to 40 percent of value, and that factor incomes were one half of the profits.

There were a number of sectors of the underground economy for which we could not obtain any estimates. These areas included sales tax evasion, hijacking, forgery, protection and extortion, and pirating of records and tapes. We believe that the "earned income" from these activities is quite low and consequently that they add very little to the national income of the underground economy.

In order to compare the size of the underground economy with the standard measures of recorded economic activity, we have used the same national accounting techniques with which recorded activity is measured to estimate the size of the underground economy. Table 14-1 summarizes these efforts. We have included a figure of $5–$10 billion in the next to last line in Table 14-1 to take into account the unestimated sectors that we listed in the previous paragraph. On the bottom line, we estimate that the total national income of the underground economy in 1974 was between $100 billion and $180 billion. Since the reported National Income for 1974 was $1,141 billion, we estimate that the national income of the underground economy was 9 to 16 percent of the reported National Income in 1974.

We have used 1974 as the base year for this study because it is the most recent year for which we have reasonably reliable figures for most segments of the underground economy. Since it is clearly worthwhile to use our analysis of the sectors to estimate the size of the underground economy in 1980, we have tried to project our

Table 14-1 Estimated National Income for the Underground Economy in 1974

Sector	Estimate (in $ billion)
Tax Evasion and Avoidance	
Federal income and profits tax	56.7–75.7
Excise taxes	0.3–0.5
Illegal Aliens	5.9–7.6
Illegal Transfers[a]	
Stolen goods	5.4–8.9
Fraud arson	.2
Other fraud	2.2–20.1
Counterfeiting	.001
Embezzlement	0.1–1.3
Bribery	6.5–13.0
Production and Distribution of Illegal Goods	
Drugs	
Heroin	3.2–5.0
Cocaine	5.6–6.2
Marihuana	1.5–2.4
Other drugs	2.8–4.4
Smuggling of goods other than drugs	0.2–0.3
Pornography	1.3–2.0
Production and Distribution of Illegal Services	
Illegal gambling	1.0–2.0
Loan sharking	.2–3.2
Prostitution	1.7–14.4
Other	5.0–10.0
Total national income	99.8–177.2

[a] In estimating the national income of the illegal transfers sector, we have attempted to estimate payments to the factor used (such as, return to a thief's labor and capital) and to exclude pure transfers where no labor, capital, or natural resources were utilized.

1974 figures to 1980 in Table 14-2. In the columns in the middle of the table, we estimate the annual growth rate of each sector between 1970 and 1975 and between 1975 and 1980, based on our analyses of these sectors. In the last column, we use these rate estimates to derive reasonable figures for the national income of many of these sectors in 1980. Noting that the national income of these sectors grew at an annual rate of 10 percent between 1974 and 1980, we project that the entire underground economy grew at this rate and that its national income was between $170 and $300 billion in 1980. This 10 percent annual growth rate is a little slower

Table 14-2 Estimated National Income for the Underground Economy in 1974 and 1980, with Growth Trends (reliability indices in parentheses)

Sector	Estimated 1974 National Income (in $ billion)	Estimated Average Annual Growth Rate (%) 1970–1975	Estimated Average Annual Growth Rate (%) 1975–1980	"Guesstimated" 1980 National Income (in $ billion)
Tax Evasion and Avoidance				
Federal income and profits tax	56.7–75.7 (moderate)	5 to 10 (low)	8 to 12 (very low)	98.2–130.9 (very low)
Excise taxes	0.3–0.5 (moderate)	10 to 15 (moderate)	−5 to 5 (moderate)	0.3–0.6 (moderate)
Illegal Aliens	5.9–7.6 (moderate)	12 to 16 (moderate)	15 to 20 (moderate)	15.1–19.4 (low)
Illegal Transfers				
Stolen goods	5.4–8.9 (moderate)	10 to 15 (moderate)	10 to 15 (moderate)	10.9–18.0 (low)
Fraud arson	.2 (moderate)	20 to 30 (moderate)	25 to 35 (moderate)	.9 (moderate)
Other fraud	2.2–20.1 (very low)	(unknown)		
Counterfeiting	.001 (moderate)	11	6	.001
Embezzlement	0.1–1.3 (unknown)	(No estimate found)		
Bribery	6.5–13.0 (unknown)	(No estimate found)		

Production and Distribution of Illegal Goods				
Drugs				
Heroin	3.2–5.0 (moderate)	10–20 (low)	10–20 (low)	7.4–11.6 (very low)
Cocaine	5.6–6.2 (moderately high)	0–5 (moderate)	5–10 (moderate)	8.2–9.1 (moderate)
Marihuana	1.5–2.4 (moderate)	5–10 (moderate)	10–20 (moderate)	3.2–5.2 (moderate)
Other drugs (hashish and synthetic drugs like PCP)	2.8–4.4 (very low)	(No estimate found)	(No estimate found)	
Smuggling of goods other than drugs	0.2–0.3 (unknown)	(No estimate found)	(No estimate found)	
Pornography	1.3–2.0 (unknown)	(No estimate found)	(No estimate found)	
Production and Distribution of Illegal Services				
Illegal gambling	1.0–2.0 (moderate)	5 to 10 (low)	−5 to 5 (low)	1.1–2.2 (moderate)
Loan sharking	0.2–3.2 (low)	−5 to 5 (low)	−10 to 10 (low)	0.2–3.2 (low)
Prostitution	1.7–14.4 (high)	0 to 5 (low)	−5 to 5 (low)	1.7–14.8 (moderate)
Other	5.0–10.0 (low)			
Total national income	99.8–177.2	10%		170–300

than the 10.9 percent annual growth rate of the reported National Income between 1974 and 1980. We have also indicated under each entry of Table 14-2 our estimate as to the reliability of the indicated figure.

As this table indicates, the largest sector of the underground economy in terms of national income is the nonreporting of legal income, with a figure that is roughly one-half of the total national income. The largest sectors in the illegal goods and services part appear to be the cocaine and heroin distribution networks (in that order), although the prostitution industry may be even larger. The fastest growing sectors appear to be the employee theft portion of the stolen goods market and the fraud arson industry.

Our estimates are in line with those of Peter Gutmann, an economics professor at the City University of New York, who used a macroeconomic approach to estimate a "GNP" of $176 billion for the underground economy in 1976.[11-13] According to *U.S. News and World Report*,[14] Gutmann's estimate for 1978 was $220 billion, of which as much as $70 billion was illegal-source income. He based these estimates on his study of the ratio of currency in circulation to the total amount of all demand deposits. He calculated that this ratio increased from 21.7 percent in the 1937–1941 period to 34.4 percent in 1976—a difference of 12.7 percent. Assuming that the earlier ratio is a normal one and that most of the relative increase in paper money in circulation has been used for underground transactions, Gutmann estimated that 12.7 percent of the currency outside banks in 1976 ($28.7 billion) was used to "lubricate the underground economy." Assuming further that only cash was used in underground transactions and that the number of times that money changed hands each year in the underground economy was the same as in the regular economy (6.15), Gutmann obtains his estimate of $176 billion for the size of the underground economy ($28.7 billion $\times$ 6.15 $\simeq$ $176 billion). Although Gutmann's hypotheses are controversial, his work and that of James Henry[15] brought to public attention the alarming size of the underground economy. (For critiques of Gutmann's hypotheses and/or methods, see Endnotes 16–19.) University of Wisconsin economist Edgar Feige[20, 21] has also used a macroeconomic approach as the basis for his claim that the underground economy may be twice as large as we and Gutmann estimate it to be.

We believe that our microeconomic approach provides a point of view that complements these macroeconomic studies. It may also have some advantages over them. For example, through its sector by sector analysis, it can more easily lead to policy considerations than the macro approaches do. Furthermore, while the macroeconomic studies often treat the underground economy as some sort of coherent entity, our microeconomic approach can illustrate and deal with the diversity and heterogeneity within the underground "economy." Certainly many sectors, such as those which produce and distribute illegal goods and services, do appear to have the coherence and interaction of a complex economy. However, their structures are rather diverse—from the monopolies and oligopolies that characterize the heroin and loan-shark sectors, to the small proprietorships of the marihuana distribution and prostitution industries, which operate in competitive or at least monopolistically competitive environments. Some important sectors, like tax evasion and illegal aliens, are not really industries at all but special types of household activities involving very little economic structure or organization. This diversity can be effectively handled in a microeconomic approach. Finally, since the various sectors are evolving and changing at different rates, our micro approach lends itself to better estimates of the trends and growth rates within the underground economy.

All of these studies of the underground economy agree that its size is too large to be ignored and that its very existence brings a number of negative aspects to the American economy. First of all, there is the obvious loss of public revenue. The Internal Revenue Service[17] estimated that between $100 and $135 billion worth of income was not reported in 1976 and that the resulting loss of federal income tax revenue was $19 to $26 billion, an amount roughly equal to the federal budget deficit in the early 1970s. Other levels of government lose smaller but substantial amounts of revenue. Obviously, for revenue purposes alone, the government would like to bring as much of the underground economy above board as possible. The current high yield on IRS compliance expenditures indicates that much of this lost revenue can be recovered.

Another adverse effect of the underground economy is a distortion of the major economic indicators upon which policy is based. Because there is substantial underground activity, we understate the size of economic activity, such as GNP, National Income, and productivity rate, and overstate levels of unemployment and inflation, especially in periods like the late 1960s when the irregular economy apparently grew more rapidly than the regular one. Gutmann[11] estimates that an underground economy as large as that described in Tables 14-1 and 14-2 provides employment for over one million people, many of whom are listed on official unemployment rolls. Our own research leads us to believe that minority teenage unemployment is particularly overstated, since relatively large numbers of young minority group members find employment in the underground economy. Economist Paul Bullock[22] emphasizes the economic significance of illegal markets for young men in the Black and Chicano communities of Los Angeles in his book, *Aspiration vs. Opportunity: "Careers" in the Inner City.* He also quotes a 1971 Manpower Report of the President, prepared by the Department of Labor, that estimates that one of every five adult inhabitants of Harlem seemed to exist entirely on money gained from illegal sources.[23]

Indicators other than unemployment are distorted by the underground economy. When substantial numbers of people buy goods or services at a discount in the underground economy (for example, clothes or appliances from fences, painting and other household services from "off the books" entrepreneurs), official price levels are misstated. This rise in "off the books" activity also results in obvious understatements of the official productivity rate. Since the size of indicators, such as GNP and unemployment rate, affects government policies, the underground economy may provide a partial explanation for the failure of some of these policies in recent years. For example, if we have markedly overstated the unemployment rate, we may have been pursuing more stimulatory economic policies than necessary.*

Finally, the underground economy is a source of concern to the general public and to political leaders because of the strong belief that its recent growth may be an adverse side effect of some laws and government regulations. Some political leaders have been using the existence of the underground economy as part of their argument to lower taxes, slow down income redistribution programs, and decrease government regulation. Government laws, regulations, and reporting requirements have obviously had a large effect

---

*Bullock[22] (p. 122) maintains that the existence of ample employment in the "subeconomy" was the principal reason that special government programs designed to increase employment and employability of residents of low-income areas found hundreds of thousands of their slots unfilled in the late 1960s and early 1970s.

on the size of the underground economy. They even define what "underground" or "irregular" means. Clearly, there would be no illegal alien problem if we had no immigration laws; there would be no tax evasion if we had no taxes. The underground economy would have no "illegal sector" if we did not have laws against the production and sale of certain goods and services. Other types of government regulations, such as health and safety rules, antipollution requirements, income tests for social benefits payments and services, wage and hour laws, and minimum wage laws, make "off the books" activity much more attractive. We hope that our detailed study of the structure and size of many sectors of the underground economy brings out the necessity of measuring and comparing the costs and benefits of many of these regulations and reporting requirements before they are implemented.

What can we conclude? One conclusion is obvious. Both the size and the effects of unreported activity are too large to be conveniently ignored. However, does this activity form an economy in the sense that we usually conceive of one? We think not, and believe that it is better to think of three distinct types of activities which happen to be unreported rather than of an economy. The first type of activity is the failure to pay taxes on earnings from legal and otherwise recorded activity. This is a problem of substantial size that we are unlikely to reduce below 5 percent of GNP because of the costs involved in such a reduction. However, we can probably reduce this type of activity by 30 to 40 percent by: (1) revising and simplifying our tax laws with possible evasion as one consideration, (2) increasing reporting at source, (3) improving document matching procedures, and (4) increasing compliance efforts against the self-employed, corporations, and those with rental income. Failure to pay taxes on legally earned income is a problem primarily because of lost tax revenue and should be approached as such.

The second type of activity is informal economic activity which exists in every economy, but is more prevalent in countries that are less developed,[24] where it often provides as much as one-third of urban employment. This type of activity does not exist primarily to evade taxes, although it generally does so. Rather, it exists because people either cannot find employment in the recorded (formal) sector because of unemployment or illegal status (illegal aliens) or cannot find jobs in the formal sector with real incomes as high as those in the informal sector. Many of those in the second category also value the informality and personal contacts involved in their job in the irregular sector. (Ferman and Berndt[25] survey the characteristics, motivations, and activities of the diverse group of people involved in this sector.) The correct approach to this sector needs to be carefully considered. Many people working in this sector are poor and ill equipped to cope with life in the formal sector. We could destroy a good part of this type of activity by adopting President Reagan's recent proposals concerning illegal aliens. What we should do about the domestic portion of this type of activity is more problematic. Many underdeveloped countries, including Brazil, have chosen to support and strengthen this type of activity, finding it a valuable source of employment and a place of safety for those who are not able to or choose not to cope with modern technological society. Perhaps the United States would be well advised to consider such a policy, which might decrease welfare rolls and, if carefully constructed, add color and diversity to a world that at times can be all too homogeneous. This type of activity is increased by government regulation and does have an effect on major indicators. Much of this activity could be surfaced by outreach efforts and exemptions from reporting and tax requirements.

The final type of unreported activity is the activity that we have declared illegal. Unless we are willing to change our laws, we will probably have to live with a substantial amount of it. More efficient law enforcement efforts can reduce the amount of most of these activities. But, given current laws, this type of activity will not be reduced by much more than 25 percent as a whole. In addition to health, safety, and productivity considerations, this sector is a problem because it reduces tax revenue and distorts some economic indicators (primarily unemployment) that should include this type of activity as currently defined. We can probably increase the tax take from this sector above the approximately 5 percent of reported income currently estimated by IRS, but we are unlikely to increase it markedly without some legalization. In addition, given current laws, we will probably be unsuccessful in encouraging the drug sellers, thieves, pimps, prostitutes, fences, etc. of this sector to report their employment status accurately to the interviewers of the Current Population Survey. Perhaps the approach of the National Income Accountants (that is, to ignore this sector as not estimable) is most realistic if we are not willing to change laws and improve methods of estimating this type of activity.

Endnotes

1. Chamber of Commerce of the United States. 1974. *White Collar Crime: Everyone's Problem, Everyone's Loss.* Washington, D.C.
2. Key, Jack. 1980. "Testimony of Jack Key, Staff Investigator, Permanent Subcommittee on Investigations," in *Illegal Narcotics Profits: Hearings before the Permanent Subcommittee on Investigations of the Committee on Government Affairs, United States Senate.* Washington, D.C.: U.S. Government Printing Office, pp. 368–375.
3. From figures of the American Management Association.
4. From the 1980 Congressional Record. •
5. From the 1977 hearings before the Subcommittee on Energy, Nuclear Proliferation and Federal Statistics.
6. From 1977 Joint Economic Committee work.
7. From General Accounting Office work.
8. As reported in U.S. Senate, Permanent Subcommittee on Investigations, Committee on Government Affairs. 1980. *Illegal Narcotics Profits.* Washington, D.C.: U.S. Government Printing Office.
9. Pennsylvania Crime Commission. 1980. *A Decade of Organized Crime: 1980 Report.* St. Davids, Penn.: Pennsylvania Crime Commission.
10. As reported by Howard Hoffman in U.S. House of Representatives, Subcommittee on Commerce, Consumer, and Monetary Affairs, Committee on Government Operations. 1979. *Subterranean or Underground Economy.* Washington, D.C.: U.S. Government Printing Office.
11. Gutmann, P.M. 1977. "The Subterranean Economy," *Financial Analysts Journal* 33 (Jan./Feb.):26–27, 34.
12. Gutmann, P.M. 1978. "Off the Books," *Across the Board* 15 (August):9–14.
13. Gutmann, P.M. 1979. "The Subterranean Economy," *Taxing and Spending* (April), pp. 4–11.
14. *U.S. News and World Report.* 1979. "The Underground Economy: How 20 Million Americans Cheat Uncle Sam Out of Billions in Taxes" (October 22):49–52.
15. Henry, James. 1976. "Calling in the Big Bills," *Washington Monthly* (May), pp. 27–33.
16. Laurent, R.D. 1979. "Currency and the Subterranean Economy," *Economic Perspectives:* Federal Reserve Bank of Chicago 3 (March/April):3–6.
17. U.S Department of the Treasury, Internal Revenue Service. 1979. *Estimates of Income Unreported on Individual Income Tax Returns.* Washington, D.C.: U.S. Department of the Treasury, Publication 1104 (9–79).
18. U.S. House of Representatives, *Subterranean or Underground Economy.* (See especially the comments by Nancy Teeters.)
19. Simon, Carl P., and Ann D. Witte. 1980. "The Underground Economy: Estimates of Size, Structure and Trends," in U.S. Congress, Joint Economic Committee. *Government Regulation: Achieving Social and Economic Balance,* Vol. 5. Washington, D.C.: U.S. Government Printing Office.
20. Feige, E.L. 1979. "How Big is the Irregular Economy?" *Challenge* (November/December), pp. 5–13.

21. Feige, Edgar L. 1980. "A New Perspective on Macroeconomic Phenomena: The Theory and Measurement of the Unobserved Sector of the United States Economy: Causes, Consequences and Implications," Working Paper, Department of Economics, University of Wisconsin at Madison.
22. Bullock, Paul. 1973. *Aspiration vs. Opportunity: "Careers" in the Inner City.* Ann Arbor, Mich.: University of Michigan Institute of Labor and Industrial Relations.
23. U.S. Department of Labor. 1971. "Report on Manpower Requirements, Resources, Utilization, and Training," in *Manpower Report of the President, 1971.* Washington, D.C.: U.S. Government Printing Office.
24. For a recent survey of this type of activity in less-developed countries, see Patricio de Araujo, T., Aldemir do Vale Souza, and Jacira Dulce da Silva Xavier. 1981. "A Pequena Produção Urbana, Uma Proposta Conceitual," Texto para Discussão No. 101, Curso De Mestrado en Economia—PIMES, Departmento de Economia, Centro de Ciencias Socialis Applicadas, Universidade Federal de Pernambuco, Recife, Pe, Brasil.
25. Ferman, Louis A., and Louise E. Berndt. 1981. "The Irregular Economy," in Stuart Henry, ed., *Can I Have It In Cash?* London: Astragal Books.

Additional References

Key, Jack. 1980. "Testimony of Jack Key, Staff Investigator, Permanent Subcommittee on Investigations," in *Illegal Narcotics Profits: Hearings before the Permanent Subcommittee on Investigations of the Committee on Governmental Affairs, United States Senate.* Washington, D.C.: U.S. Government Printing Office, pp. 368–375.

New York Times. 1981. "New policy on aliens to omit a worker-identification card." (July 20, 1981).

U.S. House of Representatives. Subcommittee on Oversight. Committee on Ways and Means. 1980. *Hearings on the Underground Economy.* Washington, D.C.: U.S. Government Printing Office.

U.S. Senate, Permanent Subcommittee on Investigations, Committee on Governmental Affairs. 1980. *Illegal Narcotics Profits.* Washington, D.C.: U.S. Government Printing Office.

INDEX